PORTFOLIO
THE POWER OF OPPORTUNITY

Richard M. Rothman is the founder and MD of Open Mind Opportunity Consultancy, the world's first and only opportunity consultancy. For over thirty-two years, he has expanded business opportunities for hundreds of companies around the world. His Indian clients have included Zee Entertainment, Onida, Aptech, Metro Shoes and Essel Propack. His first book, *Master Opportunities and Make it Big*, won wide acclaim and was a national bestseller. Prior to starting his consultancy, Richard served as trade commissioner of the United States in India, Italy and Indonesia.

The POWER *of* OPPORTUNITY

YOUR ROAD MAP TO SUCCESS

o••••••••o

RICHARD M. ROTHMAN

PORTFOLIO
PENGUIN

An imprint of Penguin Random House

PORTFOLIO

USA | Canada | UK | Ireland | Australia
New Zealand | India | South Africa | China

Portfolio is part of the Penguin Random House group of companies
whose addresses can be found at global.penguinrandomhouse.com

Published by Penguin Random House India Pvt. Ltd
7th Floor, Infinity Tower C, DLF Cyber City,
Gurgaon 122 002, Haryana, India

Penguin
Random House
India

First published in Portfolio by Penguin Random House India 2019

ISBN 9780143447535

Typeset in Adobe Garamond Pro Manipal Technologies Limited, Manipal
Printed at Thomson Press India Ltd, New Delhi

www.penguin.co.in

MIX
Paper
FSC FSC® C010615

To my late father,
Maurice Rothman

Contents

Part I: What's in It for You?

1

Where Opportunity Begins

Why do so many success formulas fail? Why are opportunities essential and powerful for creating success? Why are the best opportunities available to everybody? Is there a process to see, evaluate and choose those opportunities? Why shouldn't you wait for opportunity to knock? What can we learn from those who have made the most of their opportunities?

It was 11.30 a.m., and Ramesh Babu was taking a mid-term exam in the second standard when the classroom door opened. He was asked to step outside. At just eight years old, he received the worst news of his life: his father had suffered a massive heart attack. He had passed away.

Ramesh's voice catches in his TEDx talk when he recalls the death of his father and, standing on the stage in 2014 at Christ University in Bangalore, it takes him a few minutes to recover. Holding back the tears, he describes how his mother was left with no savings and no inheritance other than his father's small barber shop. She decided to rent the shop out and found someone willing to take it on. The tenant, though, refused to pay more than five rupees a day.

Eventually, Ramesh's mother, with little choice, took a job as a maid. With her small salary and the little rent from the barber shop on Brigade Road's St Patrick's Complex, she raised Ramesh, his brother and his little sister. They had just enough money for one meal a day.

Somehow, Ramesh stayed in school. He took a job delivering milk to apartments, and after leaving school in class ten, registered at an evening college. Life was hard but with the family's small income, they just about survived.

One day, Ramesh came home to find his mother in tears.

'The shopkeeper is torturing us,' she said.

The tenant was refusing to pay any rent. Ramesh had had enough.

'Why can't I take the shop and run it?' he asked his mother.

Ramesh's mother wasn't impressed. 'You are very vain,' she told her teenage son.

But Ramesh insisted. There could be no harm in trying, he told her.

Ramesh took over the shop. Each morning at 6 a.m., he would open the doors. He would provide hair-cutting services to customers until 5 p.m. and then head to college. When his classes were over, he would return to the shop and continue working until midnight or even beyond.

Those sixteen-hour days paid off. After a few years, and with his grandfather's help, he was able to take a loan from the Karnataka State Finance Corporation to buy a car. He bought a Maruti van, but the monthly payments came to Rs 6800, more than he could afford to pay with his earnings from cutting hair. To cover the expenses, he started renting the van out. That gave him another income—and a new opportunity. He borrowed more money, bought more cars, and rented those out too. By 2004, ten years after he had walked with his grandfather into the bank to buy his first car, Ramesh owned six more cars. He then noticed that there was a growing demand in Bangalore for luxury rentals but a shortfall of luxury vehicles. 'So I thought, "Let me do something different that no one has done,"' he recalled during his TEDx talk. He bought a Mercedes, and in 2011, he took the biggest risk of all. He bought a Rolls Royce Ghost. It cost Rs 3.11 crore. His fleet grew. He bought car after car, growing his business in line with Bangalore's growing demand. In 2018, Ramesh Babu, the billionaire barber, owned 400 luxury cars, minivans and buses. His business clients included Bollywood stars like Aishwarya Rai and Shah Rukh Khan. And he was still cutting hair every day in his two barber shops, even on Sundays.

Are you inspired by the story of Ramesh Babu? Would you like to achieve his level of success—or more? *Of course, you would.* Instead of riding in a rickshaw, wouldn't you prefer the luxury and comfort of your own chauffeur-driven Rolls Royce? *Of course, you would.* It's universal, our desire to achieve success. Everyone aspires to achieve prosperity and financial independence—yet so few of us succeed. Would you like one day to be in the wealthiest 10 per cent, or even in the top 1 per cent? *Yes, of course you would.* And why not?

Are you likely to achieve this sort of success? Unfortunately, the odds seem to be against you. The fact is that wealth is becoming more concentrated. Globally, between 2006 and 2015, while ordinary workers saw their incomes rise by an average of just 2 per cent a year, billionaire wealth rose almost six times faster. The top 10 per cent of Indians now own over 80 per cent of the nation's wealth. Are you a member of this prosperous 10 per cent? If you're not already rich, can you overcome these daunting odds and achieve outstanding success? *Yes, you can.* It is certainly possible. Many others have done it. It doesn't matter whether you are starting with nothing: no money, no education, and no contacts. You can still do it. Others have started from zero and reached the heights of success. In 2018, a new dollar billionaire was created every two days.

The billion-dollar question is: how can you achieve success? Is there a process you can use that works?

There is. This book describes that process.

The Success Strategies That Usually Fail

Business gurus have been selling success formulas for eighty years or more. Dale Carnegie told us 'how to win friends and influence people' back in 1936. Stephen R. Covey has revealed 'the seven habits of highly effective people'. Books like these tell us how to improve ourselves. They suggest that success lies within us. Change what we *do*—how we behave each day or how we relate to others—and success will flow. These gurus offer useful information, and becoming a better person with more friends is certainly a worthwhile goal.

But will your friends give you pots of money simply because they like you? Certainly not. Other gurus tell us how to *think*. Robert T. Kiyosaki's *Rich Dad, Poor Dad* told us that there is magic in thinking rich. Napoleon Hill argues that we can *Think and Grow Rich* because 'thoughts are things' and if we harness 'the power of positive thinking' and of our 'unconscious mind' we can activate the powerful 'law of attraction'.

Again, these are books filled with interesting ideas, but are they practical? Do they work? Do they bring the success that we can envision? Not really. Everyone dreams and any dreamer can dream bigger. How many of our sweet dreams of success become reality? I may wish with all my heart and soul to be as rich as Mukesh Ambani, but will desire alone attract his riches to me? I may want to be as brilliant an investor as Rakesh Jhunjhunwala. Is that wish enough to give me his skills? Millions longed to win the heart of Priyanka Chopra. Did Nick Jonas win it because he yearned more than anyone else? His good looks, successful career, winning personality—and the fact that he had an opportunity to meet her—probably had more to do with it.

Business school professors like to help us improve our competitive strategy. They toss around terms like 'sustainable advantage', 'disruptive innovations', and 'swimming in blue oceans'. But how many innovations actually sell? In 1992, IBM introduced a device called Simon. The phone with a touchscreen was innovative, disruptive, launched into a blue ocean . . . and sank without trace. It would be another fifteen years before the iPhone made touchscreen phones ubiquitous. A good idea is a good start, but success demands even more.

Finally, there's no shortage of people who believe that criminality is the easy route to riches. There are abundant examples of people who have accumulated wealth by giving or extracting bribes, by working their connections or by putting their cronies into place. But India is changing and changing fast. Financial criminals once feared only the hand of God. In the coming decades, those who resort to dishonest methods will find it increasingly difficult to avoid severe punishment at the hands of both the courts and the market. In the long run, true and sustainable success predominantly comes from honest work. The corrupt paths that remain are growing longer and more dangerous. It is indeed time for a far more unique, practical and effective approach to success. There has got to be a better way, and there certainly is.

What Does All Success Have in Common?

We all know of famous people who made the leap from rags to riches. Dhirubhai Ambani started as a petrol pump attendant in Aden (Yemen), then a part of the Bombay Presidency under the British Raj. He built the world's largest oil refinery and India's greatest fortune through Reliance Industries. How did this man from nowhere get his start? *By capturing a series of breakthrough opportunities.*

Abdul Lateef Jandali was born to an unwed mother and given up for adoption to a blue-collar couple. They had nothing to give him but a loving home and a new name: Steve Jobs. At Reed College, Jobs collected Coke bottles for the deposit money, slept on sofas, and ate the free weekly meal at the local Hare Krishna (ISKCON) temple. How did he rocket himself to the stratosphere through Apple Inc.? *By bagging the opportunity to make technology simpler so everyone could use it.*

Subhash Chandra came from a bankrupt family of commodity traders in rural Haryana. He started his career with Rs 17 and went on to form the Zee TV empire, earning a personal fortune of over Rs 20,000 crore. How did a man who started with only Rs 17 in his pocket manage to fly so high? *By taking an opportunity that even industry insiders failed to see.*

Sachin and Binny Binsal came from middle class families in Chandigarh, and studied Computer Science at the Indian Institute of Technology Delhi. They were both set for regular jobs in the hi-tech sector, writing code for companies like Amazon and Techspan. Together they began their journey in a garage in Bangalore by creating Flipkart in 2007 and rewrote the rules of e-commerce in India, giving tough competition to Amazon, until they were bought over by Walmart in 2018 for $16 billion. Similar is the example of Kiran Mazumdar Shaw, who started her journey with a seed capital of Rs 10,000 by establishing Biocon India in 1978 in the garage of her rented house in Bengaluru. Forty years later, she is a billionaire. How did the Bansals and Kiran leap from being salaried workers to billionaire entrepreneurs in the e-commerce and biotech space? *By building opportunities that others had ignored.*

Are these individuals—and others like them—in some way special, somehow endowed with superpowers that you or I can never hope to have? Of course not. They started out just like you and me—with nothing but empty wallets and strong ambition. How can people with no money, no team and few resources achieve such immense success? It takes more than honesty and diligence to build wealth from nothing. It takes more than determination, desire, or even a dream to climb a ladder so high and so slippery with no support. It takes something far more valuable. It takes something far more powerful. It takes something that is available to everyone, from orphaned seven-year-olds eating one meal a day in Bangalore to college dropouts with bagfuls of discarded Coke bottles in California.

It takes opportunity. Opportunity is the universal starting point and the essential factor in all business and career success. Opportunities are the seeds from which all wealth grows. Regardless of where you are in life, whether you're a businessperson, an employee earning wages, an aspiring entrepreneur, a student or a professional, your ability to capture the best opportunities will be the most crucial factor that determines your success. Hard work, diligence, persistence and a positive attitude are all very useful if you want to succeed. They're essential, and business gurus are right to talk about them and explain how to develop them. But they're insufficient. None of them will deliver success unless you also harness the power of opportunity.

Why Opportunities Are Immensely Powerful

Here's some good news—opportunity is abundant and available to everyone. Sure, the rich and the connected will always have more opportunities than most but even if you have nothing but a shirt on your back and an empty belly, you can still have opportunity. Poverty alone can never stop you from profiting from opportunities. That's because all opportunities are free. This fact is so important that I'll repeat it: *All opportunities are absolutely free.*

How much did Steve Jobs pay for the opportunity to pioneer the personal-computer industry? *Nothing.* How much did Dhirubhai Ambani pay for the opportunity to dominate the Indian polyester industry? *Zilch.* How much did Subhash Chandra pay for the opportunity to start India's satellite TV industry? *Not even a penny.* How much did Jeff Bezos pay for the opportunity to create Amazon, the Internet's everything store? *Not one red cent.* You can't go to the local opportunity shop to buy opportunities even if you want to because no such shop exists. *How can you buy something that's always free?* Yet remarkably, opportunities can be even better than free. They can actually pay you. Seize the best opportunities and even the poorest people can gain tremendous leverage and attract virtually unlimited resources. Finding a great opportunity can literally be like striking gold . . . if you notice it.

Is Every Idea an Opportunity?

Tiger Global is an international investment firm. The company has interests in Stripe, a payments firm valued at $23 billion, in fitness start-up Peloton, and in Panda Selected, a Chinese shared-kitchen company that has raised more than $80 million. It has poured around $2 billion into India, investing in firms including Flipkart and Ola. Investment firms like Tiger Global are in the opportunity business. They meet with young entrepreneurs, view their pitch decks and they ask themselves two questions: has the team identified a big opportunity; and can the team harvest that opportunity? Of those two questions the first is the most important. If the team lacks the experience or the know-how to build the product they've envisioned, they can always hire the people with the skills required. What matters most is whether the opportunity the team has identified is the real thing. If Tiger Global and other investment firms believe that the opportunity is huge, they'll throw money at the people who have found it.

As a consultant, I've met Indian entrepreneurs in their early twenties who had raised over $20 million from US venture capitalists like Tiger Global. Those investors weren't giving those young entrepreneurs money because they were impressed by their track records. They didn't know who the founders' parents were or whether they had grown up in a shack in Uttar Pradesh or a Mumbai skyscraper. All they saw was the size of the opportunity these kids were pursuing. I've also met plenty of highly experienced executives who told me that they couldn't get funding or find the team members they needed to grow their businesses. These people had a track record. They had skills. What they lacked was a great opportunity.

The better the opportunity, the more resources it can attract. The best opportunities are like powerful magnets that attract all the resources needed to transform a concept into a scalable business. Smart capital always chases the best opportunities. As famed investor Prem Watsa of Fairfax Holdings said recently: 'I have found in my life, if you have opportunity, money comes.'

Naveen Tewari Turned a Nopportunity into an Opportunity

Nopportunities that suck up time and resources without giving anything back are hard to identify. Even the best can fall for them.

When Naveen Tewari teamed up with his old IIT college mate Abhay Singhal, and they persuaded Amit Gupta and Mohit Saxena to join them, the first product they developed was mKhoj, an SMS-based search engine for deals.

It didn't work. For nearly a year, they tried to make it work before realizing that using SMSs to find bargains might not have been the golden opportunity they believed it was. So they thought again. They looked for a better opportunity, a more useful tool for an increasingly digital age. They launched InMobi, a mobile advertising business that went on to become India's first unicorn—a privately held business worth more than a billion dollars with SoftBank, KPCB and Sherpalo as their key investors.

You will see many nopportunities as you look for opportunities. You might even work on some. But you don't have to keep working on them or stop looking for real opportunities.

And it's not just money that a good opportunity attracts. It can also bring a team. When others see that you're chasing an opportunity that has big potential, they'll want to join you. They'll even be willing to share the risk with you in order to share in the gain.

All opportunities are not alike. In fact they can be as different as night and day. Golden opportunities that can attract huge resources are as rare as goldmines. You may think you've discovered a big opportunity, when in fact all you've stumbled upon is a worthless idea. As my father used to say, 'Ideas are a dime a dozen'. That fact is that most ideas are not opportunities at all; they are what I call '*nopportunities*'. The best opportunities attract resources like bees to honey. Nopportunities are the opposite: they waste your precious resources, especially the one you can least afford to lose—your time.

Don't Wait for Opportunity to Knock

As we'll see in this book, opportunities are all around us. We must look for them, and we have to recognize them. What we can't do is wait for them. Too many people do that—and they get nothing. It's because we've been told that 'opportunity knocks', and that all we have to do is open the door and let it in. In practice, opportunity just doesn't work that way. To leverage the immense value of opportunities, you can't wait for opportunities to knock at your door. What if opportunity never knocks? What if you don't hear it knocking? And what if the opportunity that does turn up isn't right for you . . . but you take it anyway because you waited so long? Opportunity is far too important to leave to chance. *It needs a process.*

If you're starting to feel that you've already missed opportunities in the past, you're not alone. Most industry leaders have missed opportunities. The best opportunities are often captured by upstarts who came out of nowhere and started with nothing. Rovio was a small Finnish company best known for a game called King of the Cabbage World when it brought out Angry Birds. The success of that game showed firms as large as Ubisoft and Nintendo the opportunity in mobile gaming.

I've been a consultant for twenty-eight years. I've worked in four countries and advised the leaders of hundreds of companies large and small in over sixty-seven different business sectors. Virtually all the leaders agreed that their choice of opportunities was absolutely crucial to their success. It is the responsibility of a company's leaders to identify and choose these opportunities. In fact, that opportunity hunt should be their primary area of focus. After all, if they don't do it, no one else will. And yet, I've found that most business leaders actively avoid focusing on opportunities. Their days are spent firefighting operational problems that they would be better off delegating to others. They pour human and financial resources into squeezing the last drops out of old, mined opportunities in a never-ending battle against the forces of irrelevance.

New opportunities can certainly seem risky. To mitigate risk, people often wait for someone else to make the first move, look at what others are doing, and copy them. But the wisdom of crowds rarely applies to opportunities any more than it does to investing. Buying a stock after everyone else has bought it rarely makes you money. The same logic applies to opportunities. You need to find opportunities yourself and turn them into the foundation of your success.

All Opportunities Have a Lifecycle

A few years ago, I attended a speech in Mumbai by Professor J. Bruce Harreld of Harvard Business School. Professor Harreld has studied businesses of every size and in every sector around the world. He found that only 1.7 per cent of companies last more than forty years. Within half a human lifespan, a company will be born, will grow and die. In theory, a company should be able to last forever. There's no reason that a firm can't outlive its founders.

The Nisiyama Onsen Keiunkan is a hot-spring hotel in Yamanashi, Japan. It was founded in the year 705 AD and is still going strong. You can book it at Booking.com. You couldn't do that a thousand years ago. Just as products have lifecycles, so do opportunities. While some can remain relevant for decades—or in the case of the hot spring, for centuries—others can fizzle out in months or years. These days, even iconic consumer products such as Coca-Cola are grappling with irrelevance and looking for new opportunities.

All companies have to invest in new opportunities. They must try to replace those opportunities that once served them well but are now facing irrelevance. Professor Harreld's study found that while all corporate leaders are constantly on the lookout for great new opportunities, most fail to capture them. The business graveyard is littered with the memories of once great companies that failed to overcome the forces of irrelevance.

Remember Polaroid or Kodak? Remember Nokia or Blackberry? How about Toys"R"Us or Blockbuster? In 1991, Polaroid sold nearly $3 billion worth of cameras and instant film. The company had found an opportunity. It knew that consumers wanted their pictures instantly, without having to wait for them to be developed. It also knew that professional photographers like Ansel Adams wanted small cameras that they could carry easily into the wilderness. Models like the SX-70 met both needs. They produced high-grade photos, and they did it instantly, putting prints in the hands of photographers right away.

Within a decade, the company's main advantage disappeared completely. Digital photography lets people see their images immediately, and they no longer had a need for print. Between 2001 and 2009, Polaroid filed for bankruptcy twice and churned through six CEOs in four years. The company had failed to see that its opportunity was reaching the end of its lifecycle, and it failed to find a new opportunity.

On the other hand, we constantly witness vibrant new companies like Oyo Rooms and InMobi popping up, seemingly out of nowhere. They make it big by taking advantage of mammoth new opportunities. They find a hole in the market, and figure out how to fill it.

How Coca-Cola Adapts to a Changing Market Environment

Coca-Cola is one of the strongest brands in the world. The company generated over $31 billion in 2018 and is active in more than 200 countries and territories around the world.

But at a time of increasing concern about health and rising obesity, the company's best-known product is a fizzy drink containing about seven teaspoons of sugar. It's no surprise that the corporation's income has been falling. In 2014, Coca-Cola's revenues were around $46 billion. It lost about a third of that income over the following five years as customers turned their backs on sugary drinks.

In the first quarter of 2019, however, the company earnings beat market expectations. It had grown by 5.2 per cent in comparison to the first quarter of 2018. What happened? Part of the growth was down to raising prices. But much of it was also due to adaptation.

The company now owns a number of tea, water and juice brands that are not just healthier but can also charge a premium. In 2018, Coca-Cola bought Costa Coffee, a coffee chain popular in the UK and increasingly in China. It even has stores in select metro cities of India.

Big brands are built on opportunities, and they survive by continuously adapting to changes in their environments.

Ritesh Agarwal was just eighteen when he launched Oravel Stays. The son of a storekeeper from Odisha, Agarwal moved to Kota in Rajasthan in the eleventh grade to prepare for the entrance exams for the Indian Institute of Technology (IIT). He wasn't accepted to IIT but while he studied, he travelled frequently and found that the standard of low-cost hotels in India was variable. One hotel could be comfortable and air-conditioned. Another might be dirty and filled with cockroaches. Oravel Stays was initially a clone of Airbnb, but Agarwal soon realized that what Indian hospitality really needed was both a marketing platform and a universal standard. Oravel Stays became OYO. Agarwal dropped out of college and won a Thiel fellowship worth $1,00,000. Later revenue rounds brought in $24 million, then $100 million from SoftBank, followed by $250 million from Hero Enterprises. In September 2018, the company took another $1 billion to fund further expansion in India and China. Agarwal was just twenty-four years old and his company was worth $5 billion.

When you find an opportunity, your age doesn't matter. Only the opportunity does.

The Penalties for Choosing Opportunities without a Process

Processes are the foundation of our modern world. Would you choose a surgeon who doesn't follow a proven process? *Of course not.* Would you run a factory without processes? *Never.* Would you choose a wealth manager who used a blindfolded monkey to pick stocks? *Nobody would.* Every time a pilot steps into the cockpit, he must follow a process that takes him through the engine checks and the preparations for take-off. Every time a surgeon steps into an operating theatre, she must follow a process to make sure that the patient is prepped, and the team is ready. Every time a wealth manager sits at his monitor, he must follow a process to track stocks and predict their movements.

Yet, few people choose opportunities—the most valuable resource in the world—with a process. They choose their career opportunities without a conscious process and suffer years of frustration. They choose their business opportunities without a process, and waste crores of rupees on concepts that won't work. Based on my experience, more than

99 per cent of Indian companies find, evaluate and choose opportunities without using a systematic process. They leave opportunity to chance.

The penalty for choosing opportunities blindly can be severe. Business can suffer from years of stagnation, if not outright failure. You waste time and resources on failed initiatives. You struggle and fail for years without understanding why.

Learnings from the World's First and Only Opportunity Consultancy

Opportunity is simply too important to be left to chance. That's why I started OpenMind, the world's first and only opportunity consultancy: to create a systematic process for opportunities.

My six-step OpenMind Process uncovers, recovers, and discovers opportunities for sustained, profitable growth. This process was developed over a thirty-two-year period. It's built on the experiences of thousands of successful entrepreneurs and professionals, most of whom started with nothing but an opportunity.

This book provides, for the first time, a proven, systematic process and the tools to help you see, evaluate, choose, and implement the best opportunities. Whether you use this process for your business or career, it will provide you with a clear road-map to achieve the success that you've always dreamed of earning. By using a systematic 'opportunity process' you can benefit from the learnings—and mistakes—of thousands of successful people who have come before you. Your own journey to success will be faster, more confident, and contain fewer missteps and false starts.

What You'll Learn in This Book

This book is about opportunity: how to look for it, identify it, evaluate it and use it.

You'll start by looking at the nature of success—the reward that opportunity can bring—and you'll explore the key drivers of that success. In the second part of the book, you'll increase your understanding by exploring the key forces, the nuts, bolts and engine that can power your own opportunity process to success. Next, you'll learn the process of seeing, choosing, evaluating and implementing opportunities that can get you success.

By the time you've finished reading this book, you will know how to:

1. **Actively, consciously and relentlessly pursue opportunities,** rather than waiting for them to knock.
2. **Sort through the clutter and see the best opportunities.** Naturally, golden opportunities are not easy to see. In fact, most people routinely miss them, even when they're right in front of them.
3. **Properly evaluate potential opportunities,** so that you can choose the best.
4. **Effectively implement opportunities.** Opportunities are like seeds. If you plant them and nurture them properly, they can grow tall and be fruitful. But you must know how to do it efficiently and effectively.

Ask yourself: is there any reason you don't need valuable opportunities for success? Is there any reason you don't need a systematic process to find, evaluate and choose opportunities? *Of course there isn't.*

Let's get started.

Where Opportunity Begins

1. Opportunities are for everyone, because it is free

All opportunities in the world are free. You can't buy them even if you want to. Better yet, great opportunities are like powerful magnets that attract all the resources and team needed to scale them. You don't need experience, connections or the right background to make the most of an opportunity.

Eighteen-year-old Mark Zuckerberg didn't need any money to start Facebook in his Harvard University dorm room. Find the right opportunity and the resources you need will soon follow.

2. Don't wait for opportunity

Opportunity is a good thing, but it doesn't come to those who wait. It's captured by people who look for it, identify it and know how to make the most of it—like Ritesh Agarwal, who founded OYO Rooms.

Whether you're building a video game company or looking for an edge in a crowded market for legal services, there are always opportunities for those willing to go out and find them.

3. Opportunity has an opposite

Nopportunities waste time, energy and resources. It's vital to know the difference between an opportunity and a nopportunity (like Naveen Tewari did for InMobi)—but don't expect that knowledge to always save you. Understand that although a nopportunity is a mistake, it's not the end of the road.

Once you turn your back on a nopportunity, you might find that your next opportunity is worth a billion dollars—if you can see it.

2

Seven Lessons for Success

What is success? Can the rewards of success be shared equally? Why do we waste most of our efforts? Where should we focus to generate the best returns? What are the key drivers of success? Is there a success equation that can help you to create success?

Our tribe of Homo sapiens—let's call us humans for simplicity—has been around for only about 2.5 lakh years. That may seem like a long time but it's a mere heartbeat of history, given that the earth is about 350 crore years old.

Although we humans have had our ups and downs, over the long run we've been amazingly successful. We've learned how to make weapons, work in groups, hunt and gather. We discovered how to plant seeds, domesticate animals and maintain herds. Instead of roaming endlessly across the plains, searching for game and shelter, we found that we could stay in one place, build simple houses, and wait for the crops to grow until they were ready to harvest. We created a new sedentary lifestyle that formed small communities. The communities grew into towns, and the towns grew into cities, creating new problems and new opportunities that we solved together and benefited from.

As cities developed, people found they needed a way to store value, so they could exchange it for the goods they needed but couldn't produce themselves, such as food or clothing. So, we invented money. Together we used some of the money we didn't need for food and basic shelter, to build palaces and temples, to pay for art and culture, to create libraries and fill them with the lessons we learnt so that knowledge would be kept and passed down, allowing each generation to live better than the generation before.

The history of humankind is the story of success. It's the story of how one species identified opportunities and harvested those opportunities to build better lives for themselves and for their children. The result is that we now live on average longer than ever before. Life expectancy in

India is now nearly sixty-nine. For the world as a whole, it's seventy-two—up from less than fifty-three as recently as 1960. We've eradicated killer diseases such as smallpox and polio. We've built machines that can fly, opening the entire world to travel, settlement and exploitation. We've been to the moon and back, and we now carry small computers in our pockets that can access almost all the knowledge and culture that humans have produced over the last 2.5 lakh years. We have succeeded in ways that previous generations would have struggled to imagine.

This chapter is about that success. It's about the rewards of the success that opportunity can bring. In a series of seven lessons, we'll explore the nature of success, examine why it's so rare—and explain what it takes to achieve the success we all crave.

Lesson #1: Success is the control of resources

Success can come in many forms. For an athlete, success could be a gold medal, or a world record, or just beating their personal best. For a student, success might mean a passing grade, the highest grade, or the offer of a good job after graduation. For a company executive, success could take the form of a new investment, a new product, or the meeting of sales targets.

However you define success, there is one *sign* of success that has been present throughout human history. We find it in ancient graves in the Indus Valley, in the tombs of Tutankhamen—and in the homes of today's oligarchs and billionaires. *Success is defined by the accumulation and control of resources.* That desire to control resources has always been the key driver of human prosperity. When we control the resources we need to live, we survive. When we control more than the resources we need to live, we prosper—and we can transform the excess into energy and power.

A resource is anything of value that can be traded. It might be crops growing in a field; commodities like gold, coal and oil; real estate; intellectual property; or money in your bank account. Even your education is a resource that you can convert into items of value that you can use or trade.

All life on earth is a struggle for resources. We all want the resources that will give our families a more comfortable, more prosperous, more successful life.

Lesson #2: We live in a world with a permanent inequality of results

Although poverty overall is decreasing and fewer people lack the resources they need to live, the distribution of excess resources—of wealth—remains unequal. A small number of people and companies reap most of the resources produced by the world's efforts. All human beings compete for control of those resources.

Most of us work eight to ten hours a day, five or six days a week. But while most of us make a more or less equal amount of effort, equality of results is extremely rare. In part, that's down to ability. We all have different skills. Few of us can play cricket as well as Sachin Tendulkar or run as fast as Usain Bolt. If ten runners line up at the start of a race, even if they all try as hard as they possibly can, only one will finish first. The same applies to all human efforts, from running businesses to picking stocks. There is always an unequal distribution of ability and an inequality of results.

Societies have sometimes tried to change those results. Russian soviets, Israeli kibbutzim and Chinese collective farms have all tried to fix the unequal results of equal effort to ensure that citizens received what they needed, not what their sweat earned, or their skills made. The result, inevitably, was a reduction in effort and fewer resources for everyone. None of those societies have continued in the form they were first imagined.

There will always be people who are poorer than you or richer than you—sometimes much richer. So how do you measure your own prosperity? If you're like most people and companies, you compare yourself with others who are like you. Compared to your friends and family, are your earnings and wealth *average*? Or are you a bit above average or below average? If you have your own business or manage one, are your profits around average for your industry? Are you happy with that? In India, according to a report by Azim Premji University, if you're earning more than Rs 10,000 a month, you're doing better than most. Are you satisfied with that?

You may be familiar with the *normal distribution* or *bell curve* of efforts and results, as pictured below. If you're one of the 68.2 per cent of people getting average results in the middle of the curve, you may feel satisfied.

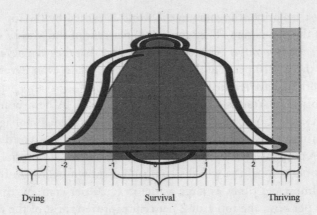

Dying   Survival   Thriving

More than two-thirds of people are in the middle. Until Ramesh Babu started renting out cars, his family would have been close to the middle of this curve, earning just enough to live from day to day. Average returns on effort allow you to survive. They don't allow you to thrive. Only the tiny proportion of people on the far right of the bell curve are thriving and prospering. In fact, the bell curve provides a poor representation of the true distribution of effort and results because the people on the right of the scale aren't just doing better than everyone else. They're doing *much* better than everyone else. They're soaking up far more of the world's resources.

Inequality of Wealth Distribution

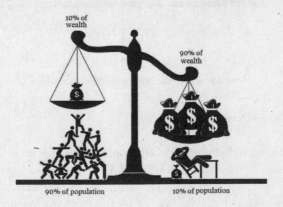

The vast majority of income in the world is earned by the top 10 per cent of the population. They control 90 per cent of the world's wealth.

The vast majority of income in the world is earned by the top 10 per cent of the population. They control 90 per cent of the world's wealth. *Where would you rather be?* Most people believe that they can never make it into the top 10 per cent, but they're wrong. Many who have started with nothing have reached the top, *and so can you*.

Corporate results are also highly unequal. A few years ago, McKinsey & Company,, the world's most prestigious management consulting firm, conducted a study of the profits of the world's 3000 largest companies. They found a similar pattern. The profits of the top 20 per cent of the world's companies, shown below on the left, were almost ten times as large as the next 20 per cent. Within that top 20 per cent, the top 1 or 2 per cent captured most of the profits. The bottom 40 per cent of the companies actually lost money.

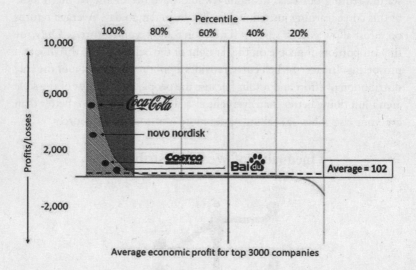

Average economic profit for top 3000 companies

Source: McKinsey Quarterly, October 2013.

The same unequal distribution of effort and results applies to the Indian market. Look at the Profit after Tax (PAT) of the 100 largest Indian companies by revenue in the 2015–16 financial year and you'll see a very similar unequal distribution of profits. The top twenty firms in India earned 68 per cent of post-tax profits. More remarkably, the top twenty companies earned ninety-five times more post-tax profit than the bottom twenty!

Largest 100 Indian Companies Ranked by PAT, FY 2015-16

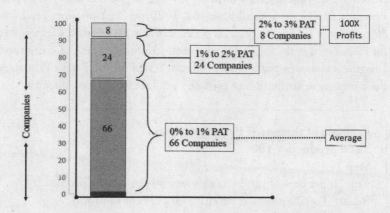

You might think this is unfair. You might believe that the distribution of resources should be made according to effort or need, and not some other uncontrollable factor. You might also believe that summers should be cooler and the Chennai Super Kings should win every game they play. It doesn't mean that any of this will happen. The question isn't how to change a distribution of profits that exists in every industry and every region. It's how much of the distribution you want to receive. Many of the people receiving the lion's share of profits started with nothing and achieved success—*and so can you.*

Lesson #3: Most of your efforts are wasted

Vilfredo Pareto (1848–1923) was an Italian economist who noticed that 80 per cent of the land in Italy was owned by just 20 per cent of the population. The Pareto Principle has now been applied to just about every aspect of life. Business owners find that 80 per cent of their revenues come from 20 per cent of their customers. Teachers spend 80 per cent of their time on 20 per cent of their students. The healthcare sector puts 80 per cent of its resources into 20 per cent of the population.

Are these numbers exact? Probably not. The ratio varies across different sectors but in general the principle remains true: the relationship between causes and effects is usually unequal and disproportionate.

The Pareto Principle applies to your efforts too. Only a small percentage of your efforts will provide most of your results. The Pareto Principle applies on a small scale too. If 20 per cent of effort produces 80 per cent of the results, then 20 per cent of that 20 per cent is responsible for 80 per cent of the original 80 per cent. Confused? Think of it this way: Imagine a company made 100 products. Based on the Pareto Principle, the company's distribution of profit by product would look like this:

Example of three-step Pareto Analysis
Total products = 100
Step 1:
Top 20 per cent of products produce 80 per cent of profits
Results: Top 20 products produce 80 per cent of profits
         Bottom 80 products produce 20 per cent of profits
Step 2:
Top 20 per cent of top 20 per cent of products produce 80 per cent of 80 per cent of profits
Results: Top 4 products produce 64 per cent of profits
         Bottom 96 products produce 36 per cent of profits
Step 3:
Top 20 per cent of top 20 per cent of top 20 per cent of produce 80 per cent of 80 per cent of 80 per cent of profits
Results: Top 1 product produces 51 per cent of profits
         Bottom 99 products produce 49 per cent of profits

Just one product out of a hundred often generates more than half of a company's profits, and we can see this, in different ratios, across companies and across industries. Every business has one outstanding product that drives the company's success. Google has invested billions of dollars in industries from solar power to autonomous cars. And yet in the third quarter of 2018, $24.1 billion of its $27.77 billion revenue still came from advertising. The Tata Group might have interests from chemicals to coffee but Tata Consulting Services Limited generates nearly 70 per cent of the dividends received by Tata Sons. These products, services or companies are what I call 'Pareto Leaders'.

When You Know Your Pareto Leader, You Know Your Opportunity

The history of Syntel is the story of constant adaptation. The company was founded in 1980 by Neerja Sethi and her husband Bharat Desai. Their first office was their apartment in Troy, Michigan (USA). Its initial offer was team sourcing; it was a recruitment agency. The pair started with $2000 and by the end of the year had earned $30,000. Over the years, the company shifted focus. In 1988, it started to supply businesses with lifecycle applications services. It had found a new opportunity and grew quickly. Four years later, Syntel opened its India global development centre. Two years after that, it employed its 1000th staff member and revenues topped $50 million. It took just three more years for revenues to double.

In 2017, Syntel's focus on business and platform solutions earned the company $924 million, which is when it caught the attention of Atos, a European rival. Atos offered the owners of the company $3.4 billion for the firm. By focusing on its richest opportunities, that 20 per cent that brought in the most revenues, Syntel had grown from a recruitment company to a billion-dollar IT services firm. Atos saw an opportunity to enhance its own offer, particularly in North America, and increase the value of its own Pareto Leader.

And Neerja Sethi and Bharat Desai? They're billionaires who started with a $2000 investment in a team sourcing company and ended selling a multibillion-dollar IT services firm.

Too often though, businesses waste a vast amount of effort and money on the 99 per cent of products and services that generate less than half the company's profits. They waste time trying to fix what doesn't work instead of doing more of what produces the best results. Sachin

Tendulkar might have played a lot of sports when he was young, but at 5 foot 5 inch (165 cm), he wouldn't have been very successful at basketball. Batting was his Pareto Leader and by focusing his efforts on his straight drive he became the best batsman in the world. Had he wasted time trying to improve his jump shot, he would have been no more than a moderate cricketer—and he would still have been a poor basketball player.

Lesson #4: For Maximum Success, Focus Your Efforts Carefully

We can see that the Pareto Principle tells us that there are Pareto Leaders. It also tells us that there are Pareto Losers, those products or other types of efforts that generate the lowest returns. Success comes when we carefully focus our efforts on the Pareto Leaders and not on the Pareto Losers. It happens when we invest our resources where they can produce the highest return.

Apple Corporation has always followed this principle of focus. The company used to see Microsoft as its chief rival, but it soon found that its own suite of productivity software couldn't compete with Microsoft's Office suite. Its Mac Office division now partners with Microsoft to make sure that Office works smoothly on Macs and iPads. While the company continues to develop Apple TV, Tim Cook has called the project a 'hobby' and ruled out entering the television market because, he says, the unit volumes are too small. Apple can make more money by focusing its efforts on the iPhone. In a 2010 interview with *Business Insider*, Apple's then-COO Tim Cook summed up the company's approach:

> We are the most focused company that I know of or have read of or have any knowledge of. We say no to good ideas every day. We say no to great ideas in order to keep the amount of things we focus on very small in number so that we can put enormous energy behind the ones we do choose.

Since becoming CEO, Cook has continued that policy, building the company into the most valuable in the world based largely on the sales of a single product. In 2017, Apple made only 20 per cent of the world's smartphones, yet reaped 92 per cent of the industry profits. The other 999 companies making smartphones collectively only earned 8 per cent of the industry's profits. *What a waste of effort!* Clearly, for maximum success we should be focusing our efforts. But where should we focus them and how do we do it?

Lesson #5: Focus and—Defocus—Using Key Drivers and Key Draggers

A business can be driven to succeed, and it can be driven to fail. We've seen that the key driver of success in business is the Pareto Leader, the product or service that generates most of the company's positive results. And we've seen that the key dragger of success will be the Pareto Losers, which generate the poorest results.

Clearly, success depends on identifying and focusing on the key drivers of success. It also depends on removing focus from the key draggers of success. But that's not as straightforward as it sounds. A key driver isn't only defined by the amount of money a product or service returns. A hospital might make the most money out of its cosmetic surgery department, but its key driver of success may be the survival rate in its oncology unit or the length of waiting times for surgery. The first step in identifying key drivers of success is to first identify what success looks like in that particular context.

For example, I recently bought a new car. As I assessed the dozens of models on offer, I needed to understand which of the features was most important to me. What kind of car would represent a successful purchase? What should the key driver as I made my choice be, the one feature that would generate the largest amount of satisfaction? And which features could I safely ignore?

Maybe I could have chosen a sports car and enjoyed the speed and the impressed looks that people gave me. Maybe I could have chosen a car that feels great to drive and scores highly among driving enthusiasts. And maybe I could have chosen a jeep with a four-wheel drive and the ability to go off-road so that I could explore the countryside. But a fast car isn't very useful when I'm stuck behind a rickshaw. I'm also not interested in impressing anyone, and Ferraris are expensive. Nor do I drive myself very often, I certainly don't drive for pleasure in India and

I'm never going to drive off-road—the roads are bad enough. So, as I reviewed those particular key drivers, I weighed them, and gave them a low score. They might be important for someone else, but they didn't match my idea of a successful car purchase. I removed my focus from those features.

My key driver, I knew, was back-seat comfort, which I researched on intensively. Focusing on that one characteristic, and understanding why I was focusing on it, was critical to making a decision that brought the highest reward.

In the end, I chose a Skoda Superb. Is it 'superb'? It's fine for me. It matches my key drivers and turned out to be a successful purchase. Once you know the key drivers that will bring you your idea of success, you'll know where to focus.

Lesson #6: Focus by Using the Success Equation

The value of focus is that it massively increases the ability to get things done. The challenge is knowing where to apply that focus. When buying a car, the process is relatively simple. I could use my intuition to identify my own preference. When creating a business or building a career, the process is much harder. Apple might be able to look at its figures now and understand that it's primarily a phone company. But in June 2007, it was a computer company with no idea of the size of the opportunity it was about to capture. It wouldn't have known then how much it should focus on phone development, and how much it should focus on producing new Macs.

Every company faces the same challenges: which markets will produce the biggest returns? Which price points will generate the highest value? Which features will attract the most attention? Where should the company place its focus? If you are an employee, and you want to get ahead and progress into the ranks of management, you must answer the same kinds of questions: which opportunities can take me forward? What should I focus on for greatest success?

There is an equation that you can follow to identify the key drivers on which to focus:

Your Success = Opportunities + Resources + Action

To create your own Success Equation, begin by breaking down the key elements required to achieve success:

1. First, focus on the big Opportunities that can . . .
2. . . . attract the Resources required to fuel your efforts.
3. Finally, take the Action that turns those resources into success.

The first and most important element of the success equation is opportunities. Regardless of how much action and resources you pour into the success effort, if you are not pursuing an opportunity, those efforts will fail. But if you do have an opportunity—and remember that opportunities are free and available to everyone—you'll find that it attracts both the resources you need, and the team that will help you to take action.

Urban Ladder Shows How Opportunities Attract Resources

When you find an opportunity, you'll soon discover that people with resources want to capitalize on it. They may not want to build that opportunity themselves, but they will want to profit from it. As long as they think the opportunity has value—that it's not a nopportunity—and they believe that you have what it takes to make the most of it, you'll find that resources flow to you.

In 2012, Ashish Goel and his school friend Rajiv Srivatsa launched an online furniture and home decor store in Bangalore. Neither of them had a background in furnishings or household goods. Goel had worked for McKinsey, and had been the CEO of *Amar Chitra Katha*, a comic-book series. Srivatsa had previously worked with Cognizant and Yahoo! Within a month of the launch, they had raised a million dollars of seed funding. Two years later, they picked up another $5 million. Within four years of launch, venture capital funds had given them about $77 million, and Ratan Tata, Chairman Emeritus, Tata Sons, had come on board as an investor-mentor, adding his knowledge and experience to the funds.

Opportunities attract resources, and the better your opportunity, the easier those resources flow.

Lesson #7: Defocus by using the Failure Equation

Just as there is a success equation so there is a Failure Equation:

Your Failure = Nopportunities + Resources + Action

For the Tata Group, It's the Top Three or Bust

The Tata Group, India's largest and most globalized conglomerate, has an unwritten rule. If a company does not make it to the top three of the industry in which it operates within a reasonable period of time, the group divests its stake in that company and puts its time, resources and attention into a more profitable business.

In the early 1990s, Tata Oil Mills (TOMCO) was making severe losses despite having third-generation employees on its rolls. Its market share had fallen to less than 5 per cent. Ratan Tata, who had just taken over as Tata Group chairman, took the tough call of selling Tata Sons' stake in TOMCO to a competitor, Hindustan Unilever. Besides ensuring a fair deal for the shareholders, the acquisition ensured that no suppliers or employees of the acquired entity would be laid off or contracts severed for at least three years. The result was a win-win for the company and its key stakeholders.

Instead of focusing on opportunities that attract effort and resources, too often people leverage *nopportunities*. They focus on areas that waste effort and resources. Nopportunities are not opportunities—they're the opposite of opportunities. Instead of being gateways to success, they are trapdoors to failure. Instead of helping you to focus on the things that bring the best rewards, they suck up your time and your assets without generating meaningful returns. Instead of attracting resources, they waste resources. And instead of attracting talented people to work with you, they them drive away. The first and most important element of the Failure Equation is those nopportunities. It doesn't matter how hard you work, and how many resources you pour into your efforts, if you're pursuing a nopportunity, you will fail. In order to achieve success, you must identify opportunities. But you also have to be aware of nopportunities, whether it's an Apple TV,

Apple's TextEdit, or a Ferrari that does nothing but sit in traffic. You have to know what to avoid.

What all these lessons show is the central role of opportunity. When you identify and focus on the right opportunity, everything becomes possible—including new opportunities. Apple might be a mobile phone company but as sales of mobile devices stagnate, it's started focusing on services, an opening created by the success of the iPhone. In the last quarter of 2018, revenues from services such as iCloud, Apple Music, and the App Store reached $10 billion. The company may have found a whole new opportunity. That's what we'll explore in the next chapter.

Seven Lessons for Success

1. Success is the control of resources
Success has always been defined as the control of resources. There has always been inequality in the distribution of resources. The top 10 per cent control 90 per cent of the resources of the world.

2. The Pareto Principle explains where to focus your effort
Most effort is wasted. Only a small percentage of your efforts generate the most returns. Success depends on identifying the key drivers, the Pareto Leaders that show you where to focus. You should avoid the key draggers, the Pareto Losers that waste your time and resources. The Tata Group's decision to divest TOMCO would have been difficult. But why waste resources that could be put to better use in a more valuable opportunity?

3. Success and failure have equations
Success is the combination of opportunity with resources and effort. Failure is the combination of nopportunities with resources and effort. But when you start with an opportunity, everything flows. Resources come to you, and as long as you take action, you'll enjoy success like Syntel and Apple Inc.

3

The Opportunity Equation

What exactly is opportunity? How does the constant flow of change around us generate a steady series of opportunities? What do we need to do in order to use those opportunities? When is an innovation an opportunity?

Sunil Mittal is a billionaire. He's one of the twenty richest people in India, with a personal fortune that Forbes estimated at around Rs 47,000 crore.

He wasn't born with that money. No one turned up at his doorstep one day with a giant bag of cash that they didn't need. He earned it— and he earned it the same way every successful entrepreneur earns it: by finding something of value, taking action that adds more value, and selling it for a profit. He identified and used opportunities. He went through that process several times. Each time, he found and benefited from a bigger opportunity.

Mittal's first opportunity came at the age of eighteen when he borrowed Rs 20,000 from his father to start a small manufacturing business in his hometown of Ludhiana. At first, he made bicycle parts. Then he made yarn and stainless-steel sheets which he sold to bicycle manufacturers and factories. After four years, he sold the company and moved to Mumbai. He started importing brass, zips, plastics and more stainless steel, then crossed India by train to find buyers around the country. That was his second opportunity, and while neither allowed Mittal to grow rich, each gave him a living on his own terms.

Mittal was twenty-four years old and had been running his own businesses for six years when he met a salesman from Suzuki Motors, who was in India to promote the Japanese company's electric generators. In Japan, the generators were used to power the freezers in ice-cream vans but in India, which doesn't have ice-cream vans, the generators weren't selling.

Mittal believed that India, a country with frequent power outages, would be a good market for electric generators to keep shops and homes running during blackouts. He persuaded the salesman to appoint him the country's exclusive agent in India. Mittal knew that power supplies in India could be unpredictable. He used that knowledge to identify an opportunity, and he built that opportunity into a business.

Within two years, his company had offices in four cities and a distribution network across the country. The generators were selling well—so well, in fact, that New Delhi officials awarded licenses for the domestic manufacture of electric generators to two of India's largest industrial groups and banned the import of rival products.

Mittal's opportunity disappeared but he didn't give up; he went out and looked for a new one. At a trade fair in Taiwan he came across push-button telephones. Indians were still using obsolete rotary phones then, if they had a phone at all, and he was sure that they would snap up the new touch-tone phones quickly. He saw his next opportunity. He signed a contract with a Taiwanese supplier and obtained a license to assemble the phones in India. When the government licensed the local manufacture of touch-tone phones, Mittal expanded into fax machines, answering machines and cordless phones, beating the other fifty-one license-holders to become the company's largest phone manufacturer. Soon Mittal's company was generating annual sales of Rs 25 crore. He bought his family a new house and a luxury car.

In 1992, Mittal was able to spot the biggest opportunity of all, a true Pareto Leader. The Indian government started selling licenses to operate India's mobile phone networks. At the time, less than 1 per cent of India's population had access to phone lines. The potential market was enormous.

'This was the bet of a lifetime,' he told *Fortune* magazine in 2007.

Mittal won licenses to run the mobile phone networks in four cities. Legal challenges from rival companies pared that back to just one: Delhi. That turned out to be a stroke of luck. Mittal had estimated that his Airtel company would need $25 million to build the infrastructure it needed. He was off by a factor of four.

'People told me this was a business for companies with deep pockets,' he said to *Fortune*. 'Had we known how deep; we'd never have tried it. We begged, we borrowed, we stole, but we put the project together fast.'

He wasn't alone. Other companies had also underestimated the expenses and overpaid for the licenses. When they went bust, Airtel was ready to step in and pick up the pieces. Starting with only Rs 20,000, Sunil Mittal had leveraged a series of increasingly better opportunities to become a multibillionaire. His success was a result of the 'Opportunity Equation.'

What is the 'Opportunity Equation'?

In Chapter 2, I described the Success Equation:

Your Success = Opportunities + Resources + Action

You've already learned that:

1. **Opportunities are free of cost and freely available to everyone, including you.** Sunil Mittal paid nothing for the series of opportunities that eventually brought him riches.
2. **Opportunities attract resources.** Mittal didn't have all the funds he needed to fully implement the opportunity offered by the Delhi mobile-phone license. But the mammoth size of the opportunity attracted the funding he needed to build the business.
3. **Opportunities are the key element of the Success Equation.** Regardless of how much action and resources you pour into your success effort, if you are not pursuing an opportunity, you will fail. For the first few years, Mittal pursued openings that were closer to nopportunities than opportunities. His hard work produced little value. His success came when he identified better opportunities.

In this chapter, we will look closely at the nature of opportunities, and where you can find them.

An Opportunity Is a Valuable Adaptation to Change

What is an opportunity? Opportunities are more than ideas. Business ideas are common. Good business ideas are far rarer but they're still only ideas. Nor are opportunities merely openings in a market or customers who have been underserved. You can build a business in those spaces— at least until a competitor undercuts you or finds a way to work with smaller margins or costs. The bicycle parts that Sunil Mittal made and sold met a need that other suppliers were missing but they're not what made him a billionaire. An opportunity is so much more.

Your Opportunity Equation is:
Opportunity = Environmental Change + Valuable Adaptation

Things change. They change all the time, and that change is the only constant in our world. Nothing stays the same. We are born, we grow old, and we die, and during that process everything around us alters: technology, infrastructure, nature, our friends, our families, our opinions, our countries, our culture and our relationships. Nothing remains unaffected by time.

I grew up in the United States, in the city of Boston. By American standards, Boston is an old city: it was first settled in 1630 AD. But you don't have to go back that far to see just how much time has affected it—and continues to affect it. Some of the earliest video footage of the city dates to 1903. That's little more than a lifetime ago but looking at those videos is like peering into another world. There are no cars on the streets, only horses, wagons and electric trams. The men wear grey or black suits with ties and leather shoes. The women's dresses all reach below their ankles. There are no jeans or trainers, no T-shirts or miniskirts. No one wears casual attire at all. There are no fast-food outlets, cafes with baristas or stores selling SIM cards.

Compare that scene to the world today in which we carry computers in our pockets. Our world has been utterly transformed in the last 200 years, and the pace of change continues to accelerate. That change can be frightening. The world is full of people who want to stop the clock and push it back to a time that makes them feel more comfortable, a time they can understand. They resist change or they try to avoid it by pretending that it isn't happening. Some consultants try to allay that fear by telling business owners that they can help them manage change. I don't believe that you can manage change any more than you can herd cats or manage the monsoon. Change happens, and it happens in its own way. What you can do, though, is lead change and benefit from it. How? *By benefiting from the opportunities created by change.*

Environmental Change Creates New Opportunities

Relentless change can create a sense of discomfort. It also creates irrelevance. What was once useful and popular, a product on which it was possible to build a business, falls out of date. The process can take dozens of years or dozens of months. It applies to products but also to social practices and ideas. We see it most clearly in fashion.

In old video footage of Boston, everyone is wearing a hat. People in Europe and America had been wearing hats for hundreds of years before that old movie was made. Watch any American movie from before 1960 and whenever a man walks into a building, the first thing he does is take off his hat and hang it on a coat stand.

What Business Are You *Really* In?

As Henry Ford pioneered mass production of an affordable motorcar, one industry soon fell into trouble: buggy-whip manufacturers.

For a long time, they'd had a growth industry. You couldn't drive a carriage without a buggy whip. Transportation relied on horses and carts. As long as people and goods needed to move from A to B, drivers would need buggy whips to keep the carts moving.

When the motor car came along, buggy-whip manufacturers failed to adapt to the change. They went out of business.

But that didn't have to be the result. As a seminal article by Theodore Levitt published in the *Harvard Business Review* in 1960 pointed out, what the buggy manufacturers had failed to do was recognize that they weren't in the buggy-whip business. They were in the transportation parts business. If they had adapted to the change by making fan belts or air cleaners, the companies would have survived. They'd still be making parts for the transportation industry. They just wouldn't be making buggy whips that no one needed any more.

It's a challenge that plenty of other industries continue to face. How will the oil and gas industry adapt to an age of renewable energy? How will car manufacturers adapt to autonomous car technology? How will home-appliance makers adapt to the Internet of Things? Only those that understand—that their job is to serve customers, not make products, and adapt their service to the new opportunities—will survive. New businesses that spot those opportunities first will replace the rest.

Hats are useful. In the winter, they keep your head warm. In the summer, they shield you from the sun. But in the 1960s, the environment changed. As cars became more popular, people didn't need to wear hats when they travelled from place to place—and hats became a hindrance. The roofs in cars were too low to wear hats comfortably and there was nowhere to put them when you took them off. Buildings too became centrally heated so that people would move from a warm environment where they didn't need a hat to a small environment where they couldn't wear a hat. It was easier not to wear one at all. Hats were no longer relevant, and the fancy hat industry died, going the way of makers of buggy whips and slide rules. Change like that creates an opportunity for people who are sharp enough to spot it.

Leominster, Massachusetts, had been America's comb capital since before the Revolutionary War. In the late nineteenth century, the city had dozens of companies churning out thousands of combs every year, using the new material of celluloid. As long as women had long hair and didn't want to look a mess, the comb factories had customers. It took just one woman to almost entirely destroy the industry. In 1914, Irene Castle, a ballroom dancer who had become a star of the new movie industry, decided to cut her hair short. Her bob spread across the country. With short hair, women had less need for Leominster's combs. It didn't take long before half the comb factories along the Monoosnoc Brook and Nashua River were out of business.

One factory owner though saw an opportunity in that changing fashion. Sam Foster, owner of Foster Grant, told his employees that if they couldn't make combs, they'd make something else. The new hairstyle, he realized, exposed women's faces more clearly and created a new canvas that could be decorated with accessories. He started making celluloid sunglasses, and paid movie stars to be photographed wearing them. The glasses took off. By 1937, 20 million pairs of sunglasses were being sold in the US every year, most of them to people who were more interested in looking like movie stars than being able to see in the sun.

Leveraging new opportunities requires you to embrace change instead of being scared by it, hiding from it, or hoping it will all go away. Most of the comb-makers of Leominster tried to ride out the change, hoping that long hair would come back into fashion and they could go back to making their combs. Their choice made them victims. Only Sam Foster saw that the change had created a whole new opportunity and acted on it. He saw the new challenge in his environment as an opportunity rather than a pain point. He led the change and benefited from it. His company is still a powerful sunglasses brand a century later.

In the 1980s, I went to business school with a guy whose parents were both heavy smokers and had died of lung cancer. As a result, he was an anti-smoking zealot. He wanted to open the first bar that would not allow smoking. At the time, this seemed like a completely crazy idea. A bar that didn't permit smoking? Who would go there? But within a short time, things changed. Within twenty years, virtually every bar in America, as well as India, was smoke free. The idea that you could smoke in a bar—or any other public place—began to feel crazy. This is a powerful example of environmental change.

Irrelevance is one of the most powerful forces that creates opportunity. In with the new, out with the old. People need relevant products, services and ideas. People will gladly pay for them, and you can provide them—if they're also relevant to you. Sunil Mittal followed the same path. He saw that mobile phones would make landlines irrelevant. He jumped on the opportunities this change offered, led the process of change, and reaped the benefits.

Anyone can do what Mittal did, including *you*. Changes in your environment can truly change your life and take you from rags to riches.

Don't Fear Change, Adapt to It

An *adaptation* is a modification that helps us to fit in better with a changed environment. The key driver of human success is our unique ability to *consciously adapt* to changes in our environment.

Our environment is never static. It is in a constant state of change that has gone on relentlessly for billions of years. Ours is not the only era in which climate change is a hot topic. Did you know that only 10,000 years ago most of modern-day Europe and North America were covered in glaciers? The only constant is change. Some things in our environment change quickly, such as prices and fashions. Others change so slowly that any changes cannot be measured in thousands of generations, such as laws of physics. In order to survive in the constantly changing environment, all living things either adapt or die. The process of adaptation to the ever-changing environment is called *evolution*. The rule is: adapt or perish. Only the organisms that fit in best with their environment survive and thrive.

Plants and animals adapt to their environments through a process called *natural selection*. Mother Nature selects certain features in animals and changes them to adapt to the environment. A good example is giraffes. Why do they have long necks? Natural selection. Millennia ago, the ancestors of giraffes would have had shorter necks which was all they needed to eat the leaves on their favourite trees. Those trees whose leaves were higher than others had a better chance of not being eaten. They were able to drop their seeds and spread across the land. As more tall trees survived and the leaves rose higher, giraffes with longer necks were able to eat more and had a better chance of surviving long enough to breed. Both giraffes and trees adapted to their constantly changing environment.

While natural selection is a process, it is not a conscious process. The giraffes never got together for a conference to decide what to do about those higher trees. They didn't need to. The process happened naturally.

The key driver of human success is our unique ability to *consciously adapt* to the changes in our environment. We don't have to wait for Mother Nature to do the job for us. We can see the change happening around us. We can predict where it's going to go. And we can identify the opportunities those changes create.

That's the difference between evolution and adaptation. Evolution is an unconscious process of natural selection in which an organism changes in line with the environment. The change is unconscious and unplanned. Adaptation is a conscious, human process in which we use our intelligence to make use of the power of change. The result is that over the last 2,00,000 years, human beings have progressively taken control of the environment and its resources to become by far the dominant species.

'It is not the strongest of the species that survive, nor the most intelligent,' wrote Charles Darwin, 'but the one most responsive to change.'

Nature practises natural selection. We humans are capable of adaptation. As an example of adaptation, consider how Chinese food has been adapted to fit the palates of every country. In India it's very saucy and spicy (*Chinjabi* style) but in Italy it is very bland and served in separate courses, just like Italian food. When I went to China, I didn't like the food, as it was so different from the versions I had eaten elsewhere. I complained to my wife: 'This isn't Chinese food!'

Humans are also capable of practising artificial selection. We breed animals so that they display certain traits. We select and grow seeds to achieve predetermined goals. Between 1925 and 2005, selective breeding reduced the time required to raise a chicken to a weight of 1.5 kg from 120 days to just thirty days.

Scientists bombard wheat grains with thermal neutrons, X-rays, and ethyl methanesulphonate to change their DNA and produce new mutant cereals with higher yields. When Norman Borlaug arrived in India in 1965, the country was at war with Pakistan and on the brink of famine. The selectively bred wheat seeds that he brought with him produced yields that were up to five times higher than that of local seeds. Borlaug received the Nobel Peace Prize and India hasn't faced a famine since. Humans don't just consciously adapt to the environment. We also change the environment itself. Natural selection is for the birds.

What Are the Key Drivers of Adaptation?

Why are humans able to harvest opportunities by consciously adapting to their environments, while all other creatures cannot? Because we are much better at *learning*. Learning is the key driver of human adaptation. Our ability to learn better is the single most important factor contributing to human adaptation and success. Other animals can learn to a limited extent. You may be able to teach your dog to do any number of cute tricks. But Fido can't share his learning with other dogs. He can't set up his own Doggie Cute Trick Training Academy, and pass on his wealth of expertise to future generations of the Fido clan. With animals, all learning is individual, and when they die, it is all lost. Humans are stupendous rapid adaptation machines because of our mastery of the 4 Cs of learning:

- **We learn Continuously.** We learn from the day we are born to the day we die.
- **We learn Consciously.** We can choose what subjects to learn and dive deeply into the topic.
- **We learn Collectively.** We share our knowledge with each other and learn faster by learning together.
- **We learn Cumulatively.** We build knowledge, making ourselves smarter all the time.

The 4Cs of learning are powered by these key drivers: *symbolic language* lets us communicate knowledge about different times, about emotions and about ideas. A monkey might scream to the pack that a panther is approaching. But only human symbolic language can say: 'The black panther who ate your brother last week is approaching and he looks hungry. Run away.' Our complex language skills enable us to better share what we've learned.

We are capable of *imaginative thinking*. We can think up entirely new things that have absolutely no place in nature, such as governments and countries. To make these function properly, we invent imaginary new rules and processes, such as laws and judicial systems, and we build stories around them in which we all play a part. A farmer near Chandigarh has little in common with a technology worker in Bengaluru, but both can imagine themselves as part of the story of India, a concept that allows them to work together for a shared goal. We can even analyse the past and imagine the future. Animals have no conception of the future.

When my son was born, I was amazed by how astoundingly ignorant he was. His mind was like an empty vessel waiting to be filled. Infants can't do anything but eat, sleep, cry and poop. My son had to literally learn everything from scratch. Many people believe that learning is something that is only done at school, in a classroom, with regular examinations. Do babies think like that? They have no idea what a classroom is. Their whole world is their classroom. Babies manage to learn even when they don't have a language to think with. But even without the use of language, they learn astoundingly fast. How do they do it? By using their five senses to consciously observe their environments.

How do babies learn by observing? They learn by *pattern recognition*. They notice that some reoccurring patterns are more important than others. A recurring pattern could be something as simple as a name. When my son Nicholas was a baby, he started to call me 'la'. My wife and I wondered why. Then we realized that 'la' was short for *bubula*, which is a Jewish endearment meaning 'darling' that my wife and I call each other. As my son got older, he gradually switched from 'la' to 'bubula'.

Another example of pattern recognition: when Nicholas was a bit older, he started to learn to crawl. At first, he couldn't figure out how to crawl forwards. He could only crawl backwards and kept getting stuck under the sofa, which was quite amusing. I realized that since no one else in the house was crawling, he had no pattern to follow. So, I got on the floor and crawled forward to show him, and by copying me he quickly learned to go forward.

The ability to recognize useful patterns allows us to learn increasingly complex *processes*, so that we can quickly progress from crawling, to walking, to running, and then eventually to running companies. Processes are interlinked sets of patterns featuring hierarchies, such as from higher to lower, or from general to specific. If learning is all about patterns, applying learning is all about processes.

As an example of hierarchy from higher to lower, and from general to specific:

Level 1: Conscious adaptation to the environment is a key driver of success.
Level 2: Learning is a key driver of conscious adaptation.
Level 3: Pattern recognition is a key driver of learning.
Level 4: Conscious observation is a key driver of pattern recognition.

We create hierarchical patterns of all types—even patterns of time, such as days, weeks, years and centuries. We extract lessons from these patterns. These lessons often dramatically improve our efficiency of learning and speed of decision making. Scientists have discovered that *intuition* is simply rapid and unconscious pattern recognition. The more often we repeat certain patterns, the more mastery we attain, and the quicker we can make certain decisions without conscious thought. A good example is driving. If you've already driven for thousands of hours, do you really need to think about when to check your mirrors?

Adaptation Beats Innovation

Adaptation is not the same as innovation. An innovation is something new or different.

Sunil Mittal didn't need to innovate when he built Delhi's first wireless network. He has never developed any new technology. He simply introduced existing technology to an India that could benefit from it, then innovated a new business model to extract more from that opportunity. Innovation is overhyped. Sure, it's built the fortunes of a few large companies, but patent offices are filled with innovative ideas that have never gone anywhere. Unless an innovation is also a valuable adaptation to a changing environment, it is not an opportunity. It is a nopportunity, a waste of time and resources. A study by Detecon Global Innovation Center in 2013 found that out of 3000 innovative ideas surveyed, just one produced success.

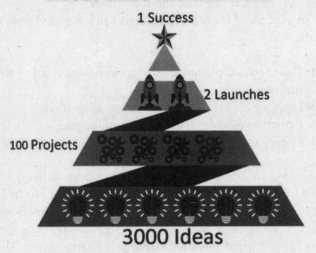

Most Innovations Fail

1 Success

2 Launches

100 Projects

3000 Ideas

New Project Failure Rate

When Google released its search engine, the technology wasn't just innovative. It was also an adaptation to a change in the knowledge environment. The growing Internet was making all knowledge available online. Sergei Brin and Larry Page were offering a way to find the specific knowledge a user wanted. That was an adaptation. When the company released its Google Plus social media network, it again offered innovative technology. Its Circles feature did a better job of organizing data and content than Facebook's lists did. But it didn't offer an adaptation to a change in the social media environment. It simply tried to give users a different way of doing the same thing they were already doing. That's not enough. It was a nopportunity, and it failed. (A social media firm that can offer an adaption to the changing interest in social media privacy, on the other hand, would have an opportunity.)

How Airtel Shows the Difference between Innovation and Opportunity

Innovation is not the same as opportunity. Opportunity is a valuable adaptation to change. Innovation is one form that adaptation may take.

When Sunil Mittal created a mobile network in Delhi, that was an opportunity. A new technology had changed the domain in which the city was operating. Whoever could make the most of that change by enabling customers to use mobile phones would make a lot of money.

But the way Mittal built his network was *innovative*. In 2004, he sold Airtel's entire network to Ericsson, Siemens and Nokia for $400 million. He then rented the network back, paying a fee based on service quality and customer flow. He also signed a ten-year contract worth $750 million with IBM, making the US firm responsible for Bharti's customer billing and account management.

At a time when Indian firms were supplying back-office services to US and European companies, Mittal reversed the model. Now, it was US and European companies supplying services to an Indian company. Mittal's reasoning was that he owned the network but not the technology. Airtel didn't make the technology and couldn't repair or upgrade it. He was better off renting it. That was an innovative solution to a problem in a valuable adaptation to change.

Valuable adaptations to changing environments are opportunities—and they can be very lucrative opportunities. Because all opportunities are free, it doesn't matter how small you are when you start. They're freely available to you and to everyone else.

You must focus your efforts. By using a systematic opportunity process, you can learn how to focus only on the biggest and the best opportunities—and there's never been a better time to do it.

In the next chapter, we'll look at the three eras of opportunity and explain why this is the best time to identify and use an opportunity.

The Opportunity Equation

1. An opportunity is a valuable adaptation to change
The world changes constantly. The products and services that allow us to adapt to those changes are opportunities. They might take the form of the implementation of new technologies, or a change in the environment that requires new forms of behaviour. But change doesn't stop so companies have to continuously understand the opportunity they're building and continue to adapt. Industries that don't, like buggy-whip manufacturers, don't survive.

2. Learning is the key driver of human adaptation
Learning enables humans to adapt and succeed. Effective learning has 4Cs: we learn Continuously; we learn Consciously; we learn Collectively; and we learn Cumulatively. We're also able to communicate what we learn and imagine what others know. That growth in knowledge and understanding ensures that we can see, evaluate and implement opportunities.

3. Adaptation beats innovation
Innovation is overhyped these days. Adaptation is not the same as an innovation. An innovation is something new or different. Unless an innovation is also a valuable adaptation to a changing environment, it is not an opportunity. It is a nopportunity, a waste of time and resources.

Part II: How Opportunity Works

4

The Age of Opportunity

Why are we living in a golden age of opportunity? How does an understanding of the patterns of history help us find the best opportunities? Why is an understanding of rules and norms crucial for achieving success? What is True Vision and how can it help us to see the future? Why is India the world's greatest land of opportunity?

Opportunity is not just a free resource. *It's also an endlessly renewable resource.* As long as the world changes, there will always be new opportunities and endless ways to use them. History creates opportunity—and one way it creates that opportunity is by changing the rules. Each historical period has its own *rules*, and they determine your ability to see and use opportunities.

Rules aren't just what you can and cannot do. They're about how, when, why and where you do it. Rules govern human action, and there are as many kinds of rules as there are grains of sand on the earth. Only if you understand history can you understand the rules that surround you and why they came about.

There have been three distinct eras of human history, each very different from the one that preceded it, with drastically different rules of opportunity. Currently, virtually all people in developed countries such as the United States live in the third and modern era of human history, which I call the *Now Era*. India, on the other hand, is a mixed country. Although much of urban India lives in the Now Era, a large percentage of Indians, particularly those engaged in subsistence agriculture, still live by the rules of centuries past. Because Indians live in different eras at the same time, it is important to understand the key drivers of each era. They have a very powerful influence on opportunity.

In this chapter, we're going to take a historical view, and assess why we are now living in a golden age of opportunity. We'll then explore the rules that both create opportunities and that prevent us from seeing them.

The Age of Exploitation

The earliest period of human history is also the longest. According to the fossil record, Homo sapiens first emerged in East Africa about 2,50,000 years ago. For most of the time that followed, in what is known as the Palaeolithic period, we were hunters and gatherers. There were no villages, towns or permanent settlements. Humans lived in small kinship groups of no more than fifty people who were always on the move in search of food. During this period, knowledge spread slowly. Small groups of humans seldom met. Writing hadn't been invented so little learning was passed from one generation to the next. This was an era defined by exploitation. As plants to pick and animals to kill ran out in one particular place, the small tribes would pack up and move elsewhere. The earth is large enough and human population was small enough for exploitation to be an effective strategy. Humans became so adept at exploitation that they wiped out thousands of species of animals during this era.

In less than a quarter of a million years, humans had managed to spread across virtually the entire planet. Because each small tribe lived off the land and required so much territory to survive, as little as 10,000 years ago there were only between 5–6 million humans. Little changed in that period so there were also fewer opportunities. When change did come though, it changed everything.

The Age of Extortion

The change that created the next era in human history was environmental. The ice age that had kept much of the planet frozen ended. As a period of warmer weather began, parts of the earth that had once been icy wastelands became more habitable. Areas that had always been habitable became ideal. River valleys, such as the area between the Tigris and Euphrates in modern Iraq, became places of abundance filled with freshwater, plants and animal life. Humans started to adapt to that change. They took opportunities that the change created. They learned how to cultivate plants and domesticate animals, and taught others to do the same. As sedentary populations grew, they also learned to collaborate beyond the family group to create infrastructure, such as irrigation networks and fortifications that benefited everyone.

Agriculture allowed humans to generate between twenty and thirty times more resources from the same amount of land than they had been able to produce from foraging. For the first time people were able to accumulate excess resources that could be collected and stored. Writing developed, initially to track and control these resources, and later to record history and lay down stories around which communities could unite in a shared identity. Within no more than 5000 years, human population jumped from 6 million to around 50 million. About 5000 years ago, the first cities and the first city states appeared. The creation and management of those larger communities also created a need for formal leadership and led to the development of institutionalized power—and the exercise of that power. As historian John Coatsworth wrote:

> For the first time there appeared on earth kings, dictators, high priests, prime ministers, presidents, governors, mayors, general, admirals, police chiefs, judges, lawyers, and jailers, along with dungeons, jails, penitentiaries, and concentration camps . . . Civilization stunted growth, spread disease, shortened life spans, and set people to killing and maiming each other on an unprecedented scale.

This was a violent age. The TV show *Game of Thrones* is based on the rules of this era. The rulers of those early cities were little different from modern gang leaders. Power flowed from above and according to a strict hierarchy. New rulers were chosen based on family lineage, not merit, or changed through force. Rulers didn't farm. Instead they extorted resources through coercion. Human labour grew crops, and the rulers took some of those crops at sword point in return for protection—both from themselves and from neighbouring gangs. The nobility was divinely ordained by a new class of priests who claimed to be intermediaries to the gods. At the same time, some people adapted to a new environment of excess resources by forming a merchant class. Unlike their rulers, merchants lacked the power to generate wealth by force; instead, they had to use finesse. They bought goods from producers and delivered them to people who didn't produce, in return for a fee. Competition between those buyers and sellers meant that they had to constantly find new ways, new products, and new markets to buy and sell as efficiently and cheaply as possible. To survive and prosper, they had to start looking for opportunities.

As rulers learned to manage larger and larger territories, cities grew into states. Powerful states conquered neighbouring states and created empires, like those of Persia and Rome. Wealth primarily increased not by productive activity and innovative adaptations, but by extorting tribute from outlying or neighbouring countries. If weaker tribes refused to pay tribute, it was entirely acceptable to attack and plunder their resources and sell entire populations into slavery. The ruling class lived by its own set of rules, everyone else was fair game. Might was right, and it was believed that God willed it.

Why was extortion the primary mode of opportunity in this era? Because growth was so slow, rulers saw little point in investing in business activities that might take generations to pay a profit. A successful war could generate wealth much more quickly than building a road and extracting a toll. Tribute-taking elites had little interest in how goods were produced and traded. It made more sense to simply invade and take away someone else's wealth, or to extort more from your own powerless peasants. Life was viewed as a zero-sum game. I win, you lose. Farmers too had little incentive to adapt to the changing environment to create new resources because those resources could be seized by rulers or invaders at any time. The only route of opportunity in this era was through loyalty and service to the ruling class as an artisan, a merchant, a bureaucrat, a soldier or a priest.

The Age of Opportunity

It took hundreds of thousands of years for foragers to spread around the world. It took about 10,000 years for farmers to spread their ideas. Since 1800, it has taken just 200 years for the Industrial Revolution to create a very different world, much to the betterment of humankind. We live in a world of unprecedented prosperity. For the first time in history, productivity has grown faster than the population: between the years 1900 and 2000, global production increased by a factor of twelve, while the world's population grew by only a factor of four. And this trend is accelerating. The old cycles of feast and famine are largely a relic of the past. According to the World Bank, more than a billion people lifted themselves out of extreme poverty over the last twenty-five years alone, and the global poverty rate is now lower than it has ever been in recorded history.

We also live in a world of unprecedented freedom. In 1863, when Abraham Lincoln described the United States as 'government of the people, by the people and for the people', it was the only democracy on earth. Today, most of the world has embraced liberty. And India is the world's largest democracy. Bottom-up or distributed networks are gradually replacing top-down rule everywhere. The Democracy Index, a rating of the state of democracy in 167 countries, now lists seventy-five countries as full or flawed democracies. The coercive methods that characterized the Age of Extortion are now considered to be criminal. International courts try to bring despots to justice and those despots pay at least lip service to ideas of democracy and freedom. The rules have changed.

We live in a world of unprecedented commerce and exchange. The discovery of the Americas and the opening of world travel since the sixteenth century has stimulated commerce, capitalism and collective learning by expanding the scale, speed and intensity of entrepreneurial activity and the exchange of information, goods and people. Adaptations of the twentieth century such as the Internet and mobile phones have made that information exchange instantaneous worldwide.

Most importantly, *we live in a world of unprecedented opportunity*. Long-standing barriers to personal and group opportunity based on class or caste, nationality or race, sex or sexual preference have steadily been eliminated. The main driver of personal opportunity has shifted from lineage to merit. Sure, it's still easier to get ahead if a fortunate birth starts you further down the road—if you're what Warren Buffett has called a member of 'The Lucky Sperm Club'. But anyone can now travel along those roads and make use of the opportunities that will power their journey, while not everyone who starts ahead stays ahead. Most countries have a variation of the saying 'Shirtsleeves to shirtsleeves in three generations'. It might not be entirely accurate but without ability and action, luck can only take you so far. Today's rule is that merit and talent beat luck and lineage.

In the Age of Extortion, it was nearly impossible for those without pedigree to attract resources. There would have been no channel through which a Ramesh Babu or a Steve Jobs would have been able to attract the resources they needed to turn an opportunity into a valuable service. In the Now Era, the dominant group is no longer an extorting ruling class. Instead, it's made up of entrepreneurs who have built their wealth by trading efficiently in open and competitive markets. The coercive empires of the past have been replaced by business empires with interests across the globe. The people of this era are largely wage earners who have to work hard and efficiently to market their labour. Businesses and employees that are the most productive have an edge in this era, a development that encourages constant adaptation. Scientific and industrial organizations pay huge sums to find innovations that will improve their productivity. Anyone who can create a valuable adaptation to change can reap the rewards—and in a world that's more connected than ever, those rewards are almost boundless. The potential for growth is limitless.

The Transition to the Rules of the Modern Era

In 1750, India and China were the richest countries, with the largest populations. They accounted for almost 60 per cent of global production, while Britain and the US accounted for only 2 per cent. At that time wealth was mainly produced by ownership of land and in most countries of the world, 90 per cent of people were peasants. One can understand why the rulers of those countries would have refused to embrace modernity when their business models were so dominant and effective.

But the trend was not their friend. The power of ancient tribute-taking empires based on agriculture rapidly evaporated. In the Old Era, power gave you wealth. In the Now Era, wealth gives you power. By 1950, the US and the UK produced 53 per cent of global output, and India and China a mere 4 per cent. Between 1913 and 1992, the gap between average income levels in the poorest and wealthiest countries grew from 11:1 to 72:1. But from the mid twentieth century, the tide started to turn once more.

Unfortunately, history is still studied using a methodology based on Old Era rules of power rather than on Now Era rules of opportunity. We read about rulers and countries and other political power formations as if these are still the main drivers of change and adaption in the world. They are no longer. We must study history with the methodology and rules that help expose opportunities rather than cover them up. The nations that benefited from modernity the fastest and most successfully did so because they rapidly adapted the Key Drivers (or General Rules) of the Now Era, and gradually discarded the obsolete rules of the Old Era. In practice, the interplay between old and new trends represents a tug of war. The shift from Old Era rules to Now Era rules has been gradual, and most countries in the world—including India—still operate under mixed rules.

To understand the rules of the Old Era, consider how gangsters operate today. They use intimidation to control territories, murdering both their customers and competitors. Loyalty to the gang is the key principle, and any rules of fair play exist only within the gang. No wonder it was considered perfectly acceptable to subjugate foreign lands for economic gain, even to the point of selling their populations into slavery. In the Now Era, this type of behaviour is considered to be highly criminal.

Once the Now Era began around 1800, the tug of war between old and new rules began to play out in the countries that were most adaptive to change. While the US and European countries moved quickly to adapt to capitalism and free markets at home, abroad they played by the old rules, best exemplified by the practice of imperialism. For example, in nineteenth-century Britain, liberal governments gradually increased the voting franchise, and allowed free markets to operate in a laissez-faire system. Yet at the same time, Britain used its enhanced wealth to build and operate a global network of colonies, run under Old Era rules, featuring exploitation of resources, authoritarian governments, and denial of opportunity based on race and nationality. Britain subjugated and exploited India and several other colonies in this way until the 1950s. Other European countries like Portugal, Spain and France did the same in South America, Southeast Asia and Africa.

In the Now Era, the increasing inequality of resource allocation provoked efforts to even out the distribution through coercive means. Although they pretended to be modern, the communist regimes that emerged in the twentieth century were fundamentally reactionary. Communism sought to replace the old ruling elite of kings and the newer ruling elite of capitalists with a better elite: 'the dictatorship of the proletariat'. The result was the creation of the most coercive and tyrannical gangster regimes in history. The individualism and opportunity of free markets was replaced by total obedience to the will of the state. Human selfishness and ambition could only be supressed through terror. Hard-core communist countries such as the Soviet Union utterly failed to adapt and compete against capitalist economies, and have deservedly fallen into the dustbin of history. China's rapid growth over the last three decades has been a result of its abandonment of communist economics and its adoption of a mixed system of free enterprise and state-supported capitalist businesses.

What Are the Patterns of History, and How Should You See Them?

Many people write off history as a boring study of the dead past. To some extent, they are right. That's because most history taught in schools is *political history*. Does it really matter who served as British prime minister in 1922, or why the Labour Party replaced the Liberals as a permanent party of government?

Many such stories of history are certainly cures for insomnia. On the other hand, the lessons you can learn from the *patterns of history* can be extremely useful. For history is above all the story of *change, and change is the mother of all opportunities.* Depending on how you focus, the patterns of history can describe the *dynamics of change* that are relevant to you. These can help you to see and understand your environment, which is the source of all opportunities, much more clearly. All history follows patterns. For example, your own environment can be divided into *levels* based on *time*, such as the one following:

Levels of History

You might ask: how is this MY environment? I'm not 13.7 billion years old! Yet in some sense you are:

- Since you live in the universe, you are influenced by the patterns of the history of the universe.
- Since you live on earth, you are influenced by the patterns of the history of the earth.
- Since you are a member of humanity, you are influenced by the patterns of the history of humanity.
- Since you live in the Now Era, you are influenced by the patterns of the history of the Now Era.
- Since you are alive, you are influenced by the patterns of the history of your own life. (That is quite obvious!)

Some of these patterns are clearly very long. Yet regardless of its length, every level of history exerts an influence over your past, present and future.

Each level of the environment is influenced by the level above it. Why? *Because long-term patterns that began in the past continue onward into the present.* As most of the patterns are enduring, they continue into the future as well. With the longest patterns, there is change, but it is very slow. The universe is always expanding, but you won't notice it. Yes, the sun will burn hydrogen and continue to shine tomorrow, and for a few billion more years. Humans will still populate most of the planet, but their numbers and ways of living will change. As the patterns shorten, the pace of change picks up a bit, but is still slow. The Now Era that began about 250 years ago with the Industrial Revolution will carry on. Your body will very likely continue to breathe. *As you move downward*, environmental change moves at a faster pace. Changes at every level have influence over you, but the lower levels have more influence.

As your own history comes closer to ground level, the rate of change speeds up, and it becomes much harder to accurately predict anything. Yes, the stock market will probably be open tomorrow. But will the price of HDFC Bank stock go up? If so, by how much? *That even Warren Buffet doesn't know.* By understanding the dynamics of enduring patterns of history, you can not only see the past and present clearly *but also make the most realistic estimates of the future, allowing you to uncover rich opportunities.* How do you do this? By learning and influencing the rules.

Can You Predict the Future like Psychic Donna?

Lately, when trying to listen to music on my phone, I'm confronted with a YouTube ad for Psychic Donna. A woman comes on and says: 'I caught my boyfriend cheating on me, and that's when I decided to see Psychic Donna.' Psychic Donna solves the woman's problems by looking into the future: she advises her to dump the scoundrel because it's clear to her that he will never stop philandering.

Fortunately, all of us can see the future just like Psychic Donna. A crystal ball is not required. It's just a matter of pattern recognition. If your boyfriend is cheating now, he's probably done it in the past, and will likely do it in the future. It's the set of rules that the scoundrel lives by. Virtually all our learning is done through pattern recognition. Dominant patterns can be quite durable, but can eventually be challenged or disappear completely. For example, the influence of the rules of Christianity over the minds, hearts and politics of much of the world has lasted for almost two millennia but has dramatically lessened in the last 200 years.

We use rules to govern and guide our thoughts and behaviour. Without rules, we'd be lost. The two major categories of rules are: 1) rules about how to believe and think; and 2) rules about how to behave. Some rules are so predictable that we think that they will never change. For example, if I stand up and put one foot in front of the other, I will start walking. That's a rule of physiology that applies to everyone and is unlikely to change anytime soon. Starting from infancy, we constantly learn rules. Open almost any children's book. What does it teach? Rules. *Don't talk to strangers. Brush your teeth.* Open any textbook. What is it full of? *Lists of rules.* Studying dentistry? Your textbook is sure to include something like *the eight most important elements to good dental hygiene*, as well as numerous other lists of rules.

Don't Mess with Mother Nature

The most predictable rules are those of nature, as described by the sciences of physics, chemistry and biology. Some rules, such as the law of gravity, apply to the entire universe. You may be vehemently opposed to the law of gravity and determined not to follow it come what may. Yet if you climb up a tree and jump, you will still fall to the ground, regardless of what you believe. That's because gravity is a *natural law*. Breaking or changing rules that are natural laws, such as gravity, is impossible. Don't bother trying!

In contrast, the vast majority of the rules that humans follow are not natural laws. All these rules have been invented by humans, and their continuing existence is based purely on our belief that past patterns of behaviour will continue to recur in the future. *That means that most rules are not set in stone.* Many rules are based on beliefs that are not necessarily true or have ceased to be true over time. All these rules can change, or completely disappear. Most rules are informal, and not written down. Sometimes you don't even realize that informal rules exist, even though they often govern almost everyone's daily behaviour. For example, whenever we meet strangers, we generally follow certain rules. We ask 'How do you do?' In India, it is a 'namaste' with folded hands. When others visit our home or office, we feel compelled to offer them something to drink. Indian culture emphasizes 'Guest is God'! All communities follow common rules of behaviour. They're not laws, and they're not written down, but they are rules, nonetheless. People who don't follow informal rules are considered to be strange, or just plain rude.

The *higher-level—or general—rules* followed by many people can also be known as *rules of thumb*. For the sake of simplicity, let's call them *norms*. In every situation, at every level of the hierarchy, there is always a *dominant rule*. This is the *Pareto Leader*, the rule which dominates the middle of the normal distribution and is so widely believed in and followed that it is the default choice, the norm. For example, shaking hands with people when you meet them. *Norms* are followed everywhere in our world, our country, our culture, our business, our family, and in our lives, *as if they were laws of nature*. No one in particular has made these rules, but most people follow them, because they are based on durable patterns of history.

In general, attempting to break or change high-level human made norms is also a difficult task. Regardless of how good your opportunity might seem, if it violates a high-level norm you could face serious opposition. For example, most sophisticated investors, such as Warren Buffett, believe that over the long run, equity has a higher return than debt. Is it true? Yes, most of the time, but not always. It's a norm of the Now Era. Let's say you want to invest Rs 1 lakh and are fortunate enough to be able to ask Warren Buffett for advice. He might guide you using these norms. He would probably advise you that *asset allocation* is a *key driver* of investment success. This is a widely believed general rule of investing. Why is it believed? Because based on *past patterns* it has generally held true. As the rule is still considered to be valid, this pattern is expected to continue into the future.

Norms simplify our lives. If we had to think about the best course of action in every situation, we'd never accomplish anything. By following norms, we are able to make most decisions without much thought, allowing us to focus on what's important. *But relying on norms can be dangerous and can limit our access to opportunities. It's when we can see beyond them that we can often find opportunities.*

In 1989, Jack Welch, then head of General Electric (GE), came to India to persuade the country to buy his company's aircraft engines. He met with Sam Pitroda, a technology adviser to India's then prime minister, Rajiv Gandhi, and laid out his pitch. According to *The Coalition of Competitors*, a book by Kiran Karnik, the former president of India's National Association of Software and Services Companies, Pitroda listened, and then made his counter-offer.

'Fine,' he said, 'But first we want you to outsource $10 million of IT software work to India.'

Jack Welch was surprised. India wasn't known for its IT service work. It was a place for cheap manufacturing and textiles. But he agreed.

GE became the first US company to outsource software work to India, and created an entirely new norm that powered a new industry led by IT bellwethers like Tata Consultancy Services, Infosys and Wipro.

Treating norms as if they are fixed laws of nature can close our mind to learning. It can make us less adaptive, too stuck in our ways to make needed changes. Old norms at every level are often challenged by new, emerging norms. For example, I once had a client in an industry in which all leading players believe that the key driver of customer satisfaction is low prices, rather than high quality. This is obviously not a natural law, although everyone in the industry treats it as if it is. When I suggested to industry players that this norm might no longer be true, they simply refused to believe me, even though my insight was based on firm evidence. (Fortunately, my client was more open-minded, perhaps because he had paid me!)

What Does It Mean to Be a Visionary?

Patterns of change that occur and recur in somewhat predictable patterns are called *cycles*. Are you familiar with the business cycles of boom and bust? An economic expansion is almost always followed by a recession. That's a norm. The length or intensity of either end of a cycle is not entirely predictable, but we know that the cycle pattern itself is very likely to continue. When asked what the share market would do, the American financier J.P. Morgan famously replied: *'It will fluctuate.'* Technical analysts try to decipher the patterns of markets in order to predict their future trends. *Trends* measure the short-term speed and direction of patterns, cycles and rules.

People often make the common mistake of believing that a short-term fluctuation will continue indefinitely into the long term. For example, in September 2008, the world's financial system crashed. The cause was sub-prime lending. Banks in the United States had been lending money to people with poor credit records who couldn't pay the money back. Fifteen banks in the United States collapsed, including the 158-year-old Lehman Brothers, America's fourth-largest investment bank. Markets crashed around the world. The S&P 500 fell 20 per cent. The Dow Jones fell 18 per cent in five days and over the next seventeen months would fall 54 per cent from its previous peak. The Bank of England's deputy governor was quoted describing the downturn as 'possibly the largest financial crisis of its kind in human history'. Millions of stock market investors sold at the bottom of the market, thinking that the sky was finally falling in. These investors disregarded the fact that the long-term trend pattern of stock markets is cyclical. Every severe downturn is followed by a recovery that exceeds its previous high. This is exactly what happened in the decade following the market meltdown. Today the Dow stands at over 26,000, twice as high as its pre-crash peak.

Few people have accumulated wealth more successfully than Warren Buffett. He is considered by many to be the greatest investor in history. Some people would call him a *visionary*. Many people wrongly believe that *vision* means the ability to accurately see the future. That is nonsense. *No one can see the future.* Not even Warren Buffett. We're not interested in predicting the future. *We are interested in creating it.* We've learned that in order to prosper, you must benefit from the valuable opportunities created by change, as Warren Buffett has. That would be easier to do if we could see the future. But regrettably, we can't. Fortunately, we don't have to.

Warren Buffett did not become rich by guessing blindly about the future. Guessing is like gambling. Speculators bet on the future like a roulette player, basing their decisions on the awful laws of luck. Like gamblers they eventually lose their resources. Buffett is not a speculator. He has become rich *by seeing the present clearly and learning from the patterns of the past.* Warren Buffett can't see the future, but he could see no reason that the rules that created opportunities and growth for him in the past won't have the same effect in years to come. Those rules have remained the same.

Those who utilized *true vision* could recognize these patterns. True Vision is simply based on seeing the *truth*. It is not about trying to predict the future. *No one can see the future.* However, it is possible for everyone to see the present situation clearly and understand the patterns of the past that are influencing the present and are likely to continue into the future. By seeing the truth about the past and present, you can better understand the future. True Vision identifies opportunities based on factual evidence and logic, not fantasy or hope. Your doctor uses a similar methodology. Before reaching a diagnosis, he examines your condition and behaviour, both now, as well as in the past. AI, machine learning and algorithms also use a similar methodology. They crunch data from the present and the past, and use algorithms to identify patterns that carry on into the future.

By using True Vision, you can more accurately see the changes that can create rich opportunities. To do this you have to look not forward but backwards. Most of the past lives on into your present and future. If you want to see the future you have to start by looking back thousands of years; 90 per cent of the truth is right behind you, lying exposed in the patterns of history.

Does the Twenty-first Century Belong to India?

In a relatively short space of time, humans have passed from an era of picking berries and sticking deer through the development of cities to the creation of global networks and rapid change. We have passed from a time when the opportunity to achieve our personal potential depended entirely on birth, to a time when success depends on knowledge and the willingness to take action. We have passed through eras of exploitation and extortion to a new age of opportunity. We have created rules in each era, and continued through history bringing those old rules with us. People who live in India today aren't just in the right time, they're also in the right place, a place with a mixture of different levels of rules from different eras and the greatest opportunities.

It's only in the last 200 years that white European men have dominated global affairs—and that period now appears to be coming to an end. China has thrown off communism in all but name. The country is now run like a business, with the Communist Party's politburo acting as the Board of Directors. The Chinese government has generated thirty years of sustained growth by building the infrastructure to attract private capital. Hundreds of millions of peasant farmers have moved off the land into better-paying jobs in cities, creating a booming consumer economy. Well-capitalized factory jobs are up to thirty times more productive than subsistence farming.

China still has some way to go. In recent years, the Chinese government has become increasingly controlling and oppressive. Limits on internal movement enforced through its hukou registration system prevent people from obtaining all the benefits of a move to a city. That's an old high-level rule that greatly influences people. The country's supply of peasants is almost exhausted, and its population is no longer growing. More recently, the government's willingness to break the rules and either demand or steal commercial technology from foreign companies has now sparked backlash from the US that threatens a global trade war.

During the first forty years after political independence in 1947, India also suffered through a failed experiment with socialism. Although not oppressive like China's communism, Indian socialism locked the country out of global commerce and collective learning. It stifled adaptation and individual initiative. In the License Raj era, opportunity operated under the rules of the Era of Extortion. Sunil Mittal saw his generator business wiped out by larger companies that were able to persuade the government to take action against any business that tried to compete with them. As a result, millions of the best-educated Indians fled abroad in search of merit-based opportunities.

Since the liberalization of the early 1990s, opportunity in India has become easier to see and easier to use. Some entrepreneurs have been able to start with nothing, identify opportunities in the changes taking place around them, attract the resources they need and build their success. For example, Nirmal Jain was able to build India Infoline (IIFL) into a financial service giant by capturing opportunities created by the liberalization of India's economy. Rafique Malik was able to grow Metro Shoes from a single store into a nationwide chain by offering relevant products to India's growing consumer class.

But it's difficult. India now has the largest population of subsistence farmers in the world. In a previous era, those farmers would have been the source of its wealth. Today, they are the source of its poverty—a problem that can't be solved through hand-outs alone. The economic model of subsistence farming is fundamentally outdated, unproductive and obsolete. Wage earners working in factories and offices are up to thirty times more productive per capita than farmers. In the Era of Opportunity, the peasant is the Pareto Loser.

That means India has both a huge amount of opportunity that can result from change, and a large number of people who will be able to benefit from that opportunity. But change is always difficult, which is why people work so hard to avoid it, stop it or hide from it instead of building adaptations to it. The government in India must finally discard the remnants of socialism and embrace an opportunity-oriented model of capitalist exchange underpinned by a rules-based system enforced by an honest and efficient judiciary. If rules are enforced fairly and quickly, they can no longer be used by government officials and their cronies as weapons of extortion. These needed adaptations will finally allow India to attract the trillions of dollars of capital required to build the infrastructure of a modern economy. If India can move its hundreds of millions of peasants away from subsistence farming into wage-earning jobs, as China has, then it can increase growth through massively enhanced productivity for decades to come. By doing so, India will have truly embraced and benefited from the Age of Opportunity. Regardless of what India does as a nation, every individual Indian can harvest the benefits of the Age of Opportunity by understanding and aligning with its rules.

The Age of Opportunity

1. We are now living in the Age of Opportunity
After the Eras of Exploitation and Extortion, we now have a new age in which everyone has the opportunity to realize their potential. But some of the old rules of previous eras remain in operation in most developing economies, including India.

2. Your opportunities are influenced by the rules at every level
While you have influence over yourself, you are also influenced by the rules of your workplace, your society, your country and the universe.

3. Know which rules you must take, which you can change, and which you can break
There are rules that you can influence, and there are rules that you can't influence. You can affect the rules around you but it's much harder to affect higher-level rules that everyone has to obey. Know what rules you can change, which you can adjust, and which you must follow . . . at least for now.

5

How to Break Rules

How do rules constrain us and limit our opportunities? When can it be an opportunity for you to break the rules? How do you become a rule maker instead of a rule taker? What are Rules for Fools?

In 2007, Brian Chesky and Joe Gebbia had a spare room and no money. Noticing that a design conference in San Francisco had filled the city's hotel rooms, they advertised their room and offered guests breakfast and a tour of the city. They took four bookings and realized that they had found an opportunity. People had spare rooms—and even spare homes—that they could rent out to travellers. They created a platform that matched those properties with those travellers. It took off. Airbnb now offers more than 6 million listings in more than 1,00,000 cities across 191 countries and regions. It has hosted around 500 million people worldwide and typically puts up over 2 million people every night. And it doesn't own a single room.

The founders of Uber saw a similar opportunity in a different field. When Travis Kalanick and Garrett Camp expanded their car rental service to allow anyone with a car to become a driver, they too created a valuable adaptation to a change. Drivers had mobile phones. Those mobile phones included real-time maps as well as a means of communication. People could contact the drivers and reach their destinations. Car owners could make money. Uber could make more money by connecting them. Uber has now completed more than 10 billion trips. It has 3.9 million drivers who make 14 million journeys every day in over 700 cities and sixty-three countries. And it doesn't own a single car.

Both of those adaptations drove straight through low-level rules: people didn't usually rent out their spare rooms to strangers for a weekend or drive people to parties for a fee. And they drove through higher-level rules: the hospitality industry and the taxicab industry are governed by anti-discrimination laws; safety and fire inspection standards; taxes; vehicle checks, and so on. Airbnb, Uber, and many of the companies in the sharing economy that followed found opportunity by challenging old rules and creating new ones. All rules *made by humans* gradually become irrelevant due to changes in the environment. Those changes create opportunity.

Can Changing the Rules Be an Opportunity?

Some norms or rules that started billions of years ago will still drive change and adaption throughout your life. Which levels have unchanging norms? Which have rules that can change? And which can *you* personally influence to drive adaptation and opportunity? Let's refer to the diagram on levels of history (on page 56) to understand this better.

Level 1: Universe—The norms of the universe *will not* change during your lifetime. Like it or not, you must obey all of them.

Level 2: Earth—The norms of the earth *may change* during your lifetime. Consider global warning. You can exert a tiny amount of influence on change.

Level 3: Humanity—Some norms of humanity *can change* during your lifetime. You can exert some influence on change.

Level 4: The Now Era—Some norms of the Now Era can change during your lifetime. You can exert major influence on change.

Level 5: Your Life—The norms of your life can change dramatically during your life. You can exert 100 per cent influence on change at this level.

Also consider your rules from this perspective:

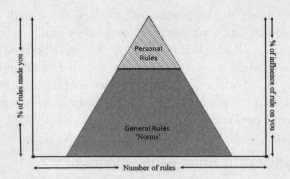

At the *You Level*, you could make all the rules (although most people choose not to). Although *Personal Rules* may be small in number compared to all the norms of your job, company, community, culture and country, they can exert much more influence over you. Your own *You Level* rules are like your own system software that dictate what you allow yourself to do. For example, if your own rule dictates: 'the stock market is too dangerous to invest in', you will not allow yourself to buy shares. You constantly follow rules at all levels of your environment. For example, imagine that you're an employee of HDFC Bank. Your rules environment at work looks something like this:

Your Rules Environment

India

Indian- Banking Industry

HDFC Bank

HDFC

Your Job Category

You Personally

Obviously, the rules at the bottom level—*You Personally*—have the most influence over how you think, feel and behave. At this level, you also have the most control over the rules. At the highest-level scale—*India*—you have virtually no influence over the rules. Yet the rules at every level of the environment influence your ability to understand change and the opportunities available to you.

What Happens When You Try to Break the Rules

Imagine that you work as a teller in the Breach Candy branch of HDFC Bank in Mumbai. You are ambitious, and dream of one day becoming CEO. Every day you strive to give the best possible service to your customers. Sometimes, they have to wait in long lines and get grumpy, especially during the lunchtime rush. Being service-minded, you hate to see unhappy customers.

One day you think: *I see an opportunity! Why don't we open a sandwich stall inside the bank branch so that hungry customers can get food during the lunch crunch? That should increase satisfaction.* You suggest the idea to your direct supervisor.

He shakes his head and says, 'You're *mad*. Do you serve coffee, or dish out money? Now go to the safe and get more cash.'

Brave and undaunted, you approach the branch manager with your nascent opportunity.

She smiles and says: 'I appreciate your initiative, but I'm fairly sure it won't be allowed.' She's never seen a bank branch with a sandwich stall and thinks that it probably violates company policy. But she's under pressure to reduce customer complaints and improve service. So she speaks to the district manager.

He grumbles: 'As far as I know, it's never been done. We're in banking, not the restaurant business. It probably isn't allowed by company policy. And God only knows about the licensing requirements.'

But her manager has been encouraged *to think out of the box*. She calls headquarters and checks with a friend in the legal department.

'There's no company policy about this at all. But serving food to customers isn't specifically allowed under our banking license,' he reports. 'On the other hand, it might be possible, if we use a caterer who has his own license. I can check on that.'

The company lawyer calls a friend who owns a chain of sandwich shops. 'Can you open a sandwich counter in one of our branches?' she asks.

'I don't see why not,' the friend replies. 'But even if I could get a license, I've never heard of any customers eating inside a bank. Indians just don't do that sort of thing.'

What can we learn from this story? You can see that your potential opportunities are influenced by *rules* at every level of the environment, from bottom to top:

1. **At the You level:** Formal and informal *rules* about what you could, should, can and will do.
2. **At the Your Job Category level:** Formal and informal *rules* about what you could, should, can and will do on your job.
3. **At the HDFC Bank level:** Internally imposed *rules* about what the bank could, should, can and will do.
4. **At the Banking Industry level:** Externally imposed *rules* about what all banks could, should, can and will do.
5. **At the India level:** Informal *rules* about what all Indians could, should, can and will do.

Your Personal Rules Environment

There are five levels in your *Personal Rules Environment*, as the following illustration shows: Mission, Model, Market, Domain, and Everything Else. All rules can change to adapt to the changing environment. Lower-level rules may generally influence only a level or two above or may have no influence at all on higher levels.

Yours Rules Environment

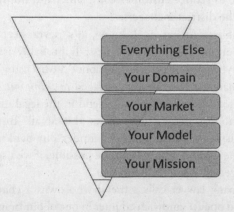

An example: Imagine once again that you're a teller at HDFC Bank. If you choose, Your Mission can be completely under your own influence. Your Model (i.e. how you do your work), however, is only slightly under your own influence. If you wish, could you change the Model, by coming to work in dirty, sweaty clothes? Can you ask all your customers to loan you money? Not if you want to stay with the bank. You have to follow their rules and have very limited ability to change them. The Model also has limited influence over the Market. If HDFC Bank decides to close all its branches and force all its customers to interact over the Internet, would the Market accept it? Probably not. You have limited control over the rules around you, but what happens when you try to break them? We'll discover that in the next chapter.

When the Rules Change, Companies Must Change Too

Higher-level rules change much more slowly than lower-level rules. Changes in higher-level rules *always* lead to changes in rules at levels below them. For example, if you are a millennial, you probably owned a simple Nokia phone as your first mobile phone. At one point, Nokia had 70 per cent of the world's cell phone market. Then you may have had a Blackberry. Now you probably own a smartphone like an iPhone or a Samsung Galaxy.

A change in higher-level rules drove the adaptation from the simple Nokia phone to the Blackberry and finally to the smartphone. Nokia failed to understand the rule change or its potential significance for adaptation and opportunity. It got wiped out like the dinosaurs getting hit by a meteorite. Blackberry took advantage of the first rule change, but then failed to adjust the next time the rules changed. It got wiped out too.

At what level of the mobile handset industry's environment did the rules change, driving dramatic change? Can you guess? A hint: the rules changed at the *domain* level of the environment. Can you guess what changed? Most people cannot. The answer: at the domain level, the dominant *bandwidth technology* shifted from 1G (Nokia phone), to 2G (Blackberry), to 3G (smartphone). A 1G phone could do voice and SMS only. A 2G phone could add email. A 3G phone could add a fully networked computer to the phone, dramatically increasing its potential utility.

> Although the mobile phone companies had no control at all over bandwidth technology, changes in this technology dramatically affected their potential choice of opportunities, for good or ill.

Rule Takers, Rule Makers and Rule Breakers

Many people and organizations are *rule takers*. They cling on to rules for too long as if they were natural laws. In order to adapt better to the quickly changing environment you can become a *rule breaker* and a *rule maker*. By breaking rules, you can adapt and innovate better solutions for human needs. This is a rich source of opportunity. If you have the right to make your own rules, they can obviously be more enduring, and you can make them so that they favour you over the competition. You can change lower-level rules, such as those of your industry or company, to make them more relevant, as long as you stay in compliance with the trend of change of higher-level norms.

The lower you go on the rules hierarchy, the more power you have to change rules, and the faster the rules can be changed. *You* are at the bottom level of every rules hierarchy that involves you. Obviously, you have the most power to change your own rules. Although you should know and follow the highest-level rules, at the *You* level, the opposite applies: blindly following *the norms of the mass* is rarely an opportunity. If you are a humble bank teller but wish to become a bank president, you must not think and behave like all the other tellers. You have to break the rules around you to reveal opportunities. As Mark Twain said, 'Whenever you find yourself on the side of the majority, it is time to reform (or pause and reflect).'

Although higher-level rules evolve more slowly than lower-level rules, they can abruptly change in a fairly significant way, generating new trends, which can be rich sources of opportunities. For example, Freddie Mercury, the lead singer of Queen, was an entertainer whose own personal rules of behaviour violated the long-standing norms of his Parsi community, his country, and of the entertainment industry. However, he was fortunate, because starting in the mid-1960s, the higher-level social trend changed. Non-conformism started to bend the norms in his favour. This allowed someone with his unique style to finally emerge as a superstar. Even ten years earlier his success—at least on his own terms—would probably not have been possible.

Some norms last much longer than others. For example, wearing clothes has become a general rule we all follow. We simply don't roam around naked anymore. But the type of clothing we wear changes constantly. Before 1960, rules dictated that women didn't wear pants in public. The vast majority of women religiously followed this rule. Then the norms abruptly changed. By examining the rules and trends around clothing, we can clearly see the following hierarchy:

Norm: *Humans must wear clothes in public*
Duration of rule: *Thousands of years*
Current relevance: *Strong*
Current trend: *Still strong*
Lower-level rule: *Women can wear pants in public*
Duration of rule: *Since 1960*
Current relevance: *Strong*
Current trend: *Trending higher*

The best way to look forward is by considering the past in the present. Always start your examination of the present by identifying the long-term trends, then the medium and short-term trends. For example, in the longer trend, women will continue to wear clothing. Therefore, although a fashion house might change styles annually, or dramatically change its look less often, it will continue to make clothing for women. Next, examine the medium- and short-term trends. Since 1960, as women have become able to work and pursue more opportunities, their clothing has become more practical. Is this trend continuing? If so, how? Is it changing? If so, how? Examine the evidence of change. This may be fertile ground for adaption and opportunities for new emergent properties. In order to find rich opportunities, it is essential for you to understand how the norms of the past are evolving. The trend is your friend. As long as you stay relevant with the higher-level trend, you can adapt properly and successfully harvest opportunities from specific trends that fall below it in the hierarchy. In fact, you can create those trends yourself.

You may think you have found a great opportunity to change the current fashion, but if you violate the norms, i.e. that humans wear clothing or that men don't usually wear dresses, you will fail to gain traction. If you violate a medium-term rule, that women can wear pants, you may also fail. On the other hand, if that trend is changing, you may succeed as a rule breaker, as Freddie Mercury did. However, if you choose to introduce adaptations that violate unchanging trends with unchanging norms, you may fail to attract resources. A line of naked clothing probably won't sell, even in our hyper-casual day and age.

Elon Musk Breaks the Rules and Makes the Rules

The start of Elon Musk's career looks like the beginning of any smart, opportunity-grabbing entrepreneur. In 1995, after dropping out of a PhD in energy physics at Stanford University, he created a software company with his brother, Kimbal. Zip2 was an Internet city guide for newspaper publishers. When Compaq bought it for $307 million, Musk pocketed $22 million. He put $10 million of that money into a new company called X.com. In 2001, he merged that company with Confinity to form a new financial services firm called PayPal.

The new company was a rule breaker. International transactions usually had to go through banks. PayPal found a way through the regulatory thickets to specialize in online transactions. It was a new adaptation to the growing needs of e-commerce. When eBay bought PayPal for $1.5 billion a year later, Musk's $10 million investment netted him $165 million.

Now Musk was rich enough not to care about rules at all. Space travel had been the domain of nation states. Musk poured money into a private satellite-launching system that used renewable rockets. It now supplies the International Space Station. The car industry was dominated by titans like Ford and Nissan who produced the same petrol-driven cars they had made for a hundred years. Musk created a new company that built an electric car that could accelerate from 0 to 60 in 2.4 seconds and drive for 370 miles. He's dreaming of Mars bases and of transport tunnels through cities.

His personal behaviour too, though, has broken rules. His announcements on Twitter have got him into trouble with the US Securities Exchange Commission. He was filmed smoking marijuana during a live interview—not the usual behaviour for a company executive. But perhaps the most interesting example of rule-breaking is the rules he made for communicating inside Tesla. Instead of staff talking to managers, everyone is told to email whoever they need—senior management, a vice-president, even Musk himself—to get things done.

'We obviously cannot compete with the big car companies in size, so we must do so with intelligence and agility,' he wrote to his staff at Tesla.

When breaking rules brings success, you get to make your own rules.

Some Rules Are for Fools

Some rules are just plain wrong. These are known as *Rules for Fools*, or *Fules*. These lead to the creation of nopportunities that destroy resources. For example, India's pre-1991 License Raj fules required all industries to ask permission from the government to start or expand production. This led to India's further impoverishment, this time at its own hands. Often, we find ourselves constrained by inflexible rules that may work for the average person, but create failure in our environment. One place that's clear is in the franchise industry. Franchises create rules that entrepreneurs can follow as they build a business. It's like buying a business in a box. As long as the rules are relevant to your environment, the business will probably succeed. But if the environment changes and the franchisor can't adjust, the business will fail and there will be nothing you can do.

Imagine that you have shifted your family to the city of Edison, New Jersey, in the US. You've purchased a nearby McDonald's restaurant franchise from its previous owner, and are running it yourself, along with your wife and teenage kids. Control isn't an issue for you. The restaurant is already fully staffed and running. McDonald's has provided you with a thorough set of Standard Operating Procedures (SOPs). Everything in your business model is covered from McSoup to McNuts. All you need to do is follow the rules, which comes naturally to you, as you're an engineer. Unfortunately, simply knowing and following the McRules is not enough for you to achieve success. You don't like most of the food you serve in your own restaurant. It's far too bland for your Indian palate, and you are a vegetarian. Unfortunately, most of your neighbours in Edison don't care for your food either. Many Indian alternatives have opened up, such as Srini's Dosa Depot, located right next door, which is minting money.

When the previous owner bought the McDonalds franchise, only 20 per cent of Edison's population was Indian. Now it is 80 per cent. You begin to realize why you got such a good deal. The market has changed, and the trend is not your friend. What can you do about it? McDonald's won't allow you to change your menu at all, and there's nothing you can do but complain. As losses mount, you realize that all you have control of is a sinking ship. You have bought the *McTitanic*, and there is no lifeboat!

Meanwhile, your next-door neighbour, Srini of Dosa Depot, has started selling franchises. The Indian population in the US is growing, and even non-desis seem to like vegetarian food. Srini seems to be much more in control of his own ability to take advantage of change than you are. As your savings evaporate, you fall into depression. You've always thought of yourself as a positive person, but now you're even questioning your control over your own interior environment. Clearly, in a changing world, just following the rules does not mean you are in control. You have to be able to change the rules as well.

Srini has now made a breakthrough: the sale of the first Dosa Depot franchise in the state of Texas. 'Can you believe it?' he asks his wife, not waiting for an answer. 'Selling dosas in Dallas?' Again, he doesn't wait for an answer. 'If I can sell them there, I can sell them anywhere.'

Life has come full circle for Srini. When he shifted his family to the US ten years earlier, he also bought a franchise: a Subway restaurant. After slaving for eighty hours a week for a couple of years, they had banked enough to buy another unit. By that point Srini's hometown of Edison had gone totally desi. His customers were requesting the specialties on the Indian Subway menu, such as Chicken Tandoori or Paneer Tikka, but he couldn't sell them. Loyal customers started to desert him for new places, such as Tarun's Tandoori Temple. Finally, Srini threw in the towel, sold his Subway franchises and, with the pittance he received, decided to create his own restaurant rulebook. He'd always loved dosas, and he had some creative ideas about how to adapt them to American as well as desi tastes. After visiting his cousin in Dallas, he invented the Tex-Mex Dosa, stuffed with refried beans and spicy salsa.

'You're bloody mad!' his wife had said. 'Tex-Mex Dosa? What *faltoo* nonsense! Idiot! You'll lose the rest of our money!'

It seemed like nobody believed in Srini, not even his kids. But he persevered. The first Dosa Depot went through some growing pains, but eventually became a hit. Within five years, he had sold seventeen franchises, and inquiries were pouring in from all over the country, along with suggestions for new dosa varietals.

'The world's first rattlesnake dosa!' he proudly announced to his vegetarian wife, who promptly fainted. 'Should sell like hotcakes in Arizona!'

At first, building a franchise system was an exercise in chaos. Srini had no idea how to do it. But as time went on, he learned how to run it. Eventually, he hired a consultant who helped him set up a complete system of SOPs. It worked like a charm. Having understood the pain of being a branch on a tree, Srini made sure to speak with each of his franchisees at least once a month to learn what was working and, more importantly, what wasn't working. His franchisees were encouraged to develop better processes and new products that were more in line with their market, such as the popular new Philly Cheesesteak Dosa in Philadelphia and Lobster Claw Dosa in Boston. Srini saw that he had prospered when he had been free to break rules. He also saw that his neighbour sank when he was unable to adapt to the changing environment. He made sure that his franchisees followed the norms that he and the market expected, but were free to make the changes they needed to stay relevant.

How to Break Rules

1. When rules change, new opportunities open
Rules and norms change all the time. What is impossible in one
era is possible in another. What is unacceptable in one era is
welcomed in another. Freddie Mercury could not have succeeded
as he did had he performed in the 1950s. But by the time Queen
was performing in the 1970s, society allowed singers to be different
and push boundaries.

2. Rules can constrain and adaptability is key
Rules can be comfortable. The rules of a franchise make building
a business easy . . . as long as they work in your environment. But
environments always change and if the rules don't change, you get
stuck. Opportunity requires the freedom to adapt just as Srini did
with the Dosa Depot.

3. Once you've broken the rules, you can make the rules
Breaking the right rules in the right way at the right time can create
a valuable opportunity. When that opportunity succeeds, you'll be
in a position to make new rules that others will follow . . . to create
new opportunities, as Elon Musk has with his electric cars and
space ventures.

6

The Fair Value Exchange

What is the most important question in the world? What is the value in an opportunity? Is value the same as money? What are the five key drivers of a fair value exchange? How do you create competitive advantage? How can you build the relationships you need to reap the benefits of your opportunity?

Imagine for a moment that you're walking down a city street and suddenly see a Rs 100 note lying on the ground in front of you. Once you see that nobody else has claimed it, you would probably pick it up, and put it in your pocket. *What a great opportunity!* You've just made yourself Rs 100 with no effort. Or was there effort? Yes. Although the opportunity cost you nothing, implementing it required a bit of work. You had to look around to make sure its former owner wasn't around, and then bend down to pick it up. In return for that minimal effort, you earned yourself Rs 100. Not a bad deal. But not such a great opportunity. Because Rs 100 is all you're ever going to get. Even if you walk down that street every day for the next 100 years, you will probably never find another Rs 100 on the ground. If you want prosperity, opportunity simply can't be avoided. The best opportunities are not one-offs, such as finding money on the road or winning the lottery. The best opportunities can provide you with a continuous stream of resources that can last a lifetime.

Now imagine this scenario: instead of walking down that street, you are pushing yourself in a wheelchair. You have a broken hip and getting out of the chair is very difficult. You spot the Rs 100 note. Would picking up that money seem like a good opportunity? Maybe it isn't worth the effort this time. You'll have to ask someone to help you, and he might expect you to share the loot. Why would you need to share? Because we live in an age in which opportunities require an exchange of some sort. *Buying, trading or selling.* Business and career opportunities require the cooperation of selfish people.

What's the Most Important Question in the World?

It's a question you ask yourself every day, sometimes several times a day, without even realizing it. Most people can't guess this. Do you know? The most important question in the world is: 'What's in it for me?' (WIIFM for short.)

There's no sense denying it: *we are all selfish*. We all want products and services that help us to meet our needs. But unless we receive good value in exchange, we are reluctant to pay the price. In fact, because we're so selfish, we generally want to receive more value than we give in return.

When it Comes to Value, It's All Relative

Whenever we ask: *'what's in it for me?'* what are we actually doing? We are attempting to measure and compare *relative values*. Humans have developed *value measurement* to determine values. There is no such concept in nature. Animals don't measure anything. If you give your dog a bowl of food, he doesn't think: 'Whoopee, he's given me 12 grams more than yesterday!' He just digs in.

What is *value*? It is relative worth—the worth of something in terms of the number of other things for which it can be traded. How much is a Rs 100 note worth? Well obviously, it's worth Rs 100, because it can be exchanged for another Rs 100 note. What is the value of your time? That's a tougher question. Things being valued can be *tangible* or *intangible*. A *tangible* thing is a kilo of wheat, a *tola* of gold or a share of HDFC Bank. Tangible values are usually easier to measure, because they are bought and sold in active markets. An *intangible* is generally harder to measure. Examples are your reputation for hard work and integrity, or an opportunity you've identified. Things whose value can be accurately measured have an *actual value*. These include a share of HDFC Bank, the dollar or the rupee rate this moment on the exchange and the current price of a kilo of basmati rice at Big Bazaar.

Most products and services are not traded on open markets and have only *perceived value*, which is more difficult to accurately measure. For example, what is the value of one hour of your labour? You might ask for Rs 10,000. But if you offer your services to different people, they would certainly give it different values, based on how they perceive the value exchange. How much do they need for what you have to offer? How urgent is the need? How much do they value your ability to carry out the service they require? Is the money available to them? What other needs do they have that are more critical at the moment?

All nascent opportunities have *potential value*. Why potential? Because the economic value of an opportunity always lies in the future. Yet, because we cannot see the future, every opportunity has to be evaluated based on the circumstances of the present. For example, if someone asks me to do him or her a favour, I must determine the value of the exchange. Is it a potential opportunity for me? To determine the value, I have to measure the value of what I'm doing for him/her and determine what sort of value s/he should give me in exchange. We make these sorts of What's in It For Me (WIIFM) calculations all the time. Whether we realize it or not, we are all constantly exchanging value in search of opportunity. Therefore, *the changes that matter most to us are the changes in value*.

Why We Must Have the Win-Win

In the Old Era, if you were the lord of the manor, it would have been perfectly fine for you to threaten to kill your peasants if they failed to hand over their freshly harvested crops. The typical nobleman certainly viewed this as an opportunity. These days we would consider that to be a criminal opportunity. Why? Because only one side gets a fair deal. Imagine for a moment that you're at a party. You are introduced to someone for the first time, and spend a few minutes talking to him. Consciously or not, your WIIFM calculator immediately goes to work, evaluating whether or not this new relationship may be an opportunity for you. If the fellow only talks about himself and never asks about you, chances are that you will not value a relationship with him, unless you discover that he can provide you with useful benefits, such as access to people or resources that you urgently need.

Business and career opportunities require the cooperation of selfish people in *relationships*. For relationships to work out, each side must feel that their selfish interests are being met better than they would be if they did not have the relationship. Relationships always involve a series of value exchanges. In every trade of value, you are trying to get something you need but don't have in exchange for something you have but don't need.

Many people think of opportunity in terms of the free Rs 100 note on the ground. They want something for nothing. This is a very short-sighted view that will deny you opportunity. For a relationship to work, the WIIFMs of each side must be balanced in a *fair value exchange*. In the Now Era, to be sustainable and successful, every opportunity relationship requires a fair value exchange. The rules require that both sides should be satisfied with the deal. There must be a *win-win*. Why must value exchanges be fair? Because if they aren't, you won't continue with the relationship. We're no longer peasants being exploited by the lord of the manor. We simply won't put up with mistreatment any longer, because we have better opportunities available to us, if we can see them.

In the Old Era, rules of fair exchange only applied within classes. Noblemen were expected to play fair with each other, but not with peasants. In the Now Era, the rules of fair value exchange apply to *all* business relationships, and one-sided *win-lose* value exchanges can provoke enormous opposition. In India, both Old and Now Era value exchange rules operate simultaneously. In relationships with your employer or with your customers, a win-win exchange is generally expected. In your relationship with government officials, a win-lose exchange may be demanded.

Opportunity Is a Free Form of Value

Opportunity is the most desirable exchangeable resource of the modern world. It is available to absolutely everyone for free. It is the number one route to prosperity for everyone, particularly for those of us who lack money. Opportunities are a resource with both perceived and potential value that can be traded for hard resources with actual value, such as cash and human resources.

Imagine what your life would be like if you were rich. Where would you live? What car would you drive? How would other people treat you differently? What could you do with your time that is more productive and enjoyable? Just think about that for a moment. Then think about all the things *you wouldn't have to do* that you're unhappy about doing now. How can you transform your dreams into reality? The fact is that you can have all of the fabulous things that you want in your life. You can get them through opportunity. Why? *Because opportunity is the bridge between aspiration and realization.* Next: stop thinking about the all the things that *you* want. Why? Because wanting money, fine things and respect won't in any way get them for you. You need to trade value for value; there must be an exchange. That involves giving other people what they want. *Giving others value..*

What Is Opportunity Arbitrage?

When I interview candidates applying to work for me, I always ask them: 'Why are you interested in this job? What do you want to get out of it?' Most of them respond: 'I'm looking for a better opportunity.' What do they mean by 'better opportunity'? Inevitably they mean more money. They want more value to be delivered to them in the form of cash. But why should anyone want to deliver more value to them? What valuable service can they provide in exchange? The best value exchanges are a form of *opportunity arbitrage*, in which each side trades something of lesser value for something of much greater value.

In a really great opportunity, each side feels that he's getting more value than the other side, or more value than he would alone. The best opportunities inevitably involve an enormous arbitrage potential. For example, according to one study, Google gives every user an economic value of around $12,000 dollars per year. You give data to Google in exchange for their services. Your ability to sell your data individually and profit from it is very limited. But when Google aggregates your data with the data of millions of other people and leverages the platforms it has created to give advertisers access to that data, it acquires tremendous value. Other examples of value arbitrage are airlines giving away empty business class seats or hotel upgrading guests to better rooms that they could not sell. It costs them nothing, but it gives a lot of value to customers, who are likely to spend more in future as a result.

Nopportunities are the opposite: you trade something of enormous value in exchange for something with the potential to destroy value for you in the future. For example, to make peace with your wife you take on her incompetent brother as your partner. You get temporary peace at home, but in a short time he destroys your business.

Don't Confuse Money with Value

In order to make a fair value exchange, it is obviously crucial to understand value; both the value you can provide, and the value you want from the other side. You need to be able to identify and measure these effectively. Most people measure value only in terms of money. They make the mistake of confusing price with value. What you want to measure and understand is the value that is being exchanged for the money. And the value is not the money. You can't eat money. You don't go into a store and exchange your money for another pile of money. Money is not a consumption item. Money is an efficient means of exchange. It is an effect, not a cause.

Everyone wants more money. So what? Wanting money will not get it for you. Goals based on money are absolutely useless. Will anyone give you a higher salary simply because you want it? Will you earn higher profits simply because you want them? Of course not. Imagine that you want to lose 5 kilos. Will simply wanting to lose weight take off the kilos? Again, no. It would be better to focus on actions that will take the weight off, such as running five times a week. It is essential for you to understand what value you deliver and how you add value. Without that information, negotiating a fair value exchange will be difficult for either side. Each side will be forced to negotiate based on price rather than value.

Sometimes even consultants can make the same mistake. Jagdeep Kapoor, MD of Samsika, India's leading marketing consultant, insists that all his consulting clients maintain a policy of selling only on a cash-in-advance basis. He will not permit any of them to offer credit to their own customers. As many industries in India operate on ninety-plus days of trade credit, this policy has saved his many clients hundreds (if not thousands) of crores of rupees in working capital costs over the years. It's quite likely that these savings have far exceeded the value of the fees paid to Jagdeep. However, since Jagdeep has never accounted for these savings, he has failed to reap the benefit in his negotiations with clients.

Key Drivers of the Fair Value Exchange

1. Empathy

Empathy is the most important driver of the fair value exchange. To be successful, it is essential to understand the other side's WIIFM. To not only understand it, but to *empathize* with it. You must be able to sympathetically see things from the other points of view. You must literally put yourself in their shoes and feel their pain and root for their gain. That isn't always easy to do. It's impossible to do if you approach a negotiation with the idea that you're going to grind the other guy down. A successful negotiation isn't one in which you walk away with everything because you could. It's one in which you both walk away with value and a desire to do it again.

For example, I recently negotiated my own consulting fees with a client whose stressed situation I understand very well. Given my knowledge of his predicament, and his need for professional help, I could have driven a hard bargain with him. But as I understand the financial challenges he faces, I offered a fee structure that would work well for him while satisfying my own value criteria. This win-win solution has helped us build a long-term relationship that benefits both of us.

2. Service

Opportunity relationships in the Now Era always involve a form of *mutual service*. Most companies, because they focus on profit as a primary goal, only truly understand service as self-service. The famed marketing guru Theodore Levitt said: 'People don't want to buy a quarter inch drill. They want a quarter inch hole.' This is a very profound statement. Whenever you buy a product, what you are actually buying is the service that it provides to you. *All forms of value are a service.* For example,

Asian Paints, India's largest paint company, obviously sells a product, paint. However, the company realized that no one actually wanted to own paint. What customers wanted is a freshly painted house. Based on this insight, they added tremendous value to the exchange by offering a complete service solution: a painted house.

Asian Paints isn't the only big company to see the opportunity in service. When Tata Steel entered the retail steel market, it became the first company in India to turn a heavy industry product into a brand accessible to customers through company and franchisee-owned stores. The company offered customized services for residential, commercial and agricultural requirements as well as steel doors with a wooden finish or complete solutions for new apartments. Over a fifteen-year period, Tata Steel's sale of branded products increased from 9 to 50 per cent of total sales of Rs 50,000 crore. They reached over 30 lakh new customers.

Asian Paints Brushes Up Its Service

'The biggest eye-opener was that no one is interested in paint.' That was the revelation described by Kanwar Bir Singh (KBS) Anand, managing director and CEO, Asian Paints, to *Forbes India* in 2016. The company had conducted a year-long customer engagement exercise and discovered that paint wasn't particularly interesting to customers. They only thought about it every three or four years, and then it was the woman of the house who did the buying. The good news was that the only brand she could recall was Asian Paints.

It helps that the company, formed by four friends in 1942, has a longer history than modern India's. Its introduction of Gattu, its distinctive mascot, in 1954, helped to multiply its sales, and by 1967, Asian Paints had become the country's biggest paint manufacturer. As the country grew and modernized, so did the company. In the 1980s, Asian Paints hired the advertising firm Ogilvy & Mather to refresh its brand. New television ads with the tagline '*Har ghar kuch kehta hai* [Every home tells a story]' focused on festivals, and reflected the country and its values.

By the start of the new millennium, the Indian public had changed. Gattu's mischievous young painter no longer represented an Indian middle class that had more money and less time. Anand noticed something else in his company's customer sessions. Customers might have thought little about paint, but they placed a high value on the *effect* the paint brought to their homes. Asian Paints had delivered its products to retailers, but it saw that the real value lay in what customers did with them. The launch of a helpline brought the brand closer to the public, while the introduction of a 'home solutions' service completed the company's move to a premium brand. Buyers of Asian Paints' premium products expected to be able to swap money for full solutions, not just paint.

All business and career opportunities require the exchange of services. There is no exception to this rule. An Indian businessman I've worked with who provides excellent service to his customers has this quotation from Mahatma Gandhi prominently displayed in his reception area:

> A customer is the most important visitor on our premises. He is not dependent on us. We are dependent on him. He is not an interruption to our work. He is the purpose of it. He is not an outsider in our business. He is part of it. We are not doing him a favour by serving him. He is doing us a favour by giving us an opportunity to do so.

The Indian law of karma sums it up well: *you give, and you receive. Seva* means service. Seva is the key to the law of karma. Apple CEO, Tim Cook, has said: 'Everybody talks about "find your purpose, find your purpose, find your purpose". The truth is we all have the same purpose. And we should all quit looking. The purpose is to serve humanity.'

It's true. Every living thing in the world is struggling to control greater energy and resources. The more we help people obtain these, the more we are rewarded with prosperity. That is opportunity. It comes from asking the questions:

1. 'How can I be *most useful* to myself?'
2. 'How can I be *most useful* to others?'
3. 'How can I align these goals so that 1 + 1 = 3?'

Service is particularly important if you are an employee. You might think of yourself as pursuing a career, but actually you are pursuing business opportunities. You are selling your services on the market and people are buying them. There is a two-way value exchange going on for your services, regardless of what type of services you are offering. Of course, service must always be tempered by the value exchange. It must be a service to *you* as well. Service to you can be much more than simply earning more. A service to you allows you to *learn*, and improve, and therefore be able to adapt and grow. The exchange should ideally help you to successfully and continuously adapt. It also helps the other side of the exchange to do the same thing.

Most people have trouble benefiting from change. We all have our different skills and abilities and circumstances and resources. We can uniquely help others to adapt based on those. Many of the best business opportunities are adaptations that help others to adapt as well. Services of this type can create immense value for the other side because they have found it very difficult to adapt or have not even noticed the need to adapt. Imagine the delight of the person first using an iPhone. Imagine the amount of value created by the smartphone. The smartphone is an adaptation to the environment that very few people would have developed themselves. It doesn't necessary deal with what the other side wants in terms of service. They might not know what they want. To provide excellent service, you should discover: what jobs are crucial drivers of success for others, and how are they failing to get them done? How can you be of service to get these done?

The Value of the IKEA Effect

IKEA sells furniture that improves people's homes. But the furniture is cheap and while that makes it competitive, it also gives the product a low perceived value. The value increases though when customers have to put it together themselves. Researchers call the value added through customer effort the IKEA effect, and it's seen in other industries.

When flour companies in the United States started introducing cake mixes, they found that sales numbers quickly peaked. Home bakers felt that adding water to a mix and putting it in the oven wasn't really baking. It was too easy, which lessened the value of the cake when it was served. So on the advice of a psychologist and marketing consultant called Ernest Dichter, the food companies changed the recipe. They removed the dried eggs from the ingredients and told home bakers to add two eggs and water. Bakers now *felt* that they were making a cake. The food manufacturers empathized with that feeling and were able to offer a service with greater value. When customers served the cake, they might have been serving the same cake they had served before, but they put more effort into it, and therefore assigned it a greater value. In order to accurately value an opportunity, you should find out what your buyers really value the most from the transaction.

Everyone is fighting daily battles. You need to help the other side to win their most difficult battles. If you give such effective service, the other side will give you amazing latitude. They'll have such trust and faith in you that they'll turn their secrets over to you for safekeeping. Durable competitive advantage does not come through differentiation or low cost, as has been propagated by Western management gurus. Differentiation is a result, not a cause. Anyone can copy these strategies. True competitive advantage comes through service to your customers. This is the foundation of a deep and unique relationship, which cannot be copied by anyone.

3. Relationships

Business and career opportunities are team sports. To find and implement opportunities, you need to create and maintain all types of win-win relationships: with buyers, sellers, bosses, employers, employees, suppliers, channel partners, investors, and so on. In order to create durable relationships with these diverse stakeholders, you need to be able to balance the value you deliver against the value you receive. The WIIFMs on both sides of the opportunity exchange have to be held in a firm handshake. It's a totally symbiotic relationship. What tightens the handshake? Increased WIIFM. What loosens the handshake? Decreased WIIFM. You should always aim to give more value to the other guy than he expected.

Relationship acquisition is very expensive and requires both of you to overcome the biggest barrier, that of trust. Relationships are very valuable. The longer you can maintain them, the longer you can capitalize the cost of obtaining them, the more you can both learn, the more you can grow. Your objective is to learn together with others on a long-term basis. For example, Metro Shoes has grown into India's second-largest shoe store chain by nurturing its relationships with its employees. Early on, managing director, Rafique Malik, decided that Indians made better entrepreneurs than employees. When they run their own businesses, he felt, they work harder and look for sales. When they have a salary, they hardly work and hope that sales come to them. Instead of paying his staff a salary, he converted his managers to owners. His company's new entrepreneurial model meant that the more shoes they sold, the more money they earned. Now instead of turning up late, closing early and delivering poor customer service, they arrived on time and worked hard to make sure the customers came back. Most importantly, the relationship between Malik and his managers changed. Now they were colleagues working together towards a common goal: to sell as many shoes as possible and earn as much money as possible for everyone.

4. Mutuality and Reciprocity

You cannot force people to buy from you; they need to be convinced of the value you are offering them. The key driver of exchange relationships in the Now Era is *mutuality*. Both sides must feel that the value exchange is fair. *All successful relationships in the modern era are based on mutuality.* Mutuality is connected to the principle of *reciprocity*. I do for you; you do for me equally. Relationships can only be sustained if they deliver equal value to both sides. Your success is 100 per cent dependent on the joy of others. Everyone wants to be rich. Ironically, the best way to get rich is to help others become rich. You may have belief in yourself, but to succeed in career and business, you must build an army of supporters. The best way to get successful is to help other people get what they want.

Hindustan Unilever's Shakti Project Brings Sales to the Company . . . and Rural Women

Around the turn of the millennium, Hindustan Unilever (HUL), India's largest consumer products company, had a problem. The Anglo-Dutch conglomerate has a broad range of health and hygiene brands such as Lux, Annapurna, Ponds, and Lifebuoy soap, items that could be used by anyone. Reaching customers in the cities was simple enough and eight out ten urban Indians used one of their products. But getting their products into the hands of customers in the media-dark rural areas was a challenge.

The solution came in the form of Project Shakti. Like the West's Avon Ladies and Tupperware party organizers, rural women were encouraged to make sales directly, and earn a percentage of commission on sales for themselves. The project, which started in 2001, has created more than one lakh micro-entrepreneurs called 'Shakti Ammas' across eighteen states. In addition to giving women access to a sellable product, HUL also provides entrepreneurial training, and help with inventory and distribution management. The company also came up with sachets of shampoo and washing powder, as they realized that the per unit consumption in rural areas and the capability to store these products was much smaller than that of their urban counterparts.

According to HUL, the incomes of a Shakti entrepreneur increases by about 30–40 per cent in comparison to other households in the same area. Because the sales commission goes directly to the Shakti Ammas, they also benefit from greater social empowerment. As one Shakti Amma from Bihar told the company: 'Earlier, I was dependent on my husband. Now I am self-dependent and not a burden on anyone. I can educate my children without help; I manage expenses on my own and I take my own decisions.' And the company, of course, gets plenty of extra sales, especially in the Indian media-dark hinterland.

The definition of success in any process of opportunity is not only defined by how well you're meeting your own goals but also by how well the other side of the opportunity exchange is meeting its goals. *Growth comes through collective winning.* The value exchange is a form of mutual service. Ninety-nine per cent of people have an inner-directed attitude. You must balance that with an outer-directed attitude. First and foremost, you need to understand the other side of the value exchange as much as your own. You need to deliver the services required by the other side of the exchange, not just the services required by you. Ideally, both sides should feel that they got the better deal.

5. Co-opportunity

The typical attitude of most business people with their employees, customers and suppliers is a battle for resources. The attitude is like the old-fashioned marketplace of haggling for a limited amount of money available; each side thinks of it as a zero-sum game. I win, you lose. *That is a fundamentally Old Era attitude, which will deny your opportunities.* Donald Trump, for example, is said to be famous for not paying contractors, for paying late or for trying to renegotiate a price long after the contract had been signed. The result was that contractors were said to apply a 'Trump tax' when they bid on his projects. They took his reputation into account and demanded more than they charged other buyers. He might win the occasional discount, but in the long run, he paid more than his competitors for the same goods.

McDonald's Builds McPartnerships

When McDonald's contacted Amit Jatia in 1994 to ask whether his family would consider investing in a venture that would bring the American fast food chain to India, the decision wasn't easy. The company would face several logistical problems. India, for example, didn't have a lettuce supply chain, a key ingredient in McDonald's burgers. Restaurants that offered burgers put cabbage on the buns instead. Nor was there a cold chain distribution infrastructure. Jatia would need to create a way to deliver both fresh and frozen ingredients directly to stores. And then there was the problem of the menu. Jatia, like much of India, is vegetarian. 'What convinced us was that McDonald's was willing to localize,' he told the BBC in 2014. 'They promised that there would be no beef or pork on the menu.'

Amit and his partners introduced, instead of the Big Mac, the Chicken Maharajah Mac. To bring in customers looking for cheap street food, India's McDonald's developed the twenty-rupee Aloo Tikki Burger and gave customers who wanted a spicier dish the McSpicy Paneer. In short, the McDonald's that Jatia envisaged was very different from the franchises across America and Europe. The menu would be localized, and so would the supply chain.

Jatia worked with Radha Krishna Foodland to create the distribution infrastructure. He built a local network of forty suppliers and fourteen core or Tier-1 suppliers that could deliver almost everything the stores needed, including lettuce, kitchen equipment and restaurant furniture. The only items that McDonald's India imports are cooking oil and fries.

The result isn't just a successful business that has made Amit Jatia rich. It has created the infrastructure for an entire industry that has benefited many companies and consumers across India.

A company must deal with many types of value exchanges with competitors, customers, channels, suppliers and other stakeholders. Haryard Business School professor Michael Porter has warned that you are in ferocious competition with these *five forces* for a limited pool of profits. *I completely disagree.* Michael Porter is a leading guru of *strategy. Unfortunately, the field of strategy limits rather than encourages opportunity.* Strategy gurus such as Porter view business as an army general views warfare—a vicious *competition* in which you can only win by wiping out your enemy's ability to fight. This is a fundamentally Old Era mindset, which is increasingly irrelevant and counterproductive in the Now Era.

In Porter's view, there are only limited profits to be had in an industry and your goal is to capture more of them. While profit is obviously important, having an overall goal of profits in no way helps you to achieve them. Remember this: *profits are a score, not a goal.* In addition, Porter's strategy model is based on conflict rather than cooperation. *But modern business is not like a war.* You do not need to wipe out your competitors in order to thrive. Business is also not like a poker game or football match. It is not a zero-sum game in which there is only one winner. In business, everyone can win. Putting primary focus *on your competitors* leads you to neglect the stakeholders who you need most: the ones who provide you resources and cooperate with you to provide value and identify and implement opportunities. These are your customers, employees, channel partners, suppliers and investors. Viewing these partners as competitors for a limited pool of profits is a foolish and potentially fatal mistake.

Instead of focusing on strategy, focus on opportunity. Opportunity requires *Co-opportunity* rather than competition. We must recognize that we are interdependent with our stakeholders. Without their cooperation, we cannot survive and thrive. We are together on a journey of opportunity and collective learning. Conflict destroys resources. Co-opportunity creates them. All sides can grow and benefit. We are not fighting for control of a limited pie. *There is no limit on growth through opportunity.* Everyone can be a winner.

As an analogy, think of marriage. Should marriage be a vicious competition over resources? Some people go into marriage with that attitude. For a marriage to succeed, it requires co-opportunity. It must be a fair value exchange relationship that creates opportunities. If the two people in a marriage compete on only one thing, it should be on how to serve the other one better. We are not competing with our environment; we are adapting to it. There's a huge difference. We need to emphasize adaptation and cooperation, not competition. Creating valuable adaptations to change requires a continuous, cumulative effort of collective learning. Conflict disrupts learning; co-opportunity fosters it.

Imagine this scenario: you are forced to hire a lawyer to resolve a dispute with a valuable customer. Which type of lawyer would be better—one who is in favour of a fair value exchange and co-opportunity or a shyster attack-dog who creates more conflict? You are obviously better off co-operating with the people you truly need rather than fighting with them.

Competition for resources can be very positive as it forces everyone to raise their game and to learn and adapt better and faster. Without competition you get stagnation. (All communist economies have failed because of a lack of competition, not an excess.) Competition benefits everyone. Ideally you should strive for alignment and co-opportunity both within and between the four segments of your opportunity environment: mission, model, market and domain. Conflict within these translates into a nopportunity.

The Fair Value Exchange

1. Know what's in it for you . . . and your stakeholders
Every transaction—and every action—needs to include an understanding of the benefits that will be won by every stakeholder, as Amit Jatia envisaged while introducing McDonald's in India.

2. Value is subjective
Different parties value different things in different ways. That creates an opportunity for arbitrage. Internet users place a low value on their personal data. Internet advertisers place a high value on that data. Merchants who collect that data in return for Internet services and sell it to advertisers can become like multi-billion-dollar business Google. Where the same items have different values to different people or in different contexts, there is opportunity for arbitrage.

3. Opportunity is a team sport
In the Now Era, opportunity always requires the creation and nurturing of numerous win-win relationships. The key drivers of the fair value exchange are empathy, mutual service, reciprocity, long-term relationships and co-opportunity.

7

How to Negotiate Fair Value

What is the purpose of a negotiation? How do you negotiate fair value? Is price the key driver of assessing value? Should you aim for a win-win result or can a negotiation only have one winner? How can you extract more than you put in and still walk away with a fair value exchange?

Ajay Sharma found an opportunity. He saw that an increasingly mobile Indian population wanted high-quality hotel rooms. But he also saw that they wanted those hotel rooms to feel unique and special. Not everyone, he realized, wanted to stay in a hotel room that looked like any other. Many travellers wanted to stay at a venue that was exciting and fun. So he broke a rule. Instead of designing hotel rooms that looked like standard boxes, he built and designed the *Bollywood Design Hotel* in Andheri, in the western suburbs of Mumbai. Guests could stay in studio apartments decorated with pictures of movies stars and designed with a Bollywood theme. It wasn't the Hilton, but it was comfortable clean, and fun. The business has grown. The opportunity that Ajay Sharma thought he had found quickly started to bear fruit.

One sign of that success was the interest that Ajay generated from OYO Rooms. South Asia's largest hotel chain, OYO Rooms wanted to add Ajay's hotel to its 'Capital O' collection. They made Ajay an offer: a guaranteed revenue of Rs 25 lakh per month, regardless of how many rooms they rented. They also wanted to give him an interest-free loan of up to Rs 1.5 crore to enable him to fix up the hotel. OYO would even provide a full-time salesperson, at its own expense, to sell the hotel to its stable of corporate clients. It was an interesting offer. Ajay would have a guaranteed income and he wouldn't have to work so hard to fill his rooms. His own sales and distribution bandwidth were very limited. If he were to team up with OYO, he could use their online platform and tap the company's huge corporate customer base. He could also increase his revenue per room by using OYO's sophisticated rate-management software. OYO's sophisticated sales platform is an adaptation that the hospitality industry has made to online marketing. Ajay could now use that adaptation too. Opportunity often works that way. One opportunity leads to another, and the deal included benefits that Ajay valued highly.

However, Ajay resisted. OYO Rooms has a reputation for offering low-budget hotel rooms at bargain prices. Since launching its elite Capital O product, the company hadn't been able to entice a single hotel in the area to join. Ajay was concerned that an association with the chain would damage his brand. He also had a dream. Though he owned only one hotel, he saw the Bollywood Design Hotel as the first of many across India. Being part of the OYO stable would be one opportunity, but Ajay believed that a more valuable opportunity might be to partner with OYO in a new chain. He could manage the hotels while OYO would find investors and handle the marketing.

As Ajay considered his decision, he had to place a value on each of the opportunities before him and the benefits they contained. As he built his business, he also had to negotiate those values. *As you build your opportunity, you'll have to make the same kind of valuations and engage in the same kinds of negotiations.*

How to Fill Your Value Bubble

Whenever you negotiate value with someone, a *value bubble* pops up in your mind. What's in the bubble? Your WIIFM—what you want, and how much you think it's worth.

We're used to seeing comic strips with dialogue bubbles in them. Instead of spoken dialogue between people, we fill the bubbles with our own *internal dialogues* weighing relative value. Imagine that you would like to buy a used car. You've responded to an ad and visit the dealer. You inspect the car that was advertised. Your value bubble pops up in your head and tells you how much you think it's worth, and your justification for this value. Let's say the price listed on the windscreen is Rs 3.5 lakh. Based on your own evaluation criteria, your value bubble puts the fair value at Rs 2.5 lakh. A salesman approaches. You can see that he's sizing you up. He has his own value bubble, which tells him how much money he wants to get in exchange for the car, and how much he expects you to deliver. Unless both your value bubbles can intersect, you won't reach a deal.

Unfortunately, most negotiations fail. Why? Because the value bubbles that are negotiating contain only one key driver of assessing value: price. *Putting price as the key driver of value will damage your ability to properly evaluate opportunities.* It will deny fair value to your own opportunities and limit the resources you can attract to them. Even worse, it will deny you opportunities that are simply based on reaching a fair value exchange.

There Is a Better Way to Negotiate Fair Value

In India, there are numerous small businesses whose only strategy is to copy someone else's model and compete on price. They survive by cheating on their taxes or cutting corners or negotiating unfair deals. Since their quality is substandard, they put price first and consider any negotiation to be a win-lose haggling session. You must *not* copy this strategy, as it is almost always a nopportunity. Instead, you can and must consider negotiation to be an essential form of *research*. The objective for each side is to determine which opportunities are worth pursuing, what resources they require, how to evaluate these resources, what and how much to trade for them, and how to obtain them. Your research will also help you to determine who to trade with and the relative value of trading with one party rather than another.

To harness opportunities, you must learn what you want and need. The only way to do this effectively is to trade insights with people with relevant expertise. The people you negotiate with should ideally have similar needs. Every stakeholder is looking for the right trading partner, the right long-term potential relationships in which you both can learn and thrive; relationships in which each side is balancing and complementing the other. *At the same time, negotiation is obviously not an exercise in altruism.* Your actions should be based on your own *intelligent selfishness*.

You don't necessarily strive to reach a fair deal because you want to. You do it because you have to. You do it because you recognize that win-win relationships are a key driver of opportunity. You need an integrated, holistic approach to create an effective Opportunity

Model. Finding and building long-term working relationships with the right partners is essential. In order to create your Model, you will need to create effective value exchanges along the entire route of your value chain. A failure to do this—transparently—will result in friction, delayed learnings, a failure to adapt and a waste of resources.

What's the Best Way to Start a Negotiation?

The general objective of all negotiations is to 1) gain required resources while 2) preserving current resources. You wish to gain as much value as you can while giving up as little as possible. But remember—it's not just about *you*—you must also strive to be *fair*. Negotiating a fair value exchange may not come naturally to you. Many of the tactics may seem counterintuitive. You may have grown up in the ruthless Old Era culture of tit-for-tat haggling, in which both sides primarily focus on their own selfish interests. A fair value exchange negotiation is exactly the opposite. For example, to carry out a successful fair value negotiation you *must not* start out by trying to get what you want. Why? Because it's likely that whatever you think that you *want* or *need* at the beginning of any negotiation is incorrect. *Instead, you should start out by learning what the other side wants, and why they want it.*

Your initial objectives are 1) to learn whether the opportunity you are pursuing is a potential Pareto Leader which merits the creation of a Model; and 2) to learn what you need to do in order to build an effective Opportunity Model, one which will eventually carry you across your Opportunity Bridge from aspiration to realization. You will learn this through interaction with other people. These people are not just potential cooperators. *The people you negotiate with are your teachers.* You may want them on your team because they are specialists, with expertise that you lack. You'd like to gain a reasonable understanding of what they do and why and how they do it so that you can integrate their learnings into the process of evaluating your opportunity and creating your Model. Therefore, your negotiations should never begin with any discussion of money. Discussions should initially determine whether the opportunity would create sufficient value for both sides.

The key questions to answer are: Could this relationship be an opportunity? If so, why and how? Can it add enough value for both of us? When starting out, your first aim is to learn HOW to learn. What is the methodology of learning in that industry? You need to learn the rules that the other side follows. This is crucial because many of the best opportunities come from changing the rules. How can you possibly determine what to change if you don't understand the rules? Your counterpart may be able to unlock great value for you by helping you to discover and explore your opportunity environment, as well as to focus and evaluate your inventory of potential opportunities.

What if You Want to Play by the Rules, But . . .?

Imagine a value-exchange spectrum in which your needle is on the far left and the other guy's needle is on the far right. Each of you is trying to move your needle toward the middle. In an unprincipled negotiation, each side is struggling to move the needle as far to his side as possible. The ideal situation, however, is for each side to attempt to move the needle to the exact middle, where a win-win value exchange can be achieved. You may believe wholeheartedly in the virtues of the fair value exchange. Unfortunately, it's quite likely that all your exchange partners don't play by the same rules. All people, without exception, are selfish. That's why you use *intelligent selfishness*. Finding out what the other side wants is like buying good stocks at the bottom of the market. *You can't lose.*

When we're negotiating with someone on value, we should first make them feel that we are looking after their value *before our own*. That's a cardinal rule. That will increase our perceived value to them at no cost. Rather than thinking only of what you need and want and disregarding the other person, start by *regarding* the other person. To put it another way, you should make the other side feel that you're more interested in helping them than you are in helping yourself. And you should do this sincerely because it's in your best interest to do so. In any exchange relationship, it is entirely normal for each side to try to improve the terms of trade to benefit his side. But one must balance this tendency by building the understanding that over time, cooperative long-term learning relationships can massively increase the resources available to all sides. It is the difference between day trading and the long-term value investing done by Warren Buffett.

You should assume that the other side does not know your rules of engagement and is not striving for mutuality. They are not necessarily seeking the same goals in the same way. That's why you need to lead with a *learning approach*—not a *teaching approach*. People feel honoured to be sought out for advice. You respect their knowledge and want to learn from them. For example, if you are a career aspirant, you should seek out potential bosses who would be ideal mentors for you. There are effective ways to deal with people who have a win-lose mentality. Even if the other side doesn't want to negotiate fairly on a win-win basis, you can convince them to be fair by appealing to their selfishness. You should strive to understand what they value and how much they value it. You should also understand their rules for negotiation better than they do. That will allow you to offer something that is valuable to them but that isn't particularly valuable to you. In other words: *value arbitrage.*

Governments often conduct value arbitrage to turn a win-lose negotiation into a win-win negotiation when they make procurements. Offset agreements are contracts attached to procurements, usually from the defence industry. For governments, defence purchases are always controversial. Defence equipment costs a great deal of taxpayers' money and the industry is dominated by giant corporations such as Northrop Grumman, Thales and BAE Systems from countries such as the UK, France and particularly the US. If India wants to buy a new top-of-the-range missile system, it can expect to have to send millions of dollars outside the country. To extract additional value from that giant foreign purchase, the government will ask potential sellers to present a second offer to offset the cost of the procurement. Sellers will have to state how much of the purchase price they plan to reinvest in the country. They'll be expected to source raw materials locally, build maintenance plants, train local technicians, form joint ventures, or license technology to local firms.

Are Canadian French Fries More Valuable Than Silicon Chips?

In 2015, when Irving Shipbuilding signed a CAD 2.3 billion contract with the Canadian government to build six Arctic Offshore Patrol Ships, both sides knew they had won a valuable agreement. For the shipbuilders, it was a large contract that would keep their yards busy for some time. For the government, it meant not only six new boats for the navy but also 1000 jobs in Halifax, Nova Scotia.

Under Canada's industrial and technological benefits policy, Irving was also required to perform work in Canada equal to the price of the contract value. But in Canada the definition of 'work' in offset agreements is kept flexible to enable sellers to find projects. The government hopes that businesses will build hi-tech plants or conduct defence research to fulfil their requirements. But they might not.

Irving invested CAD 425 million in a frozen potato processing plant that's used to make French fries. The government awarded it CAD 40 million worth of credits for the investment. The result was a discussion among officials about the value of different kinds of jobs and investments. Is a hi-tech French-fry factory less valuable than a hi-tech silicon-chip firm?

The Benefits of Value Arbitrage

In general, each side's typical objective during negotiations is to deny the other side value. We all want to get as much as possible and pay as little as possible. This is more or less a general rule of all human value-exchange relationships, so we will find it difficult to change.

The Values of Amazon Prime

Loyalty programmes aren't new in the retail industry. Stores have been handing out discounts to regular customers for decades, encouraging them to return. But Amazon has broken the rules. It charges customers a monthly fee to join a special club for regular customers. In return for that fee, Prime members get a host of benefits: free, fast delivery; discounts; movies and songs; exclusive deals, and so on.

For customers who believe that they might use the site at least once a month, it looks like a good deal. They put a high value on fast delivery and Prime delivers that. For Amazon, the marginal cost of delivering those benefits is small. Prime membership in the US costs $12.99 per month (₹ 999 per year in India) and includes streaming video. The streaming video alone is available for $8.99 per month. All the other benefits cost just $4. And Amazon can expect the discounts to increase its sales. Customers get something they value at a low cost. Amazon delivers something that it knows its customers value. Customers pay more than they would otherwise and are more likely to regard Amazon as their outlet of choice. Both sides benefit from the value arbitrage.

What we can do is increase the perceived value of what we are giving the other side so that they will be willing to pay us more and still feel that they're getting a better deal than we are. Amazon has done a magnificent job of this with their Prime programme. They give something on which they place a small value to people who value it highly. They use *bargaining chips*, things that are not very valuable to you, something you can trade away and not be harmed—something you can use as leverage to trade for something you need.

A bargaining chip is not an essential, it's not a requirement. Requirements are things you cannot trade away. Both of you can win if you discover things that are more important to you than the guy that you trade with. Both sides can do it knowingly. You need to discover the other side's bargaining chips so that you can ascertain true value.

Trying to give people exactly what they want is speculative because people keep changing what they want, particularly if the negotiation is a learning experience. Wanting is a future-oriented activity. Often people don't really know what they want, because it doesn't exist yet. It's not tangible.

More important than what the other guy wants is the reason why he wants it. If you discover why the other side wants something, you can help them solve their problem. By doing this, you can render an amazingly useful service to them.

Service Sells Better Than Salesmanship

How can you best be of service to the other side? It's simple: always behave like a consultant, instead of acting like a buyer or (even worse) like a salesperson. The stereotypical salesperson is someone you avoid, because he's trying to sell you something you don't want, just so he can make a killing. He doesn't want to listen to you. He doesn't care about you. He's a bloodsucking mosquito. People swat mosquitos away, or kill them. *The best salespeople in the world do not sell.* What do they do? They behave like consultants. What do consultants do? They are trusted advisors. They are experts. They help solve people's problems. They help get their jobs done. Especially the tricky jobs that they can't figure out themselves. *They provide service rather than sales. They ask questions. They listen. They add value.*

The perfect consultant would never seek an unfair value exchange. That's what it means to be honest. People say, 'I like him because he's honest,' but what they really mean is that he would never even consider seeking an unfair value exchange. Your objective is not to have a high score; it is to provide a useful service to others. If you do that, your score will increase. As we ideally want our relationships to be durable, we must treat others as we would like to be treated. In other words, we must follow the golden rule. If the other side doesn't know how to negotiate fairly, you can train them by setting the right example.

Negotiate to Identify Obsolete Rules

In the classic manual on negotiation *Getting to Yes* by Roger Fisher and William Ury, the authors recommend striving for agreement over interests, rather than positions. That's good advice. The authors say that understanding standards is crucial to successful negotiation. This is true. But it is even more important to understand values. Your values, and the other side's values. Standards tend to be a benchmark for certain types of value that are more standardized. For example, if you were negotiating over a hotel room, the size of the room would be a standard you could refer to in assessing value. There are certainly many other elements of value beyond standards. For example, rules can be a form of value. Rules are values that are often considered to be less negotiable, i.e. we can't or won't or shouldn't do this or that. Rules need to be examined to see if they can be negotiable. Or should be negotiable.

As mentioned before, our own rules can often become irrelevant, but we don't realize it. One of the benefits of the negotiation should be to expose and test the relevance of your rules. Often people don't even clearly understand their own rules. These can be vague and informal rules of thumb. Rather than trying to convince the other guy that his rules are wrong, you'd be much better off letting him convince you that *your rules* are obsolete. *He may be right!* Identifying irrelevant rules can be a big opportunity for you, and lead to valuable adaptations that the other side can help you to implement.

In order to create a value exchange that is effective and durable, it is essential for each side to understand what they value. The process of exchange itself, and the negotiation that takes place to create it, should help to advance the learning that each has about what they value. In order to meet in the middle, there must be an understanding about the mission in a joint perspective. That is impossible unless each side accurately and transparently understands what it values and what it needs. You should ideally examine your values, even prior to the negotiation, in order to understand who you should ideally be negotiating with.

Your Main Competitor is Your Customer

You are constantly negotiating and bargaining with your customers. The biggest success you gain is acquiring and holding onto the customer. The biggest jeopardy you face is losing the customer. You could have no major competitors, and still have problems with your customers. This is generally due to the quantity and quality of the value exchange.

If the customer relationship can be transformed from competition to co-opportunity, both sides will benefit. If you are an employee, your employer is your customer, and the same rules apply. With customers or employers, you must know how to demonstrate your own value. If you don't understand your value, how can you exchange it? How can you specifically help the other side to get what they want? Many people don't even understand what they truly want or need. Or what they want is not what they need, or why. You can help them to understand. This adds tremendous value for both of you. And in the bargain, you find out what they want and how much they value it.

The ideal situation is one in which the customer values the relationship so much that he wants to increase it. This allows the company to obtain more value from the customer. But companies that accomplish this must be very careful of going too far. The goal is a fair and equitable value exchange with the customer, combined with the steadily growing relationship in which both sides are able to learn and adopt better over time. The goal is not to squeeze more and more profits out of your customers. This is a consequence, not a goal. The score is not the goal.

Harley-Davidson Turns Customers into Fans

Imagine a business whose customers value their relationship with it so much that they're prepared to spend large sums telling people about that relationship. Those customers become more than sources of revenue. They become channels for marketing and partners in the growth of the company. That's the situation for Harley-Davidson. The motorcycle company goes out of its way to find and develop new riders. It's More Roads to Harley-Davidson plan aims to create 2 million new riders in the United States, grow international business to 50 per cent of annual volume, and launch 100 new motorcycles 'profitably and sustainably' by 2027. It plans to do that with a multi-channel retail experience but also by running a Harley-Davidson Riding Academy by giving riders the chance to trade their motorcycles up to new models, and by tripling its product placement, including in movies and television shows including *A Star is Born* and *Mayans*.

Those moves have all helped Harley-Davidson do more than simply promote its products' fuel efficiency or price. They help to promote a brand with which customers can identify. The degree of that identity can be measured. In 2018, Harley-Davidson sold nearly $4 billion worth of motorcycles. At the same time, it also sold nearly $240 million worth of merchandise such as jackets, helmets and shirts. These products are emblazoned with the company's logo. For customers, they're a sign that they're members of an exclusive group. For Harley-Davidson, their free advertising won with the cooperation of dedicated fans.

It's Not Just About the Money, Honey

People who do not understand their values well tend to measure progress based on dollars and rupees. *Unfortunately, monetary goals do not help you negotiate effectively.* Opportunity is a team sport in which common goals have to be shared by everyone. If for example you have a goal of growing profit at 20 per cent a year, how can your customers share that goal? How can your employees share that goal? How can your suppliers share that goal? Your employees will feel, 'Oh, that's going to come at my expense.' The supplier will feel, 'Oh, that will come in at my expense.' The customer will feel, 'Oh, that will come at my expense.'

How can you move the other guy's needle to the middle to create a win-win value exchange? That requires both self-knowledge as well as knowledge of the other guy as well as an ability to transparently negotiate based on each other's values. *Negotiation is not about victory.* It is about creating a win-win relationship in which both of you productively collaborate to create mutually valuable adaptations, aka opportunities.

Demonstrate Fairness, Empathy and Transparency

A key issue in relationships is revealing how much you value the other side and the service that they provide to you. People are often reluctant to do this because they believe that it will reduce their bargaining leverage. This is typical of Old Era thinking.

The rules of the Now Era reward those who strive for fairness in their relationships, as well as in the entire process of opportunity. You want the other side to be empathetic to you. If you are empathetic to them, they are more likely to reciprocate and be empathetic to you. Reciprocity is a very strong force in human relationships. The more you're nice to her the more she'll want to be nice to you. It's the secret of a happy marriage.

Any negotiation method that doesn't focus on the other side's WIIFM is flawed. The key is to make the other person feel as if you really care by acting as if you really care, but most of all by sincerely caring. This is essential, even if you have to reach it from your own point of intelligent selfishness. You want people to believe, 'This guy is really trying to help me, and he's showing the value of helping.' You're helping, but you're also helping yourself. The more you can help the other guy, and create value for him, the more he can help create value for you. By seeking to understand the other side's problems and needs, you are defining their agenda for them. You may do a better job of this for them than they did for themselves. This will help them become empathetic to your agenda because you can define your agenda in terms of how it helps them. This adds a lot of gravity and value to you and increases the amount you can receive in return.

You're introducing a set of rules about how to exchange. How do you set these rules? By starting to use them right at the beginning. Starting with empathy, not demands. Don't act like a baby. Act like a mother. How do you get others to do things your way? By being of service to them. You should introduce a set of rules about how you should interact with each other before he does. You can only get away with this if you start by being empathetic and cooperative. It may be that you are doing value arbitrage, but that's okay because you want to ideally set up a situation in which he is also doing value arbitrage. You should strive to understand the key drivers of friction for the other side. How can you help convert these into value? Sometimes people just want to make more money and don't know how. In that case you can help them understand the friction of their customers or their other stakeholders, so they can add more value in partnership with you for them. That will get them a better value exchange and allow you to get one as well. This is what true service is all about.

How Zuckerberg Negotiated Fair Value

While a student at Stanford University in the mid-2000s, Kevin Systrom met Facebook founder and CEO, Mark Zuckerberg, at gatherings on campus. Though Systrom declined Zuckerberg's proposal that he drop out of school and take a job with Facebook, the two men kept in touch over the phone in the years that followed. After Systrom launched photo-sharing app Instagram in October 2010, Zuckerberg had him over for dinner at his Palo Alto, California, home a few times to discuss 'philosophy', according to *Vanity Fair*. Zuckerberg wanted to keep an eye on the potential competitor, and, at some point, he says, 'it occurred to me we could be one company.'

In April 2012, after Systrom turned down a $500 million offer from Twitter, Zuckerberg invited Systrom over to his home for a long conversation about how Facebook could help take tiny Instagram, which then had only thirteen employees, to the next level.

'This never had the feeling of negotiation, because we kind of wanted to work together,' Zuckerberg told *Vanity Fair*. The discussions quickly led to a $1 billion offer from Facebook and a promise from Zuckerberg to allow Instagram to maintain its independence.

Systrom met with his business partner, Mike Krieger, to review the offer.

'I really like Mark, and I really like his company,' Systrom told Krieger. 'And I really like what Facebook is trying to achieve.'

The pair decided to sell. The entire negotiation had lasted three days.

Coming back to the story with which we began this chapter. What did Ajay Sharma do with the offer from OYO Rooms? He realized that competing with OYO would be difficult and painful, and he saw that he had a lot of value to gain by creating a co-opportunity with the chain. Or at least with *a* chain. So he also spoke with Fab Hotels, the promoter of an OYO competitor, to see what they had to offer. In the end, he felt that the potential value arbitrage with OYO was huge and that the company could be an ideal partner for his Bollywood Design Hotel concept. Like other large hotel companies, they wanted to create new upscale brands, they had tremendous access to resources, and they could bring his current hotel extra business during low periods.

If the partnership didn't work out, he could always give it up. He used his concern that an association with OYO might damage his own brand as a bargaining chip during the negotiations and added OYO's opportunity to his own to create a new one. In the end, Ajay agreed to a three-month trial deal. He gave them his rates and he waited to see how well they built his brand. He's testing their value to see if they deliver what was promised—and he's measuring the value of the opportunity.

How to Negotiate Fair Value

1. To get what's in it for you, start with what's in it for them

Every negotiation should start with empathy. Learn what your partner values. Understand what they need from the relationship, and genuinely care about delivering it to them. When you start with empathy, you set the rules of the relationship and ensure a fair value exchange.

2. A fair value exchange creates co-opportunity

When you create a fair value exchange, you do more than close a deal. You create the foundation of greater cooperation in the future. Businesses find partners that can improve their own services. Customers get to identify with a brand. Sellers get free promotion and fanatical supporters like in the case of Harley-Davidson.

3. To negotiate successfully, understand value and deliver a win-win

The key to a fair value exchange and a long-term business relationship is to understand the values offered and desired on each side and negotiate an agreement that benefits both sides. In today's era, winner-takes-all negotiating ends with no one getting anything in the long run. When you understand what each side values, you can find new ways to negotiate the deal, as Ajay did with the Bollywood Design Hotel contract with OYO Rooms.

8

How to Attract Value

What is opportunity gravity? How does gravity attract resources to an opportunity? How can gravity bring you leadership and additional value? How do you assess the gravity of an opportunity? How does change create an opportunity and deepen its gravity?

Computer game players can be a strange bunch, but Amine Issa is stranger than most. A competitive player of World of Warcraft, he would turn up to tournaments dressed not in a wizard's hat or as a warrior but looking very nerdy. He would have a stack of notes. Those notes listed every other team's armoury profiles, how they play, what they own, and so on. The day before the tournament, he'd sit with his team and they'd go over the details like a coach reviewing another team's players. That level of research shouldn't have been too surprising. Issa was actually a researcher at the Mayo Clinic, investigating human endurance. He was researching the performance of fighter pilots and athletes, and he started to wonder whether the same kind of analysis could also be applied in the growing world of computer gaming. He met Bogdan Suchyk, an entrepreneur, at Twitchcon, a convention for the live streaming video platform, and the two found that they were thinking along the same lines: developing the technology to create a kind of Moneyball for e-sports. They formed an analytics company. Two hours before the deadline, Suchyk submitted the project to Techcrunch Disrupt, a start-up competition. They had no product, but they had screenshots of mock-ups, and it was enough.

They were accepted . . . and went on to win. After the victory, everything came easily. The team came together. The beta version attracted users and feedback. Partners signed up, and the money flowed in. Mobalytics received $2.6 million in its first round of seed funding. They had found a valuable opportunity, and it attracted resources.

How Can You Attract Resources?

Have you read the bestselling book *The Secret*, or seen the video based upon it? It enthusiastically promotes *the Law of Attraction*. The basic premise of this 'law' is that positive or negative thoughts attract good or bad things into our lives. In other words, you attract value into your life *based purely on how you think and feel*. Napoleon Hill endorsed a similar rule in his classic bestseller *Think and Grow Rich*. 'Thoughts are things,' he wrote. All you need is a burning, definite desire, mixed with persistence, and you will be successful. Most of us do indeed have a burning, definite desire: *to be rich*. Does having the desire to be rich in any way make you rich?

Imagine this: you have a burning definite desire to become the business partner of Warren Buffet. Following Napoleon Hill's advice, you focus intensely on this desire until it consumes you. You convince yourself that Buffet will surely become your partner. Bursting with positive energy, you travel to the Oracle's Omaha office.

'Mr Buffett will meet me,' you announce to his receptionist. 'He would like to become my business partner.'

Such confidence! And why not? If you believe, so can you achieve!

You wait for hours until the Oracle can finally be contacted.

Buffett asks: 'Who the hell is this guy?'

A quick check with Dr Google finds no trace of you. You're clearly not an expert on investments. Apparently, you're only a legend in your own mind; not an attractive business partner for the likes of Warren Buffett. You're politely invited to depart, but you adamantly refuse to believe that Buffet has spurned you. Security is called, and you attract a free trip to the nearest exit. The version of the Law of Attraction that is peddled to the masses is a massive tanker of snake oil. It is not a *rule*, but a *fule* that will make a fool out of you, and for one reason only: *it simply doesn't work*. Regrettably, you don't attract money just because you're needy or greedy.

A Force of Attraction That Does Work

There is a *law of attraction* that does work very reliably: it is called *gravity*. It is the prime force of attraction in the universe. Gravity is the force which created all the stars and planets. It lights up the sun, and keeps our earth in orbit around it. Gravity creates mass, density and complexity. In the same way, *opportunity gravity* is the force that can make your opportunity a star, by attracting all the energy and resources it needs to light up. Opportunity Gravity is the crucial element an opportunity needs to attract resources. Gravity is the force that attracts value. An abundance of gravity propels an opportunity up the lifecycle curve. A lack of gravity sends it downward to oblivion.

Every new opportunity begins its life as a *seed*. Most people refer to nascent opportunities as ideas, but there is a big difference between a seed and an idea. There are many ideas in the world, but few of them are seeds of an opportunity. A seed can grow into a great tree, a mere idea cannot. Imagine a storm raging through a forest and blowing millions of seeds into the wind. How many can survive to grow into great trees? Every seed must compete for resources with other seeds. It needs sun, water and nourishment. Opportunities are the same. Without resources no opportunity can grow or survive.

Gravity Increases Potential Value

A nascent opportunity by itself has no *tangible* value. It has only *potential value*. What is the potential value? Its ability to grow and create even more value. How do investors value start-ups? They are funded based on the potential value of their underlying opportunity. Potential value is the gold under the ground that can be mined and sold. But before you can mine the gold you first must see it. Then you must convince people that it is there, and that you can take it out. Then you must build the capacity to mine it at a reasonable cost. All this requires resources. In the Old Era, major resources were only attracted to tangible things such as land, armies and religions. Land could grow crops and armies could grab physical resources from others, while religion could promise you heaven. In the Now Era, we conquer markets instead of countries.

In order to succeed, you can leverage or trade the *potential value* of the intangible opportunity for the tangible resources with *actual value* that you require for growth. These tangible resources include money, team members, hard assets and intellectual property. How do you increase the potential value of an opportunity? It's simple: *you increase its gravity—its perceived potential value.* Increasing gravity is essential, because we must *attract resources* in order to transform our budding opportunity from a seed into a tree. An opportunity that cannot attract resources, regardless of how good it sounds, will be an orphan, without any friends. It will be like the seed that is planted but never watered. It will die. Obviously, if no one can perceive any potential value in your opportunity, it won't attract resources. You'll find it impossible to recruit a team to implement it, or investors to put their money behind it, or channels to sell it, or customers to buy it.

An opportunity with higher gravity has greater perceived potential value and can attract more resources. An opportunity with low gravity has less potential value and can attract fewer resources. Opportunity gravity is like money in the bank that you can spend on your side of the value exchange. An example: you are developing an Internet business concept which you believe can attract a maximum of *1 million* average monthly users in India only. Your friend Sanjeev is developing an Internet concept which he believes can attract a maximum of *1 billion* monthly users from around the world. Which concept has more opportunity gravity? Which one has more potential value that can be traded for resources? The more you can increase the perceived potential value of your opportunity by increasing its gravity, the larger and more valuable the opportunity can become. If we are pursuing a nascent opportunity, in the short term we are probably going to harvest more success from increasing its gravity than from any other activity.

Gravity in Action

Gravity is the force that draws resources towards an opportunity. It's an abstract idea but it can be seen in the real world and explained.

Union Square Ventures (USV) is one of New York's leading venture capital (VC) firms. It invested early in companies including Twitter, Behance, Etsy and Zynga. Like other VC firms, it controls the resources needed to make opportunities grow. The company also explains its funding decisions. In effect, it tells people how the elements of an opportunity act on its decision makers to draw out investments. In April 2018, the company published its Thesis 3.0, the third iteration of the set of ideas it uses to allocate funding.

USV had started by investing in network applications. It felt the greatest draw towards customer-facing opportunities whose value to users increased as more people joined the network. That focus drew its funds to Twitter, Foursquare, and Kickstarter among others. The company's second thesis expanded the elements of an opportunity's gravity to include vertical networks such as LendingClub and Circle; the technology that other opportunities need, such as Cloudfare and MongoDB; and opportunities in decentralization, such as CoinBase. Each of those forces broadened consumer access, and that is now the focus of USV's third thesis: 'USV backs trusted brands that broaden access to knowledge, capital, and well-being by leveraging networks, platforms, and protocols.'

As a definition it's vague, but that gives the VCs, one group of people who control the flow of resources, plenty of flexibility to direct that flow. One area that USV is looking at closely now is healthcare. Rebecca Kaden, a partner at USV, explained that what the company found exciting in the field is the broadening of access achieved through increased value and lower costs; a rise in the quality of care (the product); and the opportunity contained in the combination of data and human skill. Gravity is a force. But it's a force made up of real preferences that act on those who control the flow of resources.

Whether the opportunity is your own career or a business concept, increasing its gravity can provide you with many benefits:

1. Increasing gravity inflates your value in the eyes of others. It provides you with value that costs you little or nothing, which you can trade for resources.
2. Increasing gravity provides you with resources that you need to grow.
3. Increasing gravity can give your opportunity a longer lifecycle. When opportunities lose gravity, they begin to die. Lifecycles can be extended by increasing the gravity of your current opportunities.

How Gravity Can Give You Leadership

Millions of words have been written on defining leadership. I'll offer a simple definition: *leadership is the ability to attract and retain followers.* Why is a leader a leader? What is the most basic and important job that a leader has to do? He or she has to set the direction for others to follow. You may have a great opportunity and abundant self-belief, but if no one will follow you, you're not a leader. The direction you set may be over the side of a steep cliff, but as long as others are willing to follow you, you're a leader. (For example, Hitler was a very effective leader. Millions chose to follow him into complete disaster and disgrace.)

In order to successfully grow a tiny opportunity seed into a giant tree that can bear abundant fruit, you must attract an army of followers. No one can do it all alone. The first members of your opportunity army will be a small number of *disciples* who have true faith. They must have faith, because the opportunity is nothing but a promise at that point. Your disciples will spread the gospel of your opportunity and attract other disciples and soldiers to your army, who will provide funding, skills and sweat to scale a raw opportunity into a successful service. Without disciples, you are not a leader, but a *mad man*—a lonely voice crying in the wilderness. To attract and maintain disciples, you must increase the gravity of your opportunity. To attract smart, talented people, your opportunity must be very attractive. This is obvious and essential.

How You Assess the Gravity of an Opportunity?

To assess the gravity of an opportunity, use the *nine key drivers of value*. You can also customize by adding additional key drivers that are appropriate for your particular environment.

Opportunities with the following characteristics should have higher gravity:

1. They provide *utility*, i.e. *very useful service*. This is ranked first because it is the most important.
2. They are *substantial*, with large-scale potential.
3. They are *relevant*, i.e. needed now.
4. They are *unique*—one that is relevant but not unique is a commodity.
5. They are *sustainable*, i.e. have durable competitive advantage.
6. They are *accessible*, with low barriers to entry, at least for you.
7. They are *suitable*, i.e. they align well with your mission, model, market and domain.
8. They are *actionable*, i.e. feasible to execute at scale.
9. They can be *profitable*, i.e. Pareto Leaders with the potential to be in the top 10 per cent of their category.

Among these key drivers of value, utility is generally the most essential. For example, utility has been the key driver of value in the evolution of the mobile handsets industry. Even a basic handset has far more value than a landline phone simply because it is portable and therefore always available, an important addition to utility. The Blackberry further increased utility by adding email to the phone. The smartphone massively increased utility by adding a networked computer to the phone. It is very common for companies to fail to add relevant utility to their products and, as a result, to lose most of their gravity to new competitors. As a result, Nokia was wiped out by the newcomer Blackberry, and Blackberry quickly lost out to Apple, which had never made phones before. Why does this phenomenon occur?

Companies often fail to gain gravity or they lose gravity because they don't focus on *key drivers of change* occurring in their environment. This is a huge mistake, because the key source of adaptation and therefore opportunity is change in your environment. Often companies fail to identify key drivers of change because they take a myopic view of their environment. How to identify key drivers of change? Look at change that has happened in the past and ask what caused it. Look for common causes for multiple generations of change. These could be key drivers.

Changes in any aspect of your environment can increase or decrease gravity. For example, in recent years, new trucking businesses have been able to attract substantial funding in India. One such start-up, Rivigo, has been able to raise over $216 million in venture capital. What changes in India's opportunity environment have increased gravity in India's trucking industry, allowing it to attract so much investment? An examination of the environment exposes a few possible factors:

1. The construction of new national highways has reduced travel times between major cities by up to 70 per cent, allowing for a shift of goods from air freight to road freight;
2. The introduction of e-commerce has greatly increased the amount of goods to be shipped on a timely basis; and
3. The development of tech capabilities has enabled the creation of more efficient business models linking independent truckers with shippers on common platforms.

These are just a few of the environmental factors impacting the industry and creating gravity for the industry. But this gravity is only created for those who identify and exploit these key drivers of change.

When Diets Change So Do Opportunities . . . and Their Gravity

We often like to think of food as traditional. Tandoori parathas, dal and biryanis have all along been popular in different regions of India. But while dishes and cuisine may stay largely the same, diet changes constantly.

The Food and Agriculture Organization of the United Nations (FAOSTAT) looked at food consumption patterns around the world between 1961 and 2011. They found that someone living in India in

1961 typically consumed 2010 calories every day. Grains made up 43 per cent of that diet; plant produce took up another 23 per cent; dairy and eggs were 12 per cent of a daily diet, the same as sugar and fat. Meat was just 2 per cent of an Indian's diet, while 8 per cent came from other sources such as pulses and alcohol.

Fifty years later, the total number of calories consumed by an average Indian had risen to 2458. Grains had fallen to 32 per cent of that diet, while vegetable produce had risen to 34 per cent. Indians had also more than doubled their intake of eggs and dairy. They were eating a little more sugar and fat. While meat still made up only 2 per cent of the Indian diet, the amount of meat had risen from 17 grams per day to 29 grams. The beneficiaries of this change in diet in India have been the dairy and egg industry, as well as fast food chains and the sellers of Western fast food in particular.

India isn't the only place where diet has changed—and continues to change. As people around the world have become more concerned about climate change and animal welfare, they're also turning increasingly towards plant-based diets. Between 2007 and 2014, Sweden's vegetarians rose from 3 per cent of the population to 10 per cent. In Germany, the percentage increased from 9 to 11 per cent between 2009 and 2017. The number of vegans in the UK jumped by 72.2 per cent between 2006 and 2016. That change has given businesses in building plant-based opportunities extra gravity. When Beyond Meat, a maker of meat substitutes, went public in May 2019, it ended its first day of trading 163 per cent above its IPO price. The company raised $240 million to achieve a valuation of nearly $1.5 billion.

Change creates opportunity, and strong opportunities create strong gravity that suck in large amounts of resources.

Strategies to Increase Gravity

You can increase gravity by enhancing any (or preferably all) of the nine key drivers of value, ideally working in harmony. In addition, you can employ the following six strategies to increase the perceived potential value and therefore the gravity of your opportunity:

1. True Vision

Truth is a fundamental driver of the prosperity of our age. In the Old Era, power and authority were sources of truth. In the Now Era, truth based on evidence is a source of power and potential value. By utilizing true vision, we can improve our ability to analyse the value of an opportunity based on evidence filtered through multiple levels of history, greatly increasing its potential gravity.

Let's say that you've put your home up for sale and would like to increase its perceived value. How could you do it? One way would be to tell prospective buyers that the neighbourhood was the most valuable in the entire city. If you made that claim, most people would ask: 'Why do you say that?' People value claims based on facts backed by real evidence and expertise. You would need to do your homework and provide a thorough set of statistics based on actual sales data, showing that comparative homes in the neighbourhood had been selling at a higher value than in the rest of the city for the past twenty years, and that the trend was increasing. You could also refer prospective buyers to well-known market experts who would agree with your views, lending their gravity to your cause.

2. Belief

Beliefs are the systems software that drive our thoughts and actions. *However, many beliefs are opinions masquerading as facts.* Unlike true vision, belief does not require factual evidence. For example, Adolf Hitler was a man from nowhere, who started with nothing but his own insane beliefs, all based on fantasy rather than facts. Yet he was able to create and lead an army of fanatical believers; millions of them died to protect an entirely false set of beliefs. In the Old Era, mass belief could be effectively harnessed through faith in religious doctrines and myths. In the Now Era, the most effective means of building and sustaining belief is through the consistent delivery of useful service. By doing this, some companies have been able to retain believers for decades. Employees and businesses cannot retain believers through faith or fear; they must do it by meeting relevant needs. If you don't believe in the opportunity you're promoting, you are nothing but a con artist, and will eventually be exposed as a fraud. This will obviously deflate the gravity of your opportunity. An opportunity must attract you by appealing to your own self-interest, so why should it be different for anyone else?

Building viral beliefs also requires consistently fair value exchanges. Many self-help gurus claim that simply by believing in yourself, you will attract everything you need in your life. *This is not true.* If your entire belief centres on your own WIIFM, and doesn't offer fair value-exchanges, you will fail to attract or retain many followers.

3. Social Proof

The Law of Attraction as peddled by hucksters can work, but never in isolation. If you are the only one who believes, nothing will change. However, if you can recruit an army of believers, you can attract many more. There is indeed more gravity in numbers. As mentioned earlier, leadership is primarily the ability to attract followers. The larger the army of believers, the stronger the gravitational attraction of the leader will be and the greater his ability to attract and retain yet more followers.

People believe because others believe. People take action because others take action. Even leaders follow other leaders. This powerful phenomenon is called *social proof.*

Is Cryptocurrency a Social-Driven Nopportunity?

Satoshi Nakomoto's white paper that launched bitcoin envisioned the technology as an international digital currency that could maintain its value and fuel transactions instantly and cheaply. It hasn't worked out that way. The value of bitcoin has risen and fallen faster than a yo-yo on elastic. Between mid-November 2017 and mid-December 2017, the dollar price of bitcoin leapt from just over $6000 to more than $19,000. By February it was back to about $8000. At the same time, the cost of making a single transaction at one point topped $35.

With that kind of volatility and expense, bitcoin can't work as a currency. Buyers hold onto them when it rises, and sellers won't accept them when it falls. Those determined to use bitcoins to buy goods can look to the currency's early users for lessons. The first purchase made using bitcoin was for two pizzas. The buyer, Laszlo Hanyecz, paid 10,000 BTC for the meal. If he had held onto those bitcoins and sold them at their peak, he could have earned $190 million. In retrospect, it was the world's most expensive pizza!

Yet there are now more than 2000 digital coins that can be bought and sold on digital exchanges. Some of those coins may support real opportunities that need digital tokens to underpin their technology. Most are nopportunities that are supported only by the social proof created by hopeful speculators.

The world is a complex place. We have to make many decisions every day. We simply don't have the time or expertise to make thoughtful, reasoned decisions about everything. That's why, as a short cut, we mimic what others are doing, and follow the crowd. For example, how would you determine the value of a bitcoin? Only a handful of people in the world understand cryptocurrencies well enough to calculate their inherent or potential value. Yet if the media starts writing about bitcoins, and if your friends suddenly start buying bitcoins, regardless of your ignorance, you might be tempted as well. If you decide to buy because others are buying, what price will you pay? Because you lack expertise, you may listen to the advice of self-proclaimed cryptocurrency experts; or you may respect the wisdom of the crowd and pay the market price. Either way, your decision will largely be based on social proof rather than logical evidence.

People are social animals and will adapt consciously when they see that others are doing it. Most people deal with opportunity and adaption by copying others. After all, we are a species that practises collective learning. Often, we do it by using the Xerox machine. For example, in recent years, why have so many Americans stopped drinking old-fashioned low-cost beer brands such as Budweiser? Why do they suddenly prefer to drink expensive craft beers, such as India Pale Ale, which previously had virtually no market? Why are microbreweries suddenly sprouting up all over major Indian metros? Craft beers have obtained significant gravity due to social proof. The phenomenon began at an elite level and has worked its way down.

Social proof is a powerful phenomenon because most people prefer to conform to the norms of behaviour. In 1951, the social psychologist Solomon Asch conducted a famous experiment in which he found that 75 per cent of people chose an obviously wrong answer on an exam simply because others in the same group had chosen it. It is also likely that most people will choose to pursue a nopportunity rather than an opportunity if they feel that others are also choosing it. On the positive side, largely because of social proof, the entire world has adopted the rules of the Now Era within 200 years. In previous eras, social proof was not as powerful a phenomenon on larger scales. Due to isolation, it was difficult to compare your culture and practices with others. Now, regardless of where you are, you can compare your situation with the rest of the world simply by visiting Dr Google or by watching YouTube. If you see that others are dramatically more prosperous than you, it will immediately drive the question: what do I need to do to adapt? Should I copy people who are more successful than me?

The gravity that can be created by social proof is often engineered. Anyone can do it. Let's say you're a nobody. You decide to invest whatever you have into becoming a somebody. You start blogging, become a social media influencer and hire a professional PR agency to build your image and brand with whatever your earnings are. Many have done it. These days people have most of the essentials of life taken care of. But they feel the need for something new and they choose new things mainly based on what others are adapting to. Therefore, it is essential to look at how gravity can be increased for an opportunity by increasing social proof, particularly among your peer group or people who could be ideal disciples or soldiers in your opportunity army.

4. Focus

When Steve Jobs returned to run Apple in 1997, the company was on its knees, months away from bankruptcy. The first thing Jobs did was to cut the product line from 355 down to only ten. He was determined to focus all of Apple's remaining resources on big opportunities. A series of great opportunities followed, transforming Apple into one of the world's most profitable companies. Focus on big opportunities builds opportunity gravity. Why? As discussed in Chapter 2, effort and results are not distributed equally. *Inequality* is a fundamental principle; the universe is primarily full of empty space. Big stars are few and far between. For example, the economist Alan Krueger recently reported in the book *Rockonomics* that the top 5 per cent of music performers earn 85 per cent of concert revenue; the top 1 per cent take 60 per cent. Pareto Leaders tend to take it all. You need to be one of them.

In order to become a Pareto Leader, you need to specialize. You can't be an expert at everything. Whether it's for career or business, you need to focus on becoming an expert at one thing. That will give you tremendous authority and gravity, and help you provide amazingly useful service. It will allow you to use your resources as efficiently as possible, and not waste them on things you know little about. Of course, it all depends what you choose to focus on. If you focus all your energy on nopportunities, you will fail. It is unfortunate that the mass of people focus on nopportunities that provide frustration rather than gravity, simply because they fail to use a systematic process to choose them.

5. Alignment

For an opportunity seed to grow into a big healthy tree, the entire organism must work together as a unified whole. It also must get all the resources it needs to grow, not just some of them. Sunshine, water and other nutrients are required. A lumberjack with a chainsaw must not show up to chop it down. It's the same with your opportunities. In order to effectively nurture them, you need to have alignment between the four segments of your opportunity environment: mission, model, market and domain. They need to work together on the crucial task of collective learning, the key to rapid adaptation.

Imagine that you plan to go on a long road trip through rough territory. You are the main driver, but you bring along three other drivers who have specialized skills. One of them knows how to fix the engine, another knows how to deal with the authorities, and another reads the map and knows the terrain. Each individually believes that he should be the lead driver, but isn't it best if they all work together? They shouldn't fight about who drives. They should harmonize, share learnings and cooperate. From the time your opportunity is a seed, developing it as a holistic collaborative organism can build tremendous gravity.

6. Control of Rules

In the Old Era, medieval guilds controlled access to most professions, setting the rules and blocking entry to anyone who didn't follow them to their satisfaction. Although the modern exchange economy has largely wiped out the power of guilds, a few remain. Example: bar associations, which govern the practice of law. If you want to become a lawyer, you have to play by their rules. If you don't, they will refuse to admit you to the bar, or disbar you, effectively destroying your career. In America, the vast majority of legislators are also lawyers. So lawyers don't just make their own rules; they make all the laws as well. That double whammy of rule-making control provides the legal profession with immense sustainable gravity.

You obviously can't make the rules of every game. But you can make the rules of your own game, no matter how small the playing field may be. Being able to make the rules can be an immense gravity enhancer, and also helps to block competitors, providing even more gravity.

In India, BCCI controls the rules of cricket, the country's number one sport. For BCCI, creating and controlling the rules of IPL has proven to be a huge money spinner. Although entry to rule making in cricket is blocked, others have taken the opportunity to set the rules of other sports. For example, Star TV has created the Pro Kabaddi League, with a new set of rules specifically created and ideal for television broadcast. In marketing there's a saying that if you can't be number one in your category, create your own category. Microsoft has the word 'micro' in its name because it started out very small. By creating and owning the operating system rules of most of the world's computers, it built the gravity necessary to grow very large. Ideally, you should make the rules at the highest level possible. Note that Microsoft is able to control most of the world's market for office software because it controls the operating system software that governs its use. This has allowed it to effectively control the rules of lower-level software applications, particularly those used in offices, such as word processing, spreadsheets and presentations.

Tesla's Real Innovation Is Guild-Busting, Not Good Batteries

Think of Tesla, and you'll imagine a sleek, luxury car that doesn't use petrol. Its battery releases zero emissions and yet gives drivers the torque of a high-performance sports car and enough range to get them where they need to go. Elon Musk, whose company is now struggling to meet demand, has found an opportunity. He's broken the rules about how cars are supposed to function and created a valuable adaption to the change offered by the development of battery technology and concern about the environment.

But one of Musk's biggest innovations has nothing to do with the technology underpinning his cars. It's the way he sells them.

In the United States, local legislation often prohibits auto manufacturers from selling directly to the public. Instead, they have to sell their inventory to a network of third-party dealers, who sell them on to the public. The Federal Trade Commission estimates that the practice adds an average of 8 per cent to the price of a car.

In effect, car dealers act as a kind of guild. Legal rules protect them from competitors and allow them to control who can enter the market. Tesla argues that its cars are new and complex. Their different kinds of engine can't be explained effectively by dealers and promoting the benefit of an electric vehicle would be a conflict of interest for a dealer who also sells petrol cars. In some states, Tesla has gone head-to-head with dealers in courthouses. Sometimes, it has managed to push legal change that has allowed its stores to operate. In other places, the 'stores' act only as exhibition rooms. Customers can see the car and hear the pitch but have to make a purchase online. Slowly though, Tesla is challenging control of the rules that regulate America's car sales and adding gravity to its opportunity.

How to Attract Value

1. Gravity is the real force of attraction
The Law of Attraction is a fule. Thinking about something won't bring it to you. Gravity is the force that bends space and draws massive objects together. The greater the opportunity, the stronger its force of gravity, and the more resources it will attract towards it.

2. Change can bring gravity
Change brings new opportunities, and big changes can bring big opportunities with large amounts of gravity. Businesses that make the most of that opportunity can find that they attract huge resources.

3. There are strategies to build gravity
As you're building your opportunity, you'll find that a number of steps can increase its gravity. From True Vision, social proof and belief through focus, alignment and control over the rules, each opportunity comes with levers that you can pull to add gravity.

9

How to Discover Opportunity

What is friction and where do you find it? What are the key drivers of that friction? How does friction repel resources and slow your progress? Why and how can friction be a source of great opportunities?

What keeps an airplane in the air? The scientific answer has something to do with the shape of the wing and the difference in air pressure that creates lift. A more accurate answer is money. A plane stays in the air because the company or individual that owns it has the funds to buy the fuel, pay the pilot and cover maintenance and licensing bills. When money runs out, the shape of the wing doesn't matter anymore. There's no lift and the plane stays on the ground.

That's what happened to WOW airlines in March 2019. The Icelandic low-cost carrier went into receivership after acquisition talks failed to rescue it. WOW's CEO, Skúli Mogensen, who had put €5.5 million of his own money into the airline, identified four sources of friction that stopped his flights: bad publicity regarding the company's financial state; the collapse of Primera Air, a Danish airline whose failure a few months earlier had made investors wonder who was next; stricter financial terms imposed by lessors and creditors; and rising oil prices. All of those forces put drag on the airline's wings. They brought it to the ground.

Gravity will attract the energy and resources required to grow an opportunity from a seed into a huge tree. Rather than attracting resources, *friction* is the force that repels them and takes them away from you. If an opportunity seed is nurtured with friction rather than gravity, it will be stillborn and never attract the resources it needs to grow. When friction enters your 'value bubble', it deflates it. *Friction repels and destroys value and creates an unbalanced value-exchange.* Friction creates sickness instead of health. Friction wastes resources. Friction kills careers and companies. Is friction killing yours? Friction disrupts markets and relationships, emotions and rules. It can destroy long-standing relationships. Not just between people; it could be between ideas and ideologies. Friction shakes existing systems and processes. Friction is both a result of change and also drives change.

Key Drivers of Friction

What creates friction? Consider the nine Key Drivers of Value and imagine their opposites. Friction is caused by changes in the environment that result in:

- Declining utility
- Service failure
- Win-lose or lose-lose value exchanges
- Declining relevance of products, services and rules
- Commoditization and declining competitive advantage
- Diminishing scale potential
- Increasing barriers to entry
- Chasing profit instead of service
- Poor execution
- Relying on false beliefs rather than evidence
- Lack of expertise
- Lack of focus or wrong focus
- Choosing nopportunities rather than opportunities
- Wasting resources on nopportunities
- Inadequate social proof
- Poor alignment of mission, model, market and domain
- Lack of feasibility
- Obsolete technology
- Failure to adjust to trends affecting your industry

Could Better Place Have Chosen a Better Place?

Shai Agassi believed he had found an opportunity. The world was growing increasingly concerned about climate change. Battery technology was improving. If he could build an appealing electric vehicle, he would revolutionize the car industry and improve the environment for everyone. Better Place launched in 2007 with a billion dollars of funding and an agreement with Renault to develop the car.

Agassi identified one result of friction in his plan: the barrier to entry would be high. Buyers, he believed, were concerned about the car's range. The batteries, too, tended to make electric vehicles more expensive than conventional cars. Agassi had a plan for both. Before entering a market, he would first create a network of charging stations. Drivers could pull in and swap their nearly empty batteries for fully charged ones in minutes. Charging would be no harder than using a service station. But the company would also own the batteries. Drivers would buy a mileage plan, like a mobile phone usage plan, based on how far they drove each month. That would reduce the upfront costs of owning the car while still giving the company a revenue stream.

Initially, Agassi focused on two markets: Israel, a small country with concerns about energy security; and Denmark, a country with a reputation for environmental concern. He began building charging stations and introduced the cars to Renault's outlets. Six years later, the company collapsed. Assets that had cost $850 million were sold for just $450,000. Better Place had sold fewer than 1000 cars in Israel and under 400 in Denmark.

Writing in *Energy Policy* in 2016, Lance Noel and Benjamin K. Sovacool argued in effect that Agassi had misidentified one result of friction and had failed to deal with another. Range anxiety, they claimed, was a psychological barrier, not a functional obstacle. (A shortage of charging stations has not affected sales of Tesla cars in the US.) At the same time, poor execution meant that the cost of buying and owning a Better Place car was little different to owning a conventional car. Agassi also overestimated Israel's energy security concerns and Danish environmentalism. It's not enough to be aware of the key drivers of friction. You must identify the right ones in your business and deal with their results effectively.

Friction can be purely personal and internal, such as the creative friction of the artist. For example, you feel the need to write a novel, not necessarily to entertain others, but to get it off your chest, or for the sense of achievement. Many people feel friction simply because they lack the money they need to survive. Unfortunately, while the need for money may drive you to work harder, it won't necessarily help you to identify opportunities or add value to others.

Where to Find Friction

Friction is everywhere in everyone's world. Consider:

- How often are you the victim of inadequate service or shoddy workmanship? That creates friction.
- How often are you kept waiting for no good reason? That creates friction.
- How much time do you waste on firefighting tasks that others should perform? That creates friction.
- How many rules do you deal with that seem pointless and irrelevant? That creates friction.
- How often do you feel that you overpaid for something? That creates friction.
- How often does the solution provided to you fail to solve your problem or get your job done properly? That creates friction.
- How often do service providers lie to you or fail to respond on time? That creates friction.
- How often do you see people doing the wrong thing simply because others are doing it? That creates friction.

- How often are promises made to you broken or completely disregarded? That creates friction.

What does friction look and feel like? *Something isn't working.* It is a bad situation. Things are not going in the right direction. People are unhappy; the unhappiness might have just begun, or it might be full blown. Friction causes pain. Friction can create disturbance in a relationship that was previously working well. You can find maximum friction in places where you feel like you are getting the worst deal. The greater the friction, the greater the value that can be created by fixing it. You need to find the source, because it is a source of potential opportunity.

To find friction, talk to your customers. Better yet, talk to your customers' customers. Everyone has customers. If you're an employee, your company is your customer. What are they unhappy about? Examine what's causing the friction. Look deep into the whys and hows. What are the complaints? What is the fundamental disagreement or dissatisfaction over? If resources are suddenly less available to you or cost more, it is a sign of increasing friction. Someone who was friendly is less friendly. Something that worked, no longer works as well.

Friction can be the source of enormous pain, or tremendous gain. In a famous 2006 study, researchers created a hedge portfolio that bought stocks long and sold them short based on changes in the American Customer Satisfaction Index. The index tracks customer satisfaction in about 200 companies by questioning more than 65,000 US consumers every year. The companies that scored high in customer satisfaction scores performed much better than the S&P 500. Their stock returns were higher, and their values and cash flows were much less volatile.

Why Friction Can Create Opportunities

Ironically, *friction can be an immense source of opportunity.* Why? Because friction inevitably creates pain and dissatisfaction. Other people's pain can be your gain. You should always be on the lookout for friction. When you see friction, you must ask yourself—*could this be the seed of a potential opportunity?* Friction is the biggest source of opportunity because it destroys value. When it destroys value, it creates pain. Whoever was giving you value before is now giving you less.

An excellent example goes back to the year 2001, when I was posted to the US Consulate Mumbai as the Trade Commissioner. In those days, first-time visa applicants used to routinely queue up in the middle of the night outside the consulate. Many people would wait for hours, often in horrible conditions of heat or rain. But they had no choice. That was the system. Consulate management hated the lines as well, but they didn't see a better way. Their own facility was already completely overcrowded. There was no place to move the line indoors.

Early one morning, Zubin Karkaria, the India chief of Kuoni Travels, was driving past the US Consulate and noticed hundreds of miserable people standing in line. He had seen this sight many times. He thought there must be a better way. He spotted the seed of an opportunity. Zubin immediately made an appointment to meet with Fred Polasky, the head of visa services at the consulate. He had a solution to the long lines. He suggested: *outsource the line to me*. Polasky agreed to try it.

In 2001, VFS Global made a humble beginning as a pilot project. Instead of having to stand in lines outdoors, first-time visa applicants contacted VFS's new centre near the consulate and made an appointment for an interview. All the arrangements were made by VFS. The only thing the Consulate had to do was to provide the services that it couldn't outsource: *the visa interview and issuance*.

The new service of visa facilitation was a fantastic success. Large amounts of friction were removed from the visa process and replaced with gravity. The US government was delighted. Customer satisfaction greatly improved. The service was adapted by many other countries. The visa process was an adjacency to the travel process that Kuoni traditionally managed for clients. No market for visa-facilitation services existed before Karkaria invented it. Visa services were only offered by governments on a monopoly basis and both sides of the value exchange were unhappy with the service quality. Today VFS Global, headed by Karkaria, has become larger than its parent company. It is a $500 million business based in Zurich that operates in sixty-two countries around the world. Visa facilitation was only the beginning; it has taken over all types of services that are badly provided by governments.

One Employee, One Idea . . . A Multi-Billion Dollar Product

Google is famous for its 20 per cent rule. Employees are allowed to spend up to 20 per cent of their time working on a personal project. The idea, according to former CEO Eric Schmidt, is to empower engineers. When a manager demands that an employee put in more hours, the engineer is able to reply that he's willing to give 100 per cent of the 80 per cent of the time he has to give to the company. Engineers get to feel that they have some control over their time . . . and Google gets to benefit from their creativity.

Paul Buchheit was the twenty-third employee at Google. In 2001, he was working on Google Groups, and as the project came to the end of its first generation of development, he was asked if he wanted to work on an email or personalization product.

Googlers used email a lot at that time. Buchheit would receive around 500 emails every day and employees had their own methods to store and retrieve their messages. They'd put them in folders by topic but would often forget a message, and the conversation thread would split. 'There was a very big need for search,' he told Jessica Livingston for her book *Founders at Work*.

Buchheit adapted the code from Google Groups and created a new email system that could store a gigabyte of emails, knit related messages into conversation threads, and be searchable. He started working alone but was soon joined by Sanjeev Singh and Jing Lim.

For the first three years of its life, Gmail was used internally, reducing friction in Google's internal communications. At the same time though, Buchheit started working on a side-project. One Friday evening, he created the prototype of a system that could understand the content on a webpage and match advertising to the page's subject. At the time, Google could only place advertising on its search results pages. Buchheit's prototype showed that it would be possible to expand Google's advertising system across the Web, removing a major source of friction that was slowing Google's growth.

Google established a team to develop the prototype. By 2005, AdSense was responsible for 15 per cent of Google's revenues. In 2018, it generated over $5 billion of revenue.

For Kuoni, the visa line was a point of friction for his customers, which he did not control. The question was: could he improve the process and reduce friction if he had more control? The answer was a resounding yes. Kuoni assumed partial control of the rules of the visa line and evolved it to add value and gravity and reduce friction for both the customers and governments.

How to Convert Friction into Gravity

Imagine for a moment the worst situation imaginable, one which is absolutely loaded with friction. You are a woman. On an adventure trip to a remote and exotic destination, you have been kidnapped by a primitive Old Era tribe. The chief of the tribe has killed all your companions and taken you as his new wife. This is similar to the situation faced by Daenerys Targaryen, in the TV show *Game of Thrones*, who is forced to marry Khal Drogo, the brutal leader of the savage Dothraki tribe. You eventually realize that you have only four options to reduce friction: 1) to escape; 2) to kill your new husband and his warriors; 3) to wait to be rescued; or 4) to make your new husband your friend and ally.

You carefully examine your environment. Options 1 and 2 are virtually impossible. The tribe is always on the move and lives deep below the canopy of a remote jungle. It may take months or years before anyone can find you, and any rescue attempt could result in your death. Your best option may be to convert friction into gravity by cooperating with your new husband. Remember the value exchange. Rather than treating him with hostility, if you are nice to him, he will probably be nicer to you. He may even grow to love you. Given the power of reciprocity, as far-fetched as this may seem, you may actually grow to love him. There's a phenomenon known as Stockholm syndrome in which people who are kidnapped fall in love with their kidnappers. This syndrome can be quite a rational survival response to extreme friction.

You always have a choice: *you can react to friction with opposition or cooperation*. In markets, a fight to the death is often silly because competitors often share similar goals. Opponents may create more gravity through cooperation. It might be deemed illegal in some markets, and for good reason. But not all the things you can cooperate on are going to harm buyers. For example, you can start industry groups to work on common goals. Such opportunities for reducing friction and creating gravity should always be explored, even if they also help your competitors. The biggest opportunity to reduce friction and create gravity is by challenging long-standing rules that may have become irrelevant. Consider this: what rules are you and others in your industry following that are obviously wrong or outdated? Why are things being done this way? Could there be a better way? As Zubin Karkaria and many others have found, there is very often a much better way, which can be an enormous opportunity for you.

In 2011, Samsung was developing a new model of flat-panel televisions. Its One Design model would be thinner and more attractive than its competitors. The company's engineers and designers had figured out how the new screen would work and how it would look. Now they just needed to manage mass production. That was when they hit friction. Samsung's LCD panel supplier was used to placing inner covers between the screen and the components. The TV makers would then add an external cover. Samsung wanted to remove the covers to keep the television as thin as possible. The supplier didn't want to change its entire production process just to create one model for one client, so Samsung's designers and engineers came up with a solution. According to an article in the *Harvard Business Review* by researchers Youngjin Yoo and Kyungmook Kim, Samsung created an entirely new supply-chain model for LCD panel systems that not only gave it the panels it wanted, it also reduced shipping costs. Without the covers, the supplier could pack more panels into the same space. Samsung and the supplier split the savings.

Friction can be caused by the sudden absence of the key driver of value. If you can identify this key driver, you can increase gravity by providing a substitute. For example, imagine that you are one of a group of six children; all of you like different types of cake. What do you have in common? You all like cake. Why do you all like cake? Because it is sweet. Removing all the cake will create friction. Removing only the sugar from the cake will also create dissatisfaction and friction, because sugar is the key driver of value. Where's the opportunity? To create gravity, you don't require cake; you just need to feed the kids other things that are sweet, with or without sugar.

You can turn friction into gravity by cooperating rather than competing with your stakeholders. Stakeholders include employees, customers, suppliers, investors and even competitors. What friction do they suffer, and how can reducing it be an opportunity for you? If your supplier is suffering from friction perhaps there is something you can do to help him reduce it. Perhaps this can be a value arbitrage for you. You should always be looking for places where you could find common ground for mutual improvement and better value exchange. To do that you need to understand what your stakeholders' value is, and where they are suffering friction in value gaps. You also need to understand how they have found people like you to be useful. What do they use them for? What value do they deliver? Just as the children in the example above all valued sweetness, you can learn what all your stakeholders' value in common, and where they suffer common friction. That should be a strong area of focus.

Where to Discover Opportunity

1. Friction causes pain

The consequences of friction can range from bad service to high barriers of entry to poor execution. Business leaders—and employees—need to identify the drivers of friction in their fields and know how to cope with the effects.

2. Where to find friction

You can find friction everywhere. You can find it in customer dissatisfaction, in long waits, in high prices, in inefficient processes, in irrelevant rules, and in thoughtless systems. Friction is all around us—and each instance of friction can be an opportunity.

3. Why friction can create opportunities

The removal of friction creates opportunities that can be very lucrative. Whether it's the outsourcing of visa applications like VFS Global, cooperating with a competitor on a new infrastructure like BMW and Daimler or working with a supplier to produce the part you want and lower costs like Samsung, friction can show you where to create new, valuable adaptations to change.

10

The Opportunity Mindset

Do you have the mindset necessary for success? What are the keys to the Opportunity Mindset? Why should you avoid rule reverence? How can you stop being a victim of your circumstances and take control of your fate? How can you lead yourself to become the Hero of your own life?

Ma Yun should never have succeeded. He was born in Hangzhou, China, in 1964, two years before the outbreak of the Cultural Revolution. In China, the Cultural Revolution is often described as the Ten Wasted Years. Universities stopped teaching. Students denounced teachers—and their parents. Economic production took second place to political activity.

As the grandson of a small landlord and a former Nationalist government official, Ma Yun's family was targeted. The traditional Ping Tan theatre performed by his parents was banned. Life was hard. Ma Yun was not a particularly good student either. He failed his middle school exams twice. He did poorly at maths and when the time came to sit the *gaokao*, China's university entrance exams, he failed again. Three times. It was only on his fourth attempt that he received a high enough grade to study at the Hangzhou Teacher's Institute, now Hangzhou Normal University. What he studied was English, and it's here that we can see that Ma Yun, or Jack Ma, as he's better known outside China, had a very different mindset in comparison to his peers—and how it would change even more.

China in the 1970s and 1980s was a not a place with a lot of opportunities to improve your English, but Ma would cycle for miles to give tourists free tours of his area and to practise his language skills. What he earned was not just a rare fluency in English but also a new way of seeing the world.

'Those Western, foreign tourists opened my mind,' he said in an interview with TV journalist Charlie Rose. 'Everything they told me is so different to the things I learned in the schools and from my parents.'

Interaction with others with different viewpoints and experiences had changed the way he saw opportunities. The chance to use that mindset came with Ma's first visit to the US in 1995. It also gave him the opportunity to use the Internet for the first time. With the English that he had learned as a tour guide, he put that opportunity to good use. For example, when he searched for 'beer', he found information about beer from all over the world, but none from China, because China then wasn't connected to the Internet. He saw the opportunity and realized what a connected China could be. Together with a friend, he created a website in 1999.

Do you remember what I said about gravity? Do you remember how a good opportunity attracts resources? Ma's site went live at 9.40 a.m. and by the afternoon, he had received five emails, including offers from Chinese partners. Ma's Internet company, Ali Baba, went public on the New York Stock Exchange in 2014. The $25 billion it raised made it the largest IPO in NYSE history. By 2018, its total equity was worth over $90 billion. Jack Ma is now the wealthiest man in China.

What is Your Mindset?

Imagine that you are living in the world of 10,000 years ago. Your home, if you have one, has to be packed up and carried around by you from place to place. You have virtually no possessions—perhaps some basic clothing and a few simple tools. There are no towns, cities, or permanent communities of any type. *It is an entirely natural world.* Now consider your world of today. *It is an almost entirely human-made world.* How did it come about? Everything—absolutely everything—that we take for granted in our human-made world was first imagined *in someone's mind*, as an opportunity. Now open your mind as wide as possible and try to imagine the world of 10,000 years in the future. Spend the next five to ten minutes imagining this in your mind. What will it look like? Does it look very much like the world of today? Or does it resemble something out of a science fiction movie or TV show that you recently watched? If your imagined view of the future resembles today's world, or if it's based on the entertainment industry's version of the future, then I've got bad news for you: you've got *the wrong mindset* to see opportunities. It's time for an upgrade.

For my previous book, *Master Opportunity and Make it Big*, I developed an online survey tool called *OQ Insight*, which measures your Opportunity Quotient, or OQ. This tool measures how well you perform on the twelve Opportunity Accelerators—behavioural characteristics that enhance your ability to see, evaluate and implement opportunities.

How Two British Sons of a Gujarati Immigrant Saw an Opportunity That Oil Giants Had Missed

A petrol station is a simple thing with a simple business model: drivers need fuel; petrol stations sell the fuel. If the drivers are hungry, they can buy a stale sandwich from the cash counter when they make their payment. That's how petrol stations owned by companies like Texaco, Exxon and Shell have worked for decades, and it was how the father of Zuber and Mohsin Issa worked his petrol station.

Issa had moved to Lancashire in northern England from his native Gujarat to work in the declining textile industry. He later bought a petrol station instead. His teenage sons worked in the station too but when they bought their own station in 2001, they saw things differently. They realized that the biggest asset of a petrol station wasn't the pump. It was the land. If they used the land a petrol station sat on to develop retail space, they could make a lot more money than they could make selling petrol.

First, they made it easier for drivers to fill up by putting different kinds of fuel on the same pump. They also added more lights so that the space looked welcoming and safe. Finally, they attracted shops and fast food restaurants such as supermarkets, Starbucks and KFC so that the petrol stations became destinations as well as stops. Then they expanded, buying nearly 1000 sites in

---

the US in 2018, according to *The Economist*, and opening 5000 stations around the world.

The adaptations the Issa brothers made changed the company's Pareto Leader. Petrol stations traditionally made 80 per cent of their income by selling petrol. Two-thirds of the revenue at the Issa brothers' Euro Garages chain comes from retail and dining. The company made $26 billion in 2018, making it one of the biggest privately held firms in the UK.

Thus far, hundreds of my Indian readers have taken the *OQ Insight* survey. Unfortunately, most of them have consistently *scored lowest* on the single most important personal characteristic affecting their ability to have an opportunity mindset.

To take the OQ Insight Survey, visit my website at: http://oppguru.com/ oq-insight/.

What personal characteristic is the key driver of an opportunity mindset?

The key driver of an opportunity mindset is *irreverence*, or *open-mindedness*. This driver is so important that I named my consulting firm *Open Mind*. You may be the most passionate, persistent and practical person on earth. Your nose may be bent relentlessly to the grindstone. You may also have superior empathy and integrity. All these wonderful qualities are *Opportunity Accelerators*. But if your mind is not wide open, you will still not see the best opportunities. Big opportunities may sit right under your nose and let out a howl, and you will choose to close your eyes and ears to them. The villain who blocks out opportunity from your mind is named *reverence*. His brother is *close-mindedness*, and his cousin is *made up your mindedness*. They severely limit your objective awareness and critical evaluation of your environment, which is crucial to seeing opportunities.

Imagine that you are again a baby. Besides eating, sleeping and pooping, what do you do all day? With wide-open eyes and ears, you absorb everything going on around you. You suck it all in. You have no filters. Do you follow any rules that tell you: 'No! You must not listen to that!' Of course not. You're wide open to everything, without exception. *You are completely irreverent.* But of course, you need to have filters and rules. They help you to organize all the information bombarding your mind into rational patterns, and then into processes. How else could you learn to talk and to walk, or absorb the rules that your parents begin to teach you? You fit everything neatly into boxes. You learn the norms of behaviour, the Pareto Rules that everyone follows. You learn them in every arena of your life. You are a sane, normal human being because you follow these rules. Unfortunately, however, if you are *exceedingly reverent* of all these rules and boxes, and if you treat them as if they are inviolable natural laws, you will find it very difficult to challenge them or to change them.

Rule reverence is an irony of the Now Era. Faster change means rules are actually becoming irrelevant faster than ever before. Yet people tend to cling onto rules for too long, because as a general rule of the Now Era, rules are followed and respected. It is an irony as well as an opportunity.

Reverence Leads to Irrelevance

To harvest opportunities, one should be fundamentally irreverent. That doesn't mean disrespectful. You should be kind to others and follow the laws of the nation. On the other hand, you must critically question all the rules. An open-minded approach requires that you never accept the existing rules as eternally valid. Always assume that the emperor may suddenly have no clothes on.

Sears Was No Seer

Sears, Roebuck and Company was an icon of American retail. The company was founded in the 1880s by Richard Sears, a station agent for the Minneapolis and St. Louis Railway in North Redwood, Minnesota.

Sears had a side-line selling lumber and coal. So when a local jeweller rejected a shipment of gold watches, Sears bought them himself. He sold them for a profit and teamed up with Alvah C. Roebuck, an Indiana watchmaker, to buy and sell more. The company was incorporated in 1893 and initially produced a watch and jewellery catalogue. Sears and Roebuck soon saw that a catalogue that offered farmers watches and gold could also sell them household goods and supplies. At the time, farmers could only buy from local general stores. The selection was limited, and the prices were high. A delivery service could offer more at a lower cost. Sears and Roebuck's catalogue soon ran to 532 pages and included items such as sewing machines, bicycles and even cars that could all be delivered to the farmers' doors. The local stores couldn't compete.

The company grew, but in the 1920s, Ford threatened the business model. Increased car ownership meant that customers could now drive further to buy goods instead of having them delivered. The company, then owned by Sears and Julius Rosenwald, adapted by opening retail stores. By 1992 Sears' revenues had reached $59 billion, but it would soon face two giant competitors: Walmart, which was about to become the country's biggest retailer; and Amazon, which would do for retail shopping what Sears had done to rural stores a hundred years earlier. The problem wasn't that Sears couldn't see the opportunity in the Internet. As early as 1984, it had worked with IBM to create Prodigy, a kind of early online portal. But it had sold it in 1996 at a loss of $800 million.

What sunk Sears, putting it into bankruptcy in 2018, was the mindset of its CEO. Edward Lampert was a former investment manager, not a retailer. As Walmart adapted to the threat from Amazon, improving its stores and creating a unique retail experience, Lampert focused on cost-cutting, selling brands and closing outlets. He could see only Sears' figures, not the sales industry.

Excessive rule reverence can blind you to creeping *irrelevance*. For example, Blockbuster Video ruled the video rental business throughout the US for over a decade. As telecom technology evolved, leading to cheaper and faster bandwidth, the rules of the industry abruptly changed, but Blockbuster's management refused to see it. They held on to the old rules as if they were laws of nature, and they got wiped out.

Netflix, on the other hand, has consistently practised *rule irreverence*. Their original business model thumbed its nose at the rule that people had to rent videos by the day, from a retail store. They wrote a set of new rules, by setting up a monthly subscription model and delivering through the mail. Within a few years as bandwidth got cheaper and faster, Netflix management could see that even its new rules were rapidly becoming irrelevant. Adapting to change, it once again rewrote the rulebook and rapidly converted to a wildly successful online video streaming model.

Any set of rules is just a box of beliefs; they are not eternal natural laws. You can't avoid the box, because all processes are based on rules. Without these, you would live in chaos. However, what you can do is write your own rules and create your own boxes. Things change, and you must open your mind to change along with them. If you worship the box, you'll eventually be buried in the box. Never revere beliefs. *Instead, revere truth.*

Enter the Temple of Truth

Have you seen any movies or TV shows about ancient Rome? The Romans worshipped many gods, such as Zeus, that absolutely nobody believes in now. That's not unusual. We all have false gods in our lives, which we continue to worship as if they were real. Which Roman-style gods are influencing you? Which ones do you pray to? What myths and irrelevant rules do you insist on holding onto? They are blinding you to opportunity. Know this: you do not need a god on your side in order to succeed. Why?

1. Because you are not at the mercy of a higher power that is providing or denying you opportunity.
2. Because you are not a beggar or a supplicant.
3. Because you are not a helpless victim of your circumstances.

You need to stop being a victim. The Now Era is not an age of victimhood, although many people enjoy being victims and hold onto victimhood as if it were a badge of honour. The leaders in our age are not victims, nor are they beggars or supplicants, nor are they lucky. *The heroes of our era are practical self-reliant truth seekers.*

India is a country that lives in several centuries at the same time. Many Indians still have a mindset of the Old Era. It is characterized by an inflexible belief in rules that were supposedly made by God or his representatives on earth. For thousands of years, Indians believed that their station in life was predetermined. You were an untouchable or a king because God and the Law of Karma ordained it. This Old Era mindset values obedience over truth. In the Temple of Obedience, you are a powerless victim who is begging for redemption or deliverance. Or you're begging for some other favour, offering to exchange obedience and penitence—suffering of some type—in return for deliverance and forgiveness. This was the normal relationship of the common person with the Powers That Be in the Old Era. Are you worshipping at the Temple of Obedience? If so, *please stop right now!*

In contrast, the Now Era mindset favours the scientific method. It believes that all truth is available to us, and it can be discovered in a thoroughly rational way through the collection of evidence. The scientific method is based on the principle of *ignoramus*, which means *we are ignorant*, and must always search for a better and more relevant version of truth. Do you have that sort of mindset?

Remember this: in the Now Era, nobody is stuck. Your status is not fixed by God or birth. Opportunities are available to you, but the burden of their discovery and exploitation *is in your hands.* To find opportunity, you must see clearly. To see clearly, you must stop begging fictional gods for help, and seek the truth, and nothing but the truth. The truth is a good deal. It can not only set you free—*it is free!* Seeking the truth is the key driver of irreverence. *If you seek the truth, you will always question all the rules, and ask why?* There will be no sacred cows in your life. Avoid truth, and you will die.

An example: RadioShack was founded in 1921 and at one point was the world's largest electronics chain, with more than 4300 stores and over 2000 franchises. It even made the TRS-80, one of the world's first mass-produced personal computers. But the rise of competition from smartphone outlets, Amazon and Best Buy left the company flat-footed. It failed to respond or adapt, and was so focused on trying to squeeze more out of its current practices that it missed the rise of the maker movement. In 2017, the company entered bankruptcy for the second time in two years.

Are you holding on to a false version of the truth because it's politically convenient? Because you're lazy and willing to rely on what others believe? Because you see no better alternative? Instead, pay attention to things that you are inflexible or reverent about. Notice the inflexibility of people around you. To unlock opportunity, rather than challenging your competition, you must challenge the rules of the game. To do that, I encourage you to worship in a new kind of temple: *The Temple of Truth.* In this temple there are no priests. Nor are there any prayers or begging for favours of any kind. There is no one to pray or beg to; there are no gods, no idols and no saints. You cannot make a pilgrimage to this temple, because it only exists *in your own mind.* This temple has only one permanent rule: *always seek the truth.* In this age, the truth is freely available to everyone. You just need to know how to look for it. This entire book is designed to help you find it.

How Uday Kotak Challenged the Status Quo

Uday Kotak grew up in an upper-middle class family which had a successful business in agricultural commodities. As a child, he was good at maths, and his academic path took him to Sydenham College Mumbai and then to an MBA at the Jamnalal Bajaj Institute of Management Studies, a leading business school in south Mumbai, then ranked among the top. When the time came to join the family firm though, it was clear that Kotak had other interests. His focus was on financial services. His father persuaded the family to let him use 300 square feet of office space, and he looked for opportunities by talking to his friends.

He quickly struck gold. One of Kotak's old business-school classmates was working in the finance department of NELCO, part of the Tata Group. NELCO was paying banks an interest rate of 17 per cent for ninety days of working capital financing. Bank deposit rates at the time were just 6 per cent. The opportunity was clear. If Kotak could raise funds by paying more than 6 per cent and make them available to NELCO for less than 17 per cent, he could make a profit.

But there was a problem. If he could see this opportunity, surely everyone else could too? Why had no one else used it? Was there a law that blocked people from challenging the old ways of doing things? He asked his lawyers to investigate. They gave him the green light. The problem wasn't that there was no opportunity. It was that no one else had dared to challenge the banks to make the most of it. Everyone had assumed it couldn't be done. No one had asked whether it could. Kotak used Tata's brand name to raise the funds, and formed a company with the help of Anand Mahindra. The Kotak Mahindra Bank now has a market cap of nearly Rs 3 lakh crore. And Uday Kotak is among the richest Indians of his generation.

Why Are You on Earth?

It is impossible to know why we exist. Our purpose tends to be dictated by the fashion of our current society or era that we live in. In the Old Era, when things changed so slowly that innovation or adaptation were not even noticeable, most people found purpose in doing their duty. Purpose was based on fulfilling your obligations to your parents, your community, your lord, and your king. In the Now Era, familial or community duty is no longer such a strong driver of purpose. The people we look up to are the opportunity masters, the ones who have, in the words of Steve Jobs, made a dent in the universe. Those who have taken opportunities and made it big are admired as much as victorious warriors were in the Old Era. They are the heroes of our era.

Neeraj Roy Adapts and Adapts Again

In 1998, Neeraj Roy saw the future. A friend had told him about India Internet World, a conference about the Internet that was taking place in Delhi. At the time, Roy was working as a marketing manager at the Taj Group, but he knew as soon as he encountered the Web that he wanted to start his own Internet venture. On 1 April 1999, he launched Hungama, a site focused on trivia and gaming. It was fun and entertaining, and its hourly prizes helped to win it a large audience.

A year later, the dotcom bubble burst. Hungama's funding dried up. Roy needed to adapt. He pivoted the company, turning it into a digital media agency, which would go on to win more than a hundred awards over the next four years. When the mobile industry began to take off, Roy saw a new opportunity and a new chance to create a valuable adaptation to change. He partnered with music labels and bought the rights to distribute digital content that could be played on mobile devices. By 2011, Hungama was India's largest supplier of digital media and entertainment, serving nearly 100 million customers in forty-seven countries around the world.

Neeraj Roy hasn't trusted fate and he hasn't bemoaned his luck. He looks for change, predicts trends and makes sure that he's ready to make the most of each new opportunity he identifies.

Historical events are seldom caused by some mysterious force called inevitability or luck. Nothing in your life, or in your business, is inevitable either. Your future, just like your past, depends on the choices you make. Opportunities are not created randomly by luck; they are created by changes in the environment. Anyone can see these changes, if they choose. You can choose to benefit from change or choose not to benefit. That is also a conscious decision, it is not a matter of luck or fate.

In the Old Era, individuals were the product of their environment. In the Now Era, the environment can be the product of the individual. To benefit from opportunities, you must take advantage of changing circumstances, and use them to shape your environment—99 per cent of people either accept their circumstances or complain about them. They are victims who use circumstances selectively as an excuse for failure. The victim of circumstances says *I can't do it, because . . .*—so he does what he's told. S/he is a lifelong follower. To be successful, you must use your changing environment as a rich source of opportunities, and opportunities as a leverage for resources.

Therefore, a knowledge of your internal and external environment is absolutely essential for the mastery of opportunity. You need to examine your environment as objectively as possible. This includes all aspects of your environment, with particular focus on the content of your own mind. To find truth, you need conscious and directed awareness. Given the voluminous number of things going on around you, you must focus selectively and intensively by identifying key drivers. The process in this book will show you how.

By using a systematic opportunity process, you can transform yourself from a powerless victim, into a person who can change the environment for the greater benefit of yourself and many others. Any person can make the shift from negative to positive, from loser to winner, from unfulfilled and frustrated to deeply fulfilled and respected, from zero to hero. But to succeed you must take responsibility for your own success and proactively seek opportunities. *You must think and act like a hero.*

How Can YOU Be a Hero?

Imagine that you're eighteen years old. You're sitting in a packed auditorium with a large group of students. You all look more or less the same. The school principal goes to the lectern, waves the crowd into silence, then leans into the microphone. She says: 'Twenty years from now who among you will stand out? Who will be up on this stage being honoured as the hero of this class—the one who has made a real difference in this world, the one who has moulded and shaped the world? Who will be the one who everyone admires and wants to learn from? Is it going to be you? How can YOU be the hero of the class?'

You sit, stunned, unsure what to think. You? A hero? You realize that you would love to be a hero, wouldn't everybody? But what does it take to be a hero? You have only a vague idea. Who is a hero? Whether in real life or fiction, a hero is a person who doesn't accept the conditions of his world. If we look at the single factor that differentiates heroes from most other individuals, it is that they try to make a difference. Heroes choose to shape and change the world, rather than letting the world shape them. They are leaders, not victims. Why is the hero not a victim? Because he sees and evaluates the opportunity, *and he decides to take it,* although he has no resources, other than his own will. He uses the mantra: 'Although I may be small, I can tackle big opportunities.'

The hero's journey is never simple or easy. Crossing the Opportunity Bridge can be a horribly difficult task. He starts out all alone. Nobody believes in his quest. Many think he is stupid or mad. He must overcome many baffling obstacles and solve problems that he has never encountered before. But he perseveres and learns to overcome every hurdle. Along the way, he attracts a team of disciples who aid him in building the opportunity into a success. What he and his team create helps many people, and the world flocks to him.

Why can the hero succeed? First and foremost, because *he is able to lead himself.* Unless and until you can *lead yourself,* you will never be able to successfully master an opportunity or lead others. You will only succeed through opportunity if you take full and complete responsibility for your own mind. Why? Because all your behaviour and actions are driven by your mindset:

As you believe, so do you think.
As you think, so do you feel.
As you think and feel, so do you do.

You can prepare to be a hero by thinking and acting like a hero. Fortunately, you don't have to make it all up. There are plenty of great examples to learn from. Think of the heroes in films. How do they lead themselves? Are they scattered and unfocused? Are they lazy? Are they cowardly? Are they irresponsible? Are they undisciplined? Are they dishonest? Are they helpless and clueless? When they face a problem, do they give up, or do they seek out the answers to solve it? When they see a challenge, do they face up to it, or do they immediately throw in the towel, grab a beer and play video games?

Everyone would like to be a hero, and anyone can be a hero, including you. But most people fail to even get started for one reason, and one reason only: *fear of screwing up*—FOSU. In reality, FOSU is just another false belief. If you examine your situation truthfully, what have you got to lose, besides your frustration, your failure, your poverty and your ignorance? Wouldn't you be willing to give those up? The true heroes of opportunity are not at all like film heroes. They're not born perfect like James Bond. Most successful people had no clue what they were doing when they started their journey of opportunity. But one thing they had to have was *the determination to lead themselves*. The story of Dr A.P.J. Abdul Kalam, from being the son of a boatman in the small temple town of Rameswaram in south India to spearheading India's nuclear programme, being conferred the Bharat Ratna, India's highest civilian award, and ultimately being elected as the President of India, is a shining example of determination and success against all odds.

Can You Be Your Own CEO?

In order to lead yourself, you must be your own CEO—Chief Executive Officer. Even if you are in a career and have no employees below you, you are still your own CEO.

What *must* a CEO do? A CEO must make decisions. He must constantly choose between alternative courses of action. Even if he takes advice, because he is on top of the hierarchy, the CEO must make decisions *alone*. He doesn't have to do anything else; all other activities can theoretically be delegated to others. Tim Ferriss, author of *The Four Hour-Workweek*, is known for outsourcing everything he doesn't have to do himself, reducing his working week to just four hours. He even outsourced his online dating. He hired a team of people to meet women online for him and set up twenty-minute dates, one after the other, in nearby cafes. He went on thirty dates, whittled the numbers down for second dates, and then chose one person to date exclusively.

If you can outsource dating, you can outsource anything! The decisions a CEO makes are critical to the identification, evaluation and implementation of opportunities. Everything else you can leave to others.

Is your ability to make decisions as good as it could be? You may be very skilled at making some kinds of decisions, because you have a lot of experience. For example, if you're an expert tennis player, you'll intuitively know where to run as soon as the other player hits the ball. That's because intuitive decisions are made based on pattern recognition. But what if you aren't familiar with the patterns and don't know the rules of the game? If the data you are using for pattern recognition is inadequate because of lack of experience, or if you lack understanding of how to analyse the data, you will probably make bad decisions.

Should you give up on the idea of leadership because you lack the experience to make decisions? *Of course not.* If the patterns and rules aren't familiar to you, you can use a process. A process should be based upon patterns and rules created by others, ideally Pareto Leaders, who have successfully taken the journey of opportunity before you. This sort of process will help you make decisions better and quicker and to execute better. It can also provide you with the understanding of the methodology of decision making. If you understandably feel uncertain about choosing opportunities, you can start by learning and using an opportunity process, like the one described in this book. As you practise the process, your fear will be gradually replaced with mastery and confidence. Your lack of clarity and confusion will be replaced with focus.

The Opportunity Mindset

1. The key driver of an opportunity mindset is an open mind
The importance of an open mind is so great that I used it to name my consultancy. Only an open mind will let you see the opportunities that are always available and right in front of you.

2. Excessive rule reverence can make you irrelevant
If you believe that the way things are done is the only way they should be done, then you won't be able to adapt when change comes like Blockbuster. Successful entrepreneurs don't just see change; they challenge the rules and embrace the opportunities that change brings, as Netflix did.

3. Stop being a victim and focus on truth. Lead yourself
In order to take advantage of opportunities, you must never be a victim or a beggar. You must always lead yourself, be your own CEO, and seek the truth. You must recognize that your fate is in your hands. It's up to you to make the most of the opportunities, to change the rules as Neeraj Roy and Uday Kotak did.

11

The Nopportunity Mindset

Where do nopportunities come from? How can you spot them? How can you avoid getting distracted by them while looking for the right opportunity? What are the four nopportunity traps that can waste your time, money and resources? What are the five common reasons that you choose nopportunities?

The year was 1985, and Britain's Sir Clive Sinclair was changing the world. His Sinclair Research company had created three of the world's first home computers: the ZX80, the ZX81 and the ZX Spectrum. Together, those simple machines with their rubbery keyboards and single kilobyte of memory (expandable to 128 kilobytes on the Spectrum, provided the memory pack didn't fall off while you were typing) created the first generation of computer enthusiasts. They also helped to build a multi-billion dollar industry. The ZX Spectrum sold five million units after its launch in 1982 and earned Sinclair Research more than £14 million of profit from revenues of more than £77 million in 1984. As Bill Gates was preparing to launch the first version of Windows, Sir Clive Sinclair had already won a knighthood from the Queen and had three successful products under his belt. So what would he do next? Which new opportunity would Britain's most technological entrepreneur capture with his next product?

The answer was . . . the C5. It wasn't a new computer. The press called it an electric car, but it looked nothing like a car. Sir Clive himself called it a 'vehicle' but it was really a cross between a scooter and a tricycle with a single seat and handlebars that you turned under your knees. It ran on a twelve-volt lead-acid battery, had a top-speed of 15 miles an hour, and could travel no more than 20 miles. It was also open-topped, like a bicycle, but launched in an English winter. It lasted three months before production was cut by 90 per cent. Only 14,000 were ever made, and only 5000 of them were sold before Sinclair Research went out of business, brought down by a nopportunity followed by one of Britain's greatest modern inventors.

Where Will YOU Choose to Focus?

Only you—*no one else can do it for you*—can focus your own mindset on the small pathway that leads to big opportunities, the Pareto Leaders that create massive value and garner virtually all the positive results. They're the 1 per cent of products that give you half your profit. They're the 1 per cent of investments that provide 50 per cent of your returns. They are 1 per cent of beliefs that empower you to achieve your dreams of success. Regardless of your current situation, you can choose to focus on the 1 per cent. It costs you nothing, and the gains can be great.

Or, like most people, and most businesses, you can choose to focus your mindset on the rocky road that leads to dismal nopportunities. These are the Pareto Losers that destroy value, waste your time and resources, and damage your reputation. *Nopportunity Avenue* is a much wider and more crowded road that leads only to failure and the frustration of broken dreams.

The penalties for pursuing nopportunities can be very harsh, and even the mighty can fall hard. A good example: Anil Ambani. Since separating from his brother Mukesh in 2006, he's pursued a series of nopportunities that have destroyed billions of dollars of wealth. In 2008, Anil's companies were valued at Rs 2,36,354 crore. By February 2019, they were worth only Rs 24,922 crore. In March 2019, he faced ninety days of imprisonment for the failure to pay his bills to Ericsson, and had to be bailed out by his brother Mukesh. What happened? Anil invested in infrastructure, defence and entertainment businesses that earned only losses. Over Rs 1.2 lakh crore he invested in power generation is stuck; power plants that could generate 24,000 megawatts are shut due a non-availability of gas. Although his telecom business borrowed Rs 45,000 crore, it failed to properly modernize, and it has been virtually wiped out by the entry of Reliance Jio.

Nopportunities can take anyone from hero to zero very quickly. Consider the harsh nopportunity penalty paid by Subhash Chandra for his disastrous foray into the infrastructure business. He's been forced to divest his crown jewels, including the highly profitable Zee TV media empire. Chandra pledged his Zee TV shares to borrow thousands of crores of rupees that he invested in various infrastructure businesses that produced only losses. His purchase of Videocon's Direct to Home business also turned out to be a complete failure. As a result of these nopportunities, on a single day in January 2019, shares in Chandra's public companies fell by Rs 13,686 crore.

Those who choose opportunities reap the *opportunity gain*, while those who embrace nopportunities must bear the *nopportunity loss*. People who invest in nopportunities often waste years trying to fix them. The rule is: *when a nopportunity knocks, shut and bolt the door!* Think of nopportunities as vermin that are slowly draining the blood from your body. You need to see them and kill them before they suck you dry.

An Old Era Mentality Attracts Nopportunities

Thought follows belief, and action follows thought. Your own belief system dictates whether you tend to embrace opportunities or nopportunities. If you have an Old Era mindset, you'll find it difficult to take advantage of Now Era opportunities—you wouldn't necessarily want to either.

India stands in the middle between the Old Era and the Now Era. Millions of Indians still have a mentality which sees opportunity in slavish obedience to the leader. In organizations that follow the Old Era culture, such as many family businesses and government bodies, sycophantic loyalty is greatly rewarded, while disloyalty or independent thinking may be discouraged and sometimes even punished. This often has nothing to do with ethics or competence. You may feel that you have no choice but to follow the Old Era rules, because you have little else to offer, due to poor education, poor birth, poor community, poor location, or any number of factors that if not denying you opportunity outright, have massively restricted it. Or you may simply feel trapped because everyone else you know seems to be in the same boat. You look around and see people just like you, and you benchmark yourself against them.

People who feel powerless often beg for divine help. But this behavior is fundamentally disempowering, as well as highly ineffective.

It works no better for you than it does for the drought-stricken peasant who begs God for rain, when what he really needs is irrigation. The communists replaced God with a human being, the infallible leader. But infallible leaders are infinitely worse than God because they actually punish you if you disobey. Why do people feel the need to surrender their power to God or to an infallible leader? Because they don't want to take responsibility, or they don't know how to take responsibility. They feel powerless and unable to lead themselves. But there is absolutely no need for you to feel powerless. You do not need to bargain for loyalty with a leader or an idol. You can learn to adapt and can take advantage of opportunities as well as anyone else. It costs you nothing to do so, and the upside is huge. But you must adjust your mindset to accept this fact.

There is a giant force over you and around you that surrounds you wherever you go. *It's your entire environment*—begging and praying for Mother Nature to meet your selfish needs doesn't work, because you have no control over her. However, there's one part of your environment that you can have complete control over—but only if you choose to. *Your own mind.* You should replace begging behaviour with a mindset that takes personal responsibility for seeing, choosing and implementing opportunities. You can nurture this mindset by increasing your awareness of God's environment all around you, which is a veritable Garden of Eden bursting with opportunities.

Rule Reverence Can Be a Curse

Since opportunities are valuable adaptations to change in the environment, conscious awareness is crucial. The most important environment to be aware of is the one inside your own head. Most people end up pursuing nopportunities because they let the opportunity choose them, rather than choosing consciously, based on accurate awareness and relevant selection criteria. In 2011, Ivan Reedman, an Australian IT consultant living in Wales, met Barry Davies, a former Special Forces soldier working as a project manager for BCB International, a manufacturer of military equipment. BCB wanted to expand into drones. He asked Reedman if he could make an autopilot module.

The Rise and Fall and Rise Again of Boba Tea

Charlie Tan had written a 150-page business proposal. He had been interviewed and interviewed again, spent two weeks at a boot camp in Shanghai where he learned about tea leaves infused with blueberries, the right way to close a shop, and how to maintain the fructose dispenser and put away the measuring spoons.

At last, the moment came. After a practical test lasting six hours, he received his coveted authorization to open the first branch of Taiwanese boba-tea chain The Alley in Singapore. According to Singapore's *Business Times,* which reported the story, the branch, at Jewel Changi Airport, was soon selling more than 1000 cups of cold, milky tea with tapioca balls every day. The drink, also known as bubble tea, had been invented in Taiwan in the 1980s and helped by the rise of the new cafe culture, spread quickly around the world. Taiwanese emigrants took it to Los Angeles, to China, to college campuses, to just about every area with large East Asian populations.

The craze didn't last. Too many people copied the opportunity. Instead of one or two boba outlets in an area, there would be three or four or five, cannibalizing each other's businesses, competing on price, and pushing down profit margins. Stores closed. The trend faded.

But by 2016 boba tea was back. Chains opened new stores with new recipes and flavours. Analysts put the value of the industry at $1.9 billion and predicted that it would reach $3.2 billion by 2023 with much of that growth coming from the North American market. In 2018, shares in boba tea-maker B&S International Holdings tripled their HK$1 IPO price within hours.

So has Charlie Tan spotted an opportunity or a nopportunity? It's too early to say but a year after its IPO, B&S's share price had fallen to HK$0.80 and the bubble in Taiwan's tea trend might just have burst . . . again.

'It was an easy opportunity to say, yeah, I haven't done this before, but I'll certainly get into it,' Reedman later told freelance journalist Mark Harris.

Reedman expanded his team and set to work. But the drone wouldn't work. Reedman couldn't get the Wi-Fi control system to operate and the obstacle-avoiding sonar was poor. Three years and hundreds of thousands of BCB's pounds later, neither company had anything to show for the effort. BCB had lost the initiative and Reedman had put three years of his life into a technology that didn't work.

If Reedman had done his homework before choosing this nopportunity, he likely would have discovered that it was a waste of time. By plunging in with limited awareness, he was almost guaranteed to fail.

Your ability to see opportunities is largely based on the rules you personally choose to follow. Excessive *reverence* can make you cling to irrelevant rules for too long, block out the truth, and resist valuable adaptations to change. Reverence of long-lasting higher-level rules, such as the Ten Commandments or the laws of physics, is perfectly rational. Reverence for lower-level rules, such as trends, fashions or technologies, which can lose relevance quickly, can lead you to choose nopportunities. Decide to open a bar dedicated to full jar soda, for example, and you could find that your opportunity becomes a nopportunity very quickly. Instagram trends have very short shelf-lives.

Rule reverence is a deadly nopportunity mindset that stifles adaptation and drives even the large companies to collapse. It can be particularly deadly for companies that have scaled up huge capital-intensive operations. When rules that were once Pareto Leaders become gradually more irrelevant due to changes in the environment, managements can blind themselves to the point of suicide to avoid needed adaptations. For example, although Kishore Biyani's Future Group was the pioneer and leader of Indian modern retail, it completely missed the even larger opportunity in e-commerce because it couldn't adjust its mindset to go beyond the old bricks and mortar rules of retail. As a result, it lost the ecommerce opportunity to Flipkart and Amazon.

Even worse is reverence for *fules*—rules for fools. Some people follow fules with religious devotion, often to their own demise. A great example: Easter Island (aka Rapa Nui), a tiny Polynesian island that is now part of Chile, is one of the most remote places on earth. Settled between 1000 and 1500 years ago, its population grew to about 7000. At some point, its village chiefs began building the large stone statues (called gures) for which the island is famous. About 500 years ago, Easter Island society suddenly collapsed into warfare, disease and famine. Archaeologists have reconstructed much of the story. The gures were carved in the island's single quarry and moved on rollers made from trees. As villages competed to build more statues, more trees were cut down until eventually none were left. That meant no wood for boats, houses or fuel. Islanders must have seen disaster coming as they felled the last trees, but they felled them, nonetheless.

Persistence is usually a positive quality, but persistence in pursuit of fules is always a nopportunity, leading to resource destruction.

Don't Worship the Holy 'I'

We all wear blinders that can close our minds and focus us away from opportunities. The cause is one-sided WIIFM obsession, an unbalanced identification with *the holy I*—our own *egos*. Opportunities often slap us in the face, but we disregard or even resent them because we're too focused on our own needs. Because of ego, we also tend to get married to our beliefs, rather than constantly questioning their continued relevance. As a result, we often rush to judgment and toss budding opportunity seeds into the *nopportunity bin* before giving them adequate consideration. Don't expect anyone to bend a knee at the altar of your ego. Nobody besides your parents selflessly care about you. Nobody will do anything for you just because you want it, any more than you will do anything for others just because they want it. There must always be a fair value exchange. Unless you're an aspiring gang leader (which is a nopportunity in the Now Era generally leading to prison or death), you must give up the pure pursuit of ego.

You are not an island. An opportunity mindset requires an empathetic identification with *the all*; in other words, your environment, which is the source of all opportunities. Unlike your ego, your environment is never stiff—it never resents or resists change. You can force open your mind by bending your knee at the temple of truth rather than at the altar of ego.

Don't Focus on Competitors First!

Where you focus your mind first is critical. Your primary area of focus must ideally be able to yield you Pareto Leader results. Modern business strategy theory as a rule focuses first on competition; that's why it's normally called *competitive strategy*. There is a professional field called *competitive intelligence*, and large multinationals spend billions of dollars per year gathering data on their competitors. Unfortunately, focusing first on the competition is almost always a nopportunity. Do your competitors buy your products? Do they pay you? Do they help you succeed? Are they on your team? Of course not.

Imagine that you are an individual, not a business, and you are entering the job market. Where should you focus first? What is the most important issue facing you? Is your competition most important? Or would it be far more important for you to identify your mission and skills, and match these with services required by the marketplace? How much would an aspiring career-seeker need to focus on the competition? Obviously, not much, and maybe not at all.

How Adobe Premiere Became Number One by Ignoring Apple

In 1999 Matt Douglas was the product manager for Adobe Premiere, the company's video editing software. It was a good product, with a loyal customer base, but Adobe knew the company would soon face a tough new competitor.

Apple was about to introduce its own Final Cut Pro. It was a dangerous moment. Apple was a colossus with its own customer base of loyal fans. It could package its product into the Mac's operating system and was able to integrate it perfectly with the rest of Mac's software suite. And, of course, the product was coming from Apple, so it was always going to be good.

Writing on his blog, Douglas explains how Adobe tried to take the wind out of Apple's sails by announcing Premiere's new features at the same time that Apple made its own announcement. But no one was listening. Everyone was more interested in what Apple had to offer.

Final Cut Pro came out and soon started taking market share among Mac users. Adobe tried to fight back, checking their competitor's features and making sure they weren't left behind. But Apple just ignored them. It kept building its product and serving its customers as though Adobe didn't exist.

'Apple had their own strategic priorities, their own product road-map, and their own take on the world,' Douglas wrote. 'Nothing we did would stop them.'

So, Adobe copied their approach. They ignored Apple and did their own thing. They focused on what they could control and not what Apple could control. Over the next ten years, the company completely rebuilt Premiere for both Mac and Windows, improving its service and regaining the top spot in the market.

Competitive advantage is something that every company strives for. In my view, it's a false god, a nopportunity. If you fail, it is rarely because of your competitors. *Rather, it's because you failed to recognize the changing environment—and how it creates opportunities.* Competitive failure is a consequence rather than a cause, just as competitive advantage is a consequence rather than a cause. If your competitors overwhelm you it's because they adapted well to changes in the environment and you didn't.

In 1967, Keuffel & Esser, the largest manufacturer of slide rules in the US, commissioned a study of the future. The report predicted that by the year 2067 Americans would live in domed cities and watch three-dimensional television. Unfortunately for the company, the report failed to predict that slide rules would be obsolete in less than ten years, replaced by electronic calculators. By 1976, Keuffel & Esser mothballed its slide rule manufacturing equipment and sent it to a museum.

Remember Meru Cabs? In the early 2000s it was a fast-growing company, spreading its wings across Indian metros. It raised $75 million in venture capital. Meru offered air-conditioned taxis that you could order by phone. They were a big improvement over the old-fashioned taxis then plying city streets. By 2019, Meru is on its knees, as its revenue has fallen 30–40 per cent over the past few years. Why? Is there any reason Meru couldn't have evolved into Ola? Of course, it could have. Its customers started buying smartphones, Google developed maps, and Uber developed GPS-driven aggregation technology to connect buyers and drivers. But it missed the opportunity created by those changes and became irrelevant, because it focused on besting its existing competitors, who were not even a threat!

Competitors can certainly be annoying. But, like mosquitos, they are rarely life-threatening. Swatting them away will provide temporary relief, but not prosperity. Excessive focus on competitors can lead to two other dangerous behaviours: 1) copying and 2) differentiation. If you've captured a great opportunity, you can expect others to copy you. They're going to drive out your profits and create killer price competition by building cheaper, simpler or more convenient versions of your product. Is it an opportunity to disregard them or copy them? Or would you be better off focusing first on valuable adaptations as Steve Jobs did after rejoining Apple? Differentiation for the sake of it can lead to pointless innovations that waste enormous resources. Before Steve Jobs returned, Apple wasted billions of dollars being different from Microsoft and its PC partners. It created hundreds of computer models that people didn't want to buy, driving the company close to bankruptcy.

Don't worry about being different. If you sincerely work at providing useful service, if you provide a fair value exchange, and if you are irreverent about existing rules and are willing to create your own, you will be automatically be different—in a relevant way. The only competitors you should fear are the ones who are better at adapting to the changing environment to provide useful service than you. But simply being afraid of them is a nopportunity. Instead of fearing them, or copying them, or aspiring to be different from them, you would be better off learning from them. Focus on how your competitors adapt to change better than you, and how they see, evaluate and choose opportunities.

Avoid These Four Major Nopportunity Traps

Various *nopportunity traps* can ensnare people in behaviours that makes them miss opportunities. The major traps include:

1. Don't Let Rules Trump the Mission

As organizations become larger, following the rules becomes more important than the organization's mission, transforming opportunity into nopportunity. For example, when I started my first tour as the US Trade Commissioner in Mumbai in 2000, I found meagre interest in trade between US and Indian companies. To fulfil my mission of promoting US exports, I raised Rs 50 lakh from Indian donor companies and created the American Business Club, which quickly attracted thousands of Indian member companies. The Club used the funds raised to hold a series of well-publicized nationwide catalogue shows in which over 400 new-to-market US companies participated for free. This innovative and successful market promotion initiative was abruptly abandoned, and the entire opportunity lost when a single Washington-based bureaucrat questioned whether it was following all the rules. (A subsequent investigation proved that no rules had been broken.) My overseers in Washington and Delhi cared far more about following the rules than they did for the trade promotion mission of the organization.

2. Avoid Opportunities Because They're Free

Ironically, many people avoid opportunities because they're free, and prefer to pay for nopportunities because they're expensive. For example, Ray Kroc, the man who transformed a single McDonald's hamburger stand into the world's largest restaurant chain, paid nothing to the McDonald brothers for the opportunity to franchise the brand. Yet people gladly spend many crores to buy franchises that are, in comparison, very poor opportunities with limited scope for growth.

In 1981, a movie company called Amblin Productions, wanted to use some branded candy in a children's movie it was making. Amblin called Mars, the confectionary firm, with an offer: could the movie use M&Ms? The movie wouldn't pay but in return, Mars would get some free advertising. Mars thought it over and said 'no'. Amblin made the same offer to Hershey's, which agreed. Hershey's got the placement in Steven Spielberg's *ET: The Extra Terrestrial* for free, although they later agreed to spend $1 million helping to promote the film. When the movie became a blockbuster, sales of Reese's Pieces jumped 85 per cent.

Other companies were smarter. The 1969 movie *The Italian Job* was a heist story, but it was really little more than a long car chase. The stars of the movie were the Minis which were filmed racing through Rome's sewage system. But BMC, the car's manufacturer, only gave the moviemakers a small number of vehicles for free; the producers had to buy the rest themselves. Fiat saw the opportunity. They offered the movie as many cars as they needed plus $40,000. BMC was lucky. The moviemakers turned down the offer and Mini won a whole new group of fans.

3. Focus on Problems Rather than Opportunities

All business managers and owners are engaged in a constant battle, firefighting operational issues and solving problems. Our brains crave rewards. Most people will prefer the quick rewards of solving day-to-day problems, rather than tackling opportunities whose rewards may be unclear and very far in the distant future. However, as management guru Peter Drucker correctly pointed out, 'Results are obtained by exploiting opportunities, not by solving problems.'

Unfortunately, when it comes to priorities, most people place the search for great opportunities at the bottom of their to-do list. Instead, they spend most of their time trying to fix troublesome nopportunities that never should have been chosen. For example, I had a client in the travel industry who had started half a dozen businesses over the past decade, all of them failures with no potential to meet his goals. I encouraged him to shut these down and focus all his efforts on a single good new opportunity that we had identified.

If possible, you should identify and dump hopeless nopportunities and delegate problems solving to others, in order to give you more time to focus on opportunities. After all, if you don't focus on your own opportunities, who else will?

4. Focus on Profit Rather than Mission

Companies miss opportunities because they are often more focused on increasing profits by cutting costs than they are on spending on opportunities that provide customer satisfaction. Don't let your service mission be overwhelmed by your profit mission. Your service mission should become more and more intense all the time. Even from a pure greed standpoint, the better the service and relevance you can give to your customers, the more value you create. The more value you create, the richer you become.

Ironically the goal of making money becomes more intense once a company is successful. When a company is a start-up, it isn't making money so it is more likely to focus on the opportunity by creating an attractive value exchange with the customer. Once a company becomes successful, it becomes more obsessed with profits. The desire is to wring out the maximum value from the investment already made. As the environment changes and begins to make older opportunities irrelevant, companies can be hesitant to alter existing value chains and cost structures. It is always a nopportunity to prioritize profit over the mission of providing useful service. If you do so, you will only replace profits with losses.

There are abundant examples of companies that missed huge opportunities because they were more focused on wringing every penny out of existing assets rather than enhancing their service mission.

For example, when digital streaming was launched in India, the opportunity was potentially huge because the average Indian home had only one television. Zee set up a new business called Ditto TV, a platform for people to watch existing Zee TV programmes on their phones or tablets. This obviously appealed to Zee management because it could potentially wring more profit out of already paid for TV content, mainly soap operas targeted to a female audience. The service flopped, because the audience for phone streaming was mainly young men with no interest in female content. In contrast, Zee's competitor Star TV set up Hotstar, which offered free sports content which appealed to the male audience. This attracted enough viewership to be supported by advertising and premium fees. Realizing the changing environment, this strategy was successfully replicated and expanded by another competitor, Sony Entertainment Television, through SonyLiv. They expanded their OTT offerings to include a bouquet of programmes including episodes of old popular soap operas, special screening of movies, regional entertainment content, international shows and lots more.

The Dangers of Going with Your Gut

Many people think that the best way to make decisions is to 'go with their gut', also known as *intuition*. When we go with the gut, we don't evaluate a range of options before making decisions. Usually when we assess a situation, we find cues in the circumstances which match with past patterns that look like the current situation. We reason by analogy to past situations. We adapt certain rules from past experience, i.e. this worked in the past, so let's adapt to this situation. We also know what actions to reject as well. For example, you don't have to think about how to drive, or how to tie your shoes, or brush your teeth. Many decisions are required for these tasks, but they're automatic. Intuition gradually develops as you develop deep expertise in a given field. For example, my own father operated various retail businesses. Even though he had no training, he was a genius at merchandising. He could artfully arrange enormous amounts of products in a remarkably limited amount of retail space. Because he had no formal training, my father always insisted that his merchandising ability came from channelling insights from *infinite intelligence*. Well, maybe. But it's far more likely that his merchandising skill was simply the result of his three decades of experience and learning.

Reasoning by analogy often fails because we tend to focus too much on similarities between two situations and downplay the differences. We also get overly influenced by highly salient analogies that have left an indelible imprint on us, even when those analogies do not fit the current situation. Some events in life leave such a scar, or indelible imprint, that we create analogies to them even when it is irrelevant. For example, the appeasement of Hitler before World War II left an indelible imprint on politicians for decades afterwards and influenced their behaviour, even when it was not appropriate.

Relying on pattern matching can lead to nopportunities as it tends to block out new or different thinking. When you're going with your gut, you often don't surface and bother to analyse the underlying assumptions that are embedded in analogical reasoning. Sometimes the analogy is like a solution, and we go out and hunt for problems to solve with it. It's like having a hammer and going out and finding ways to use it for new problems. If that's the case, everything looks like it needs a hammer.

It's important to make the distinction between what is fact and what is assumption because decision makers often confuse the two. The objective is to separate fact from assumption, and to test the assumptions carefully to check if they are valid. For example, I invested in an Indian start-up that aimed to become the Uber of tempos. Tempos are small trucks that handle most merchandise deliveries within Indian cities. They are largely disorganized and run at only 40 per cent capacity. The promoters based the business model on the assumption that tempos could be aggregated on a tech platform, using the same rules that Uber had used to organize drivers for passenger transportation. But that underlying assumption proved to be opinion, not fact, and the model has struggled to scale.

Why Zano Turned Out to Be a No-No

You can still see Zano's campaign page on crowdsourcing site Kickstarter, and you can still feel excited by the product. It looked like a great idea, a solution to the problem faced by anyone who has ever taken a selfie: how can you take a picture of yourself doing something interesting instead of just beaming at the camera while holding out your hand?

After Ivan Reedman's drone project collapsed, he felt that he had an answer: he would continue investing in his technology and build a drone capable of autonomous flight. Set the distance to the controller in your smartphone, and it would follow you as you go about your business. When you were done, you could call it back. The promotional video showed someone being photographed as they rode their dirt bike, leaping off a rock into a lagoon, and sitting outside a bar with friends. The drone had infrared obstacle avoidance, echo-sounding sonar and an air pressure sensor to control altitude. While other drones focused on their ability to fly high and shoot beautiful pictures while being controlled, the Zano was all about set and forget while it shot selfies. Reedman was sure he could do it.

Kickstarter's audience loved it. By the end of the campaign, more than 12,000 backers had placed an order, generating nearly $3.5 million, twenty times the company's goal. It was Kickstarter's most-funded European campaign.

But things soon went wrong. Campaign updates suggested that the company was struggling to source parts. Production wouldn't scale. When the first models went out, the drone didn't work at all. It would fly for a few seconds, then crash. The video quality was poor—and there was no autonomous flight. Reedman had built nothing more than a bad drone.

Within a few months, Torquing Group, Reedman's company, was bankrupt. Kickstarter hired freelance journalist Mark Harris to find out what had happened. He uncovered a tale of ambitious promises, of overconfidence, of sunk costs, and an opportunity too large for its founders.

Making decisions through intuition can work well in an unchanging world. However, when things change, as they always do, the norms, heuristics or rules that you followed can quickly become irrelevant. My dad's expertise at retail merchandising would have been of little help to him if he had to sell products in cyberspace.

Five Common Reasons Why You Choose Nopportunities

People often choose nopportunities simply because of poor decision-making. Major reasons for choosing badly include:

1. The Sunk Cost Fallacy

The Sunk Cost Fallacy leads people to keep investing in a nopportunity, even when it's clearly hopeless. For example, I once had an Indian client with a portfolio of eight small businesses, all in different sectors, which he had inherited from his father. All were based on opportunities that may have been good in the days of the License Raj, but were now uncompetitive and obsolete. Yet even after two decades of hopeless effort, he refused to give up these nopportunities, still believing that he could turn them around.

2. Confirmation Bias

Professor Richard Wiseman of the University of Hertfordshire in England studied why some people seem to get all the luck while others never get the breaks they deserve. He carried out a simple experiment to discover whether this was due to differences in their ability to spot opportunities. He gave a variety of people a newspaper and asked them to look through it and tell him how many photographs were inside. He had secretly placed a large message halfway through the newspaper saying: 'Tell the experimenter you have seen this and win $50.' This message took up half of the page and was written in type that was more than two inches high.

Although the lucrative message was staring everyone straight in the face, a large percentage of people missed it. Wiseman concluded that *unlucky people* miss opportunities because they are too focused on looking for something else. They go to parties intent on finding their perfect partner and miss opportunities to make good friends. They look through newspapers determined to find certain types of job advertisements and miss other types of opportunities. This phenomenon is not based on luck at all. It is simply a form of confirmation bias. This refers to a tendency to gather and pay attention to information and views that confirm our existing beliefs and hypotheses, and to avoid information that are contrary to these.

People exhibit a stubborn attachment to their existing beliefs. This points out the strong need to expose existing beliefs and challenge them in light of objective evidence. In other words, sincerely seek the truth. We should attempt to poke holes in our pre-existing beliefs, pre-existing hypotheses and pre-existing assumptions to see where they are not valid. We should not defer blindly to the expert and organization, including ourselves. Just because people have been right in the past doesn't mean they'll always be right.

3. Framing as a Threat

How you frame an issue has a large influence on how you react to it. Companies tend to use a dichotomy of framing an issue as either a threat or an opportunity, because of their use of SWOT analysis. For example, when the Internet appeared, newspapers were hurt because classified ads began to migrate to specialized websites. The companies that framed the issue as a threat invested a lot of money in the Internet, but most simply put their existing classified ads onto their website in a PDF type of format that did not make use of the benefits of the technology.

Framing as a threat leads us to copy our competitors rather than looking at it as an opportunity to provide better service to our customers. The source of the threat is countered, rather than uncovering the source of the opportunity, which could be different. The newspaper companies that framed the Internet as an opportunity looked at the useful benefits of the medium, and how they could use the new technology to expand value for customers. They set up sophisticated mechanisms such as search functions, blogs and podcasts, which were far more successful. In doing so, they tended to invest much less than the newspapers that reacted as a threat.

Another problem with framing against threats is that we usually frame in terms of the mental model of the previous big threat. The newspapers framed the threat as if they were reacting to a competing newspaper. Another good example is how the US reacted to 9/11. They framed it as they would a Cold War threat because that was their mental model for threat reaction. When people frame the issue as a threat, they are more likely to put more resources into combating it. Because of the sunk cost fallacy, when things went badly, the newspapers with failed Internet strategies tended to double down on the existing course of action rather than thinking of new ways to offer useful service to their customers.

4. Anchoring Bias

Anchoring bias refers to the idea that we allow an initial reference point to distort our analysis of what could be. For example, your current growth rate could be your initial reference point for future growth potential. But your current growth rate is absolutely no indicator of how much you can grow in future if you undertake new opportunities. In the same way, we might consider it an opportunity to buy a stock simply because its price recently fell by a few per cent. But that reference point has absolutely no bearing on the actual value of the particular stock.

Similarly, when I lived in Indonesia in the late 1990s, the exchange rate was generally around Rp 2000 to the dollar. At one point the rupiah fell to 2500 to the dollar, so I decided to invest to buy a year's worth of currency. To my shock, within a couple months, the rupiah fell to 17,000 to the dollar, and I lost a fortune.

5. Groupthink

Groupthink refers to the situation in which we avoid discussion of topics or smooth them over in order to avoid conflict. It's go along to get along. When groupthink takes place, people censor themselves and are reluctant to speak. It happens even with groups full of intelligent, knowledgeable people who are devoted to their goals. For example, while serving as Trade Commissioner at the US Embassy in Jakarta, Indonesia, I attended daily meetings of the country team headed by the Ambassador. For several years, the Ambassador was an arrogant man who enjoyed publicly abusing his staff members. As a result, all the members of the country team avoided any discussion of difficult topics on these meetings, which usually made them a waste of everyone's time.

Sounds familiar?

The Nopportunity Mindset

1. It's all about your mindset
No one is going to give you an opportunity that's right for you. You have to find your own opportunities. You have to identify them, build them and ignore the nopportunities that look so inviting. If Ivan Reedman had known how to say 'no' instead of 'yes' when he was offered a nopportunity, he might still have had his business and his reputation.

2. Avoid the four nopportunity traps
Blindly following rules, believing that valuable opportunities can't be free, focusing on problems instead of the opportunities, and being distracted by profit instead of the mission are all signs of a nopportunity. Just as Zee lost out on the digital media business and Meru on the online cab business in India, nopportunities all waste your time and your resources.

3. Five reasons you choose nopportunities
We often believe we can do more than we can, have invested too much to give up, or believe that we know exactly what we're looking for. We frame things the wrong way, are led astray by reference points, and follow the crowd. They all create nopportunities but being aware of them can help—and if it doesn't, experience will.

Part III: The Opportunity Process

12

Benefits of the Opportunity Process

Why do you need a process to help you to find and assess opportunities? Who needs such a process? How can an opportunity process help you to succeed? Why should you audit your environment in order to see, evaluate and choose the best opportunities?

Faisal Siddiqui's company, Zaka Group, has served as the General Services Agent (GSA) for a major foreign airline for decades. While this business had been good, he was always looking to make his mark by developing new opportunities. Over the years, Faisal had developed several new businesses, but none had amounted to much. He felt that if he used a systematic process of choosing opportunities, he could make better choices and get much better results.

I conducted an *opportunity audit* for Faisal's company, and identified over a dozen potential opportunities. Based on Faisal's preference, these new opportunities were within the domain of the travel, tourism and cargo industries. After filtering these opportunities through nine evaluators, we narrowed the list down to three. These were then aligned with the four segments of the promoter's own environment, with specific focus on his mission. We also identified several nopportunities, businesses that Zaka Group would be better off curtailing.

The Open Mind process for Zaka Group revealed that the best potential opportunity was to launch a new kind of courier service: *the fastest in the world.* At that time, the fastest courier services, such as Fedex or Blue Dart, could only deliver parcels overnight. The opportunity that the process identified was for a courier service that could deliver a parcel to major Indian cities in only eleven hours. A package could leave Mumbai at 10 a.m. and reach Delhi by 9 p.m. This service had never been offered before. But could it be done? Was there enough friction in the market to create a gap that this opportunity could fill? During the implementation process we carefully but economically tested the feasibility and market potential of the service. It was indeed feasible and had adequate market to make at least a modest beginning. The new courier service, under the brand name Bombax was launched within one year of beginning the Opportunity Audit. It was an immediate success, and two years later has operations all over India and offices in eleven Indian cities and is expanding rapidly and profitably.

Who Needs an Opportunity Process?

Imagine that a distant relative has died and left you Rs 50 crore. Suddenly, you are rich. You no longer have to struggle for money to survive. But soon you realize that you have a new challenge: *investing*. How will you get a good return on your newfound wealth? How is it normally done? As you have never invested before, you are ignorant but eager to learn. After doing Internet research and speaking with friends, you learn that there are certain commonly followed rules of investing. For example, one should divide investments into two major categories: equity and debt. You're excited to learn that equities have a higher return over time. But how to choose individual equities or equity mutual funds to invest in? You learn that many people hire wealth managers to handle the task of choosing equities. You decide to speak to some of them to understand how they go about this task. The first few that you meet all tell you the same thing: they employ teams of researchers who are experts on the investment opportunities in various industries. These analysts' study and test various models of investing to determine which work best. Some focus on value, buying stocks that are selling at bargain prices. Others follow a process of technical analysis and select stocks based on predictable patterns of price behaviour.

Eventually, you meet a different sort of wealth manager. He says: 'I used to employ a whole team of analysts, but they weren't worth the money. Nobody can beat the average return of the market. So, I sacked them all, and replaced them with Bobo.' He pulls out his phone and proudly shows you a photo of a monkey, who is wearing a blindfold over his eyes.

'*A blindfolded monkey?*' This is not at all what you expected.

'Yes, exactly. I put the names of the stocks on the wall and have Bobo throw darts. Wherever the darts land, that's what we buy.'

You don't know whether to be shocked or amused. 'Isn't that risky?' you ask.

'Not at all. At the end of the day, the results you get are all based on luck. The monkey works as well as any other method. And he literally works for peanuts. I give the savings to you.'

Would you hire a wealth manager who uses a blindfolded monkey to choose stocks? Over the past six years, in pursuing my business as the world's first and only opportunity consultant, I have asked over 300 Indian business promoters this question; they manage businesses of all sizes, ranging from Rs 1 crore in sales to Rs 5000 crore, in all sectors. Not surprisingly, 100 per cent of these promoters replied that they would not hire the monkey to choose their equity investments. They refuse to use an investment process that is based purely on luck.

I next asked these promoters: *'Would you agree that using systematic processes creates better outcomes?'*

All of the promoters surveyed agreed that systematic processes create better outcomes. It could be argued that systematic processes are the foundation of our modern world. For example, your chartered accountant follows clear processes to manage your accounts and do your taxes. Engineers use processes, factories use processes. Would you use a surgeon who didn't follow a systematic process, who made it up as he went along, Indiana Jones style? Of course not.

I next asked these promoters: *'Do you currently use a systematic process to find, evaluate and choose the best opportunities?'*

Remarkably enough, 100 per cent of the promoters answered that they *do not* use a systematic process to find, evaluate and choose opportunities. Although all agreed that the opportunities they pursue are critical to their success, none of them used a systematic process to select them. In other words, *they were all relying on the luck of a blindfolded monkey to choose their opportunities.* Finally, I asked these promoters: 'Is there any reason you *don't need* a systematic process to find, evaluate and choose the best opportunities?' None could find a reason. They all agreed that they need an opportunity process. Why hadn't they used one? Simply because such a process didn't exist.

The Open Mind Process

To address this universal need, I have developed the six-step 'Open Mind Process', the world's first and only systematic opportunity process. Its purpose is to help anyone and everyone to uncover, recover and discover opportunities for sustained, profitable growth.

As discussed earlier, we learn through pattern recognition. By stringing patterns together, we create processes. By doing this, we can create complex systems and organizations. Processes allow us to very efficiently perform tasks and provide services to people. Better processes are the foundation of our prosperity; they have driven immense advancement and wealth creation in the modern age. Is my opportunity process perfect? Of course not. All processes can and must evolve and adapt. One of the hallmarks of the modern age is the ability to improve processes quickly based on continuous, collective and cumulative learning.

What are processes? They are, in a sense, the rules of the game. If you create the process, you create the rules. Understanding the process thoroughly will give you the opportunity to change the process and change the rules. In this book, I've suggested rules, and a general framework for an opportunity process. Everyone who reads this book can contribute and participate in improving this process. You can also be a rule breaker and a rule maker. Everyone needs opportunity. We are doing our best to build a learning community around opportunity, in order to create something truly useful that can benefit everyone in the human race. This is an open process. I hope that thousands of people, through their experiences, help to improve this process.

Why Should You Use an Opportunity Process?

Imagine this situation: you go to a doctor in severe pain. He pokes around a bit but doesn't have you take any tests at all. He says that based on his vast experience, all those tests are a waste of your money. He's 'seen it all' and 'goes with his gut'. He decides: 'You need surgery.' It will cost X and probably keep you in bed for weeks. Has he done this type of surgery before? Not really, but he has done plenty of other types of surgery. He'll figure it out as he goes along. Once he opens you up, it'll come to him, because he has vast experience and his instincts are very good.

Would you allow this doctor to operate on you? You would not want to be one of the victims of his *school of failure,* would you?

To seek the truth, you must first admit that you don't know and find a process for determining the best answer. How can you know the truth? You need to use an evidence-based scientific process of learning through systematic investigation. It is the same type of process that is used by your doctor who treats you. The questions you need to answer first are: *what do we already know? What do we need to know?*

Now imagine an alternative situation: you go to the doctor complaining of pain. She says: 'I've got a couple of ideas on what's wrong with you, but I need to collect more data on your condition.' She has you do a battery of tests and refers you to a specialist who does more tests. Your doctors take you through a complete protocol of investigation that has been developed over decades based on collected evidence and doesn't rely on 'gut'. A conclusion is finally reached using decision methodologies that have been developed over decades. Your doctor believes that the diagnosis has a 99 per cent probability. She provides treatment options, again chosen based on processes that deliver a high likelihood of success. Each comes with potential costs and negative consequences you can evaluate. Eventually you decide on surgery. You hire a surgeon who has done this particular surgery hundreds of times with a high degree of success. *Which course of action would you rather follow?*

Imagine how fearful you would be if you had to be operated on by a surgeon who had never performed that procedure before. If you have no opportunity process, that is your situation. You are flying blind and have every right to be fearful. The penalties for making bad choices can be very grave.

How to Avoid the School of Failure

If you do not use an opportunity process you may be condemned to many extra years in the school of failure. Many of the hundreds of business promoters I've spoken with in depth admit they *need* an opportunity process, yet they don't want it. Why? Because rather than a process, they want a pill. If the doctor tells you that the cure for your problem is to walk every day for one hour, give up alcohol, and always be nice to your wife, what percentage of people are going to do it? If the doctor says take this pill twice a day, 99 per cent of people would rather take it. It's much easier. Unfortunately, there is no pill available for opportunities. Simply being positive or thinking in a positive way may make you happier, but it will not help you to find opportunities efficiently. Success requires action. But how to take action? What action to take? Where and when to take action? Obviously, you must have some sort of methodology for transforming thought into effective action. In other words, a system or process. A process greatly reduces the possibility of failure. It increases the possibility of a better outcome. Why? Because a process is a school of *other people's failures—and lessons learned.*

You don't need to be a *victim of your circumstances.* Even if you don't want to control your environment, you can at least understand it in order to harvest good opportunities. Yet 99.9 per cent of business people and career seekers approach opportunity decision-making without a conscious process. Their only school is the school of failure. This is why 99 per cent of people fail. They say: 'I'll go with my gut.' What does that mean? *Unconscious decision-making.*

There are three levels of environmental consciousness. These are:

1.   Unconscious—making the decision-maker a complete victim of circumstances.
2.   Conscious—the decision-maker is consciously aware of the environment but has no process to consciously extract the best opportunities, and only does it unconsciously.
3.   Conscious—the decision-maker is able to understand the environment, both internal and external, to see, evaluate and properly choose opportunities.

The extent to which you can master this hierarchy of awareness controls your fate.

Opportunity can be difficult and confusing for many people. That's largely because the process is not yet habitual. A regular process must be practised regularly, the same way that you brush your teeth twice a day. You don't mind doing it, do you? Studies have found that if you want to go to the gym on a regular basis, the first priority is to go to the gym every day. Some days you won't do anything, you might just sit around and talk to your friends, but you must go every day. You must build the habit over time. You will enjoy going to the gym as it will become a habit, and you will exercise more and more.

Ten years ago, I had a burning desire to write a novel. But I kept procrastinating, as I was intimidated by what appeared to be a monumental task. In order to understand the best process of writing a novel, I read several books. One of the best authors suggested that I write only five minutes a day, but do it every day. Based on this advice I was able to write a novel in six months. Every day I wrote more and more, it became more and more of a habit, and the book got done.

How to Build an Opportunity 'Bird by Bird'

Writing about the difficulty of tackling a project as big and difficult as creating a book, writer Ann Lamott describes an event that took place one summer at her family's cabin in Bolinas, California.

Her ten-year-old brother was sitting at the kitchen table surrounded by paper, pencils and books about birds. He was close to tears. He had no idea what to do. All summer, for three months, he had had to write a report about birds. All summer he had put it off, believing that he would make a start the next day or the day after that. Now the summer was ending. The report was due the next day and he hadn't done a thing. The path from where he sat at that table with a blank page to the end of the project looked impossible to bridge.

Lamott's father sat beside him and put his arm around his shoulder. 'Bird by bird, buddy,' he told him. 'Just take it bird by bird.'

It was great advice and became the title of Lamott's bestselling book on writing and life. What makes the advice so powerful is that it does two things. On the one hand, it describes a repeatable process that can turn a large, overwhelming task into a series of small achievable tasks. But it also describes a habit that ensures that each of those small tasks is completed. Writing about a dozen birds in a day is hard. Writing about one bird a day for twelve days is easy. A process performed habitually gets the job done . . . though it also helps if you start early.

It's the same with opportunity. Most people are reluctant to use a process to see, choose, evaluate and implement opportunities largely because they are confused about how to do it, and they fear failure for good reason. Many experts on success urge you to improve your habits. Just telling you to have better habits is useless. But with a process, you can learn to use these habits in the easiest way possible. This success will encourage you to learn more and improve and reward you with increasing success.

Opportunities are created by change. People tend to approach change management in the same way that they approach dieting, as something you do on a periodic basis when it becomes necessary, because it is difficult and unpleasant. As a result of this approach, the results are similar to dieting. You go through a tough process, make some changes, and then revert to your previous habits. Experts know that the best way to diet is to not diet at all. Dieting should be replaced with weight management, in which you balance healthy lifestyle with healthy eating, eliminating the need to diet at all. But such an approach requires sustained effort. The process must become habitual rather than sporadic. A similar attitude needs to be taken toward change. Opportunity is the most important factor in the long-term health of both careers and companies. Therefore, change must be managed because it creates opportunity. It cannot be something that you deal with on a periodic or campaign basis.

Imagine a sea captain who only paid attention to the weather when it turned bad. He would be massively influenced by the environment without any preparation and as a result risk sinking much of the time. He would not be able to take advantage of favourable winds or advanced knowledge of weather conditions in order to avoid bad weather or go faster than other ships. So, his upside and downside would be very limited.

It's the same with you. If you are not aware of your environment, you face grave risks created by change. You will also find it difficult to consciously identify and take advantage of favourable environmental conditions before your competitors, by capturing the best opportunities.

A Process Massively Improves Our Decision Making

You are fortunate to be living in an age of vast opportunities. Not only have the types of opportunities available expanded immensely with technology and with globalization; but everything about 'opportunity' has expanded. That's good news for Indians, because they can now compete on a global playing field. The heads of Google and Microsoft, Pepsi and McKinsey, Citibank and Mastercard, and several big American corporations are or have been from India. Even the deans of leading global business schools, including Harvard, Kellogg, Cornell and INSEAD, are or have been from India. This was unheard of before. Now the range of professional opportunities, types of careers, places you can work, or the scale you can consider achieving is absolutely unlimited.

However, the scale and quality of your competition has also increased. In this kind of hyper-competitive environment, you can't possibly let opportunity be unconscious, you can't wait for it to knock on your door. It would be similar to not bothering to study for the IIT or IAS exams. Just as you must have a process of preparation for highly competitive careers, you must use a process to see, evaluate, choose and implement the best opportunities.

How to Pick an Ice Cream Flavour

As part of his research for his book *The Creative Curve*, a guide to the source of creativity, Allen Gannett went out of his way to discover how large companies identify opportunities in their markets. He visited the testing kitchens of Ben & Jerry's. The idea though wasn't just to score some free ice cream (though he did do that). It was to see the process that a large company uses to create new products that its customers will love.

'I assumed the process for creating a new [flavour] was by now efficient and direct,' he wrote. 'A food scientist would come up with a flavour idea, churn up a batch of the concoction, sample it, then supply the all-important verdict of 'thumbs up' or 'thumbs down.'

Instead, Gannett found that making a new ice cream was 'serious business'. Ben & Jerry's launches between six and twelve new flavours every year. Each flavour, from Cherry Garcia to Chunky Monkey, goes through four steps that together take between eighteen and twenty-four months. The researchers are looking for opportunities that they can use two years ahead. First, the food scientists, or 'Flavour Gurus' as Ben & Jerry's calls them, conceptualize. They check their environment. They visit grocery stores to see what people are buying and sit in restaurants to observe the dishes people are ordering. They browse the food pictures on Instagram and track current eating trends. They use that information to list 200 flavour profiles. In the second stage, those 200 ideas are reduced to fifteen by surveying loyal customers. The third stage is curation. The Flavour Gurus hand make small batches of the flavours, taste them, and score them, taking feedback from other team members and sometimes from customers too. Finally, they launch, gather feedback widely, and tweak the flavour profiles in response to customer reaction.

It's not guesswork. A successful flavour has nothing to do with luck. The fact that you can pick up a tub of Ben & Jerry's and know that it will taste good is not because the company is fortunate. It's because it follows a process when it looks for opportunities.

We often miss opportunities because we can't make up our minds. We identify the opportunity, but take no action, and eventually someone else benefits. An inability to make up your mind is caused by an insufficient or flawed process of decision-making. Using a process helps you to eliminate procrastination. Using a process also defeats your fears. Instead of being driven in our decision made by unconscious emotions such as fear and greed, we use a conscious process in which we take control and make all our choices based on rational factors.

If you use a process, you benefit from the experiences of thousands of successes and failures that have occurred in the past. You also benefit from learning from the collective learning community which uses the process. It's much easier to identify and join a formal community if one exists and you are learning its methodology. Therefore, using a process greatly improves your ability to learn and the speed of learning, which are key drivers of conscious adaptation. The beauty of the process is that you don't have to make it all up yourself, just as you didn't have to write the code for Excel or Word. An opportunity process is like a set of application software for making better opportunity decisions. It vastly speeds up progress by giving you a suggested list of decision rules which you can further customize to your own needs.

Ironically, using a process can also help you to be more flexible and creative. People say: 'You need to get out of the box.' There is always a box. The borders of the box are the rules. The contents of the box are contained by its rules. The rules are mostly human-made, so you can change them. It's difficult to effectively improve rules unless you understand what they are and why they're there. A process will help you identify the rules as well as the best opportunities to improve them.

An Opportunity Process Pays for Itself

Imagine you have a basket with 100 eggs, and only one of them is golden. Unfortunately, the golden egg *is gold on the inside, not on the outside.* You must carefully focus using the opportunity process to choose that single precious golden egg.

When people don't have a conscious process to evaluate opportunities, what do they do? They automatically adapt the unconscious rules of the mass and compete with each other based on the lowest common denominator, price. By using a process, you can completely avoid the price trap by focusing on the key drivers of value, particularly useful service. Using a process also increases your ability to attract resources, helping you pay for development, testing and implementation of the opportunities. Up to 80 per cent of your resources, both human and financial, may now be wasted on nopportunities. By using a process, you can identify and eliminate your biggest nopportunities, the ones that are no-hopers, and redirect their resources to opportunities. Therefore, using an opportunity process can greatly improve the effectiveness and efficiency of your resource reallocation.

Some people avoid using an opportunity process because they can't estimate its future value. It seems like a lot more work, with an uncertain return which might not be worth the effort. You must also consider the opportunity cost of not using a process. How much money you have lost in past years trying to fix hopeless nopportunities, or by not harvesting opportunities that your competitors have taken advantage of?

How the Opportunity Process Works

Let's say that you've landed in New York for the first time and need to know how to get from your midtown hotel to Wall Street. You pull out your trusted Google Maps to find the best route. What is the first crucial bit of information that Google Maps will ask you for? *Your location.*

It doesn't matter how well defined and passionate your goals are. To get from Point A to Point B you must first know where you are *now*. If you don't know where you are now, any route that you take will get you lost. Imagine if you were an army general in charge of defending a frontier. How well could you grasp opportunities if you have no awareness of the terrain?

The Opportunity Process Step 1: The Opportunity Audit

In order to gain awareness of your environment, you must first do an *audit*. What is an audit? An audit is a complete picture of reality. When a chartered accountant audits a company's financials every year, does he count only half its money? Of course not. An audit must be thorough. The objective of the audit is to isolate the key drivers of both positive and negative change in each segment of our environment and examine how they interact with each other. We need to understand what is denying us opportunity as well as providing us opportunity.

In order to see and understand changes that are relevant to you, it's crucial to focus on and understand your own *Opportunity Environment*. How well could you play cricket if you don't know what a cricket pitch looks like? Trying to benefit from change without understanding your own environment is like driving with your eyes closed. Why? *Because change in your environment is the source of all opportunities.* To *see* opportunities, it is absolutely crucial to examine the areas of your environment that are relevant to you. Your Opportunity Environment is everything within you and around you that can change, and therefore create opportunities. It has four distinct quadrants:

Your Opportunity Environment

Your unique MISSION: Includes everything that is going on inside your head and directing your actions—your purpose, your goals, your aspirations, your beliefs. *Your mission is why you take action on opportunities.*

Your MODEL is like your car: It's what makes you move. If you have a business, it is your team, your investors, your suppliers, your assets, your resources, your products and services, your capabilities, your intellectual property, your systems and processes, your business strategy, etc. *Your model is how you take action on opportunities.*

Your MARKET: Includes your current and potential customers, consumers, channels and competitors. Even if you're only selling yourself as an employee, you still have a market. *Your market is where, when and for whom you take action on opportunities.*

Your DOMAIN is *everything outside* your mission, model and market which influences change in all four quadrants. This includes technology, industry and macro trends, political trends, government regulations, fashions, industry beliefs, potential substitutes, emerging needs, etc. *Your domain is often the key driver of change in your environment, and therefore an enormous source of opportunities.*

For Ben & Jerry's, the *mission* is to provide useful service by producing the world's best ice cream with original, distinctive flavours. The *model* is all the parts of the company, including its products, marketing team, factories and, of course, the testing kitchen where the recipes are created and checked. The *market* is the consumers who eat their ice cream, the retailers that sell it, and the distributors who deliver it to stores and restaurants. The *domain* is everything outside of their mission, model and domain that can affect it, such as things that affect people's changing tastes in food in general, and ice cream in particular. If diabetes is becoming a problem in society, for example, Ben & Jerry's might want to make the most of that opportunity by creating more unique sugar-free flavours. In order do this successfully, they need to know what's happening in the domain.

A thorough Opportunity Audit will help you identify your Key Drivers of Opportunity. These are the crucial factors that will help you focus on your best opportunities, and align them with your mission, model, market and domain so that they can be smoothly implemented. Just as there are Key Drivers of Opportunity, there are also Key Draggers of Nopportunity, which are factors that you must stop focusing on in order to get best results.

The Opportunity Process Step 2: Create Your Opportunity Inventory

A thorough examination of your environment will reveal a whole array of opportunities that you could potentially pursue. These include:

- Opportunities that you're currently pursuing
- New opportunities that you are thinking of pursuing
- Old opportunities that you had pursued in the past that failed
- Old opportunities you thought about in the past but never pursued
- Nopportunities you should reduce or abandon
- New opportunities you have never considered before

An audit of Ben & Jerry's Model Environment would surely uncover an Opportunity Inventory that includes the flavours that it currently sells, as well as the new flavours that its Flavour Gurus are working on. It would also list the products marked in the Flavour Graveyard, an area next to the factory filled with marble headstones engraved with the names of flavours, such as blueberry lavender swirl, that have had their day, and then died. It would list the 185 flavours that are cut during each round of reduction, the flavours that are no longer selling as well as they used to, and the flavours and distribution channels that the company might pursue in the future. It produces a whole raft of possibilities.

The Opportunity Process Step 3: Evaluate Your Opportunities

Your next step is to carefully filter each opportunity in your inventory through your key drivers to determine whether they are compatible with your unique opportunity environment. Those that qualify will be filtered through the nine key drivers of value (see Chapter 18) to determine whether they are valuable enough to consider pursuing. You can also use additional customized evaluators based on your unique mission and model. So, an ice cream company like Ben & Jerry's might want to do more than simply approve a new kind of vanilla. It would want to make sure that it can produce a vanilla with an original name and a unique approach.

At the same time, you can evaluate potential nopportunities that you can remove. At the end of Step 3, you will have identified the best opportunities that you would like to implement, and the worst nopportunities that you would like to eliminate.

The Opportunity Process Step 4: Implement Your Opportunities

The key driver of implementation is alignment. First, opportunities must align with your environment. If all the pieces of mission, model, market and domain fit together, you can implement smoothly. Otherwise, you will suffer from unrelenting problems and waste resources. Second, you must align the nine sources of value so that they can effectively work together and attract resources. Third, you must align your team so that they provide all the skills you need to provide world class service. Finally, you must align your resources so they are more than adequate to test and refine your opportunities. Let's say you have identified an opportunity that looks big. How do you know? The implementation process is focused first on testing opportunities for feasibility and market potential. Opportunities have to sink or swim on their own merits. Only those that can generate sufficient value to attract adequate resources will go on to survive and thrive.

This Is a Living Book—and a Living Process

I sometimes dislike books, because they seem set in stone, unchanging, while the world evolves around them. This is a *living book*, which continues on my website, open to everyone's participation. I offer to the world an opportunity process, as I currently see it. Is it a perfect process, written by God? Certainly not, I'm no better or smarter than anyone else. Many others have written books about how to achieve success, and never updated them based on the learnings of their readers. That is the wrong approach. Every manmade set of rules must be approached with infinite irreverence. Every process requires conscious, collective, cumulative learning in order to improve. This has been the reason for human success from the beginning. Like every other process in the world, the opportunity process needs to improve, and will improve with help from people like you, through collective and cumulative learning. Others will have great ideas on how to improve this process, based on their own experiences.

You're invited to contribute to the opportunity process by visiting my website www.power-of-opportunity.com.

Benefits of the Opportunity Process

1. Successful opportunities come through a process, not luck
It's a mistake to believe that opportunities just turn up. They're not found lying on the ground or knocking on your door. They're discovered through a process that understands your environment, both internally and externally, and identifies the best opportunities. For Ben & Jerry's, identifying the opportunity in a new ice cream flavour can take up to two years. Failure can happen much faster.

2. Take control and avoid the school of failure
Failure is the price of not following an opportunity process. Most of the business people I meet do not have an opportunity process, and are hence struggling. Those two things aren't a coincidence. When you have a way to assess opportunities and implement the Pareto Leaders, you're no longer bound to your circumstances. You're in control.

3. The opportunity process has just four steps
The process starts with an audit of your opportunities. It continues with an inventory, passes through an evaluation, and ends with implementation. That's all there is to it. It's the most important process your business can undergo. Bombax is an example of a successful opportunity that this process has helped to identify and implement.

13

The Opportunity Audit: Your Mission

What do you really want to do with your life? How can you determine your life's purpose? How can you best define your mission in order to capture opportunities? How can you provide useful service to others? Why should you avoid Mission Impossible?

It's tempting to look at successful people and believe that their success was inevitable. They're so comfortable doing what they do. They're so good at what they do. They couldn't possibly have done anything else.

It doesn't always work that way. Bollywood actor Boman Irani was expected to work in Golden Bakery, his mother's 10 x 4.5 square foot wafer shop located between the Novelty and the Apsara Cinemas on Grant Road in downtown Mumbai. But he knew that a life frying potatoes wasn't for him. So, he went to the Taj Mahal Hotel and took a job as a room service waiter. He was so good at serving food that he was soon promoted to a job as a bar waiter. Until finally, he reached the top of his profession: waiting tables in the Rendezvous French restaurant. He worked there for some time, earning tips and making a living, until his mother met with an accident, and he returned to the shop.

'There was no one to take over the work,' he told the *Hindustan Times* during an interview in 2010. 'I was this Young Turk who wanted to make a difference. I sat at that shop and later, got married.'

But Irani still knew that making potatoes wasn't enough.

He had taken up photography while working as a waiter, selling children's sports photos for Rs 20–30 at a time. It was when he took his children on their first vacation that he realized that selling chips and the occasional picture wasn't enough. The hotel he had booked for his family was run down. The room was lit by a single 'zero number bulb'. Ashamed and embarrassed, he understood that he needed to do something creative. He needed to take control of his life. He called it his 'zero number bulb moment'.

Irani decided that from that moment on, he was a photographer. He was thirty-two years old. He talked his way into a job photographing the World Cup of boxing, set up a studio, and gradually did well. He received royalties for his work and interesting projects.

One day, the choreographer Shiamak Davar came into his studio for a portfolio shoot. When Irani gave Davar his photos, Davar, convinced that Irani could do even more, invited him to lunch. Instead of taking him to a restaurant though, he took him to an audition for a musical. That led to a new career path in acting. Irani was forty-two when he took his first movie part and started the career that would bring him his greatest success and satisfaction.

Boman Irani isn't the only person to discover his mission later in life. It took me over thirty-five years. When I graduated from Bates College with a BA in Political Science in 1979, although I was ambitious, I had no idea what to do with my life. For several years I drifted from place to place and from job to job, with no conscious direction or means of finding a direction. Between 1979 and 1990 I lived in Boston, Washington DC, New York, Los Angeles, Arizona, Hawaii, India and Israel. I held jobs as a salesman, construction worker, farm worker, proofreader, paralegal, dishwasher, bartender, busboy, waiter, cook, investment banker, management trainee, business manager, business plan writer and fund raiser. In 1990, I finally settled on a career as a commercial diplomat.

Why did I become a diplomat? Mainly because I took, and passed, the US Foreign Service exam. Why did I take the exam? Because the exam was free and held within walking distance. My friend Larry Andre was taking it and suggested that I go along. I had no passionate interest in the job that was eventually offered to me, or in the mission of the organization that employed me. But because I was one of only two people hired that year from a pool of 20,000 candidates, I felt obliged to accept it. It tickled my ego. I clearly made this important decision for irrational reasons. Why? Because I had no inkling of a process to identify my true calling. The usual advice to 'go with your passion' meant nothing to me, as I had no idea how to accurately identify my passions. If I had been able to evaluate the opportunity by using the 'opportunity process', I probably would have refused the job.

For twenty-three years I served as a US Trade Commissioner around the world—in Italy, Indonesia and India. Although I was good at the job, and quickly promoted up the ranks, I found the career to be deeply unsatisfying. The prestige that came with the position meant nothing to me. Working for the US government was stifling. While I'm an entrepreneurial rule-maker by nature, the US government rewards rule taking over results. While my work did help many people, our performance metrics were largely hot air, smoke and mirrors. I found many of our goals to be just plain pointless, driven by politics rather than useful service. I yearned to have the freedom to do more meaningful, satisfying work. But fear and confusion kept me in my golden cage. I had a family to support. I felt I had made a mistake in choosing this career and was scared to blunder into an even worse choice.

I decided to get out as soon as I qualified for a pension. For five years prior to my retirement, I agonized over my next move. I was over fifty years old and couldn't afford to waste any more time. I knew that rather than going with the flow as I had in past, *I had to lead myself.* I needed to create a mission for myself, one which would truly satisfy me. But how to do it?

We All Need to Be Useful

We all desire to have more than just the resources of survival, such as food, shelter and sex. We are the only animal to be consciously aware of our own impending demise. Our ego is future-oriented and would like us to somehow live on after we die. We invent an *individual purpose* which we hope will somehow give us immortality. Although our purpose is largely a creation of our own imagination, *it is the key driver of our actions.* We all want to make our mark on the world. We all strongly desire to be *useful.* Our concept of success, our desire for success, and our actions in pursuit of success are all consequences of our individual purpose.

Many of us are unclear or confused about our purpose, which limits our ability to choose the best opportunities. To get clarity, you must first define what *success* means to *you.* Why is this so crucial? Because if you don't know where you want to go, every route will get you lost. If you don't know what you want, you will pick the wrong opportunities, attract the wrong resources, and waste your time with wrong actions. Sound familiar?

Can You Slay the Dragon?

How could I understand how to lead myself to success? That was a question I failed to answer for many years. I finally decided to study many others who had achieved the kind of success I aspired to. One of the benefits of my job as trade commissioner was that I had easy personal access to the most successful people in the countries where I served. For example, in Indonesia, where I lived for eight years, I got to know virtually all of the country's 100 richest people, most of them self-made. In India, I got to personally know many business leaders, such as Mukesh Ambani, Uday Kotak, Anand Mahindra, Adi Godrej, Aditya Puri, Subhash Chandra, Rakesh Jhunjhunwala, Deepak Parekh, Dr Yusuf Hamied and Harsh Mariwala.

As a trade commissioner, I served as a matchmaker between American companies wishing to export, and foreign companies wishing to represent them. As a result, I also got to know hundreds of American businesspersons who were my clients, and the promoters of literally thousands of small- and medium-sized Italian, Indonesian and Indian companies who did business with them. They came from all sectors of enterprise. From interacting with thousands of business people in several countries, I discovered not only common lessons but also common points of friction. I learned that most people are unsatisfied. Their dreams of youth are not being met. Unfortunately, while humans collectively have progressed, this is largely due to the success of the 1 per cent. Very few people achieve the success that they aspire to.

What do you truly want? It's important to think about it. If you're like most people, you want money, respect, accomplishment and self-fulfilment. Most of all, you want a *purpose*. You want to do something that matters deeply to you, and to others. A *service* to both yourself, and to the world. Something that will be *appreciated and remembered*, even after you're gone. In other words: *a heroic mission*. In your heart of hearts, most people would like to be a *hero*. Your mission should ideally be a useful *mission of service*, to both yourself and to others.

Imagine that you're living in medieval England in the time of King Arthur and the famed Knights of the Round Table. Although you're a poor nobody, you have found an immense opportunity: to remove the magic Excalibur sword from the stone, and use it to slay the vicious dragon, rescue the beautiful princess and save the kingdom from conquest. The task before you seems impossible. To succeed, you'll have to overcome many seemingly insurmountable obstacles. If you fail, which is likely, both you and the princess will die, and the kingdom will fall into the hands of evil demons. If you succeed, you will be a true hero. You will go on to marry the princess and become a rich, beloved and respected King.

Does this sound inspiring? What if you accepted this mission for *purely selfish reasons*: only because you want to get rich quick and ravish the beautiful princess? Would you be able to succeed? It is highly unlikely. People would soon catch on to your selfish motives and deny you help. You would be viewed as a villain yourself. On the other hand, accepting the mission as selfless duty wouldn't be very satisfying either, particularly if you loved dragons, hated living in the kingdom, and considered the princess to be a spoiled ungrateful shrew. Identifying the right mission always involves difficult choices. How can you decide?

Who's the Most Important Person in Your Life?

Who's the most important person in your life? If you answered 'my wife, my husband, my mother, my father, my son, my daughter', I'm sorry, but you're absolutely wrong. Sure, they are all important, but someone else comes first. The most important person in your life is *you*. How do I know that? Because you're a human being. Like every other person in the world, *you are selfish. It is really all about YOU.* If you want to achieve success through opportunity, you need to accept the fact that you're selfish. In fact, you need to do more than accept it. You need to benefit from it.

This book is all about *you*, and how you can write your own success story. What should *your* success story sound like? If you're like many people, you've thought about success, but haven't really defined what it means to *you*. It's very important to do this. Why? You need to care deeply about where you're going, which is hard to do if you're pursuing someone else's goals and desires. Success is a journey, not an event. It can take many years of effort and struggle. The objective of this book is to make that journey go quicker and easier for you. The journey can go more smoothly if:

1.   You know where *you* want to go—*your* mission is clear;
2.   Your mission is defined by *you*, not by someone else.

Money Is Not a Useful Mission

Money is obviously important, especially when you have too little of it. But simply chasing an opportunity only because it pays you a higher salary is usually a bad move. Even if you're good at the job, unless it provides great satisfaction, you may find yourself in a golden cage, as I was for many years. Or you will bounce around from job to job, as I did for over a decade. Working without a true mission is like leaving home with no clear idea of your destination.

Chasing money instead of mission is a big reason people do not find the best opportunities. They just stumble around and get lost. Or they find an opportunity through luck and eventually it expires, and they don't know how or why.

Similarly, many companies write a mission statement, but it means nothing to them, so they pay no attention to it. In practice, they substitute a financial score for a mission. In the past six years as an opportunity consultant I've interviewed the Managing Directors of several hundred Indian companies of all sizes in dozens of sectors. Over 99 per cent have described their missions to me in financial terms, such as: 'We would like to double sales in the next three years.' In general, these leaders have consistently failed to meet these lofty goals. Why? Financial goals can be useful at a tactical level, for example to set targets for individual salespeople. However, at a strategic level, they are ineffective. Why? Because financial goals do not in any way help you to find, evaluate and choose the opportunities that can provide sustained, profitable growth. Does wanting to lose weight help you to lose weight? Of course not. But does wanting to lose weight in order to fit into a wedding dress help you to lose weight? Many women seem to think so. It's the same simple logic.

Everyone wants more money. But you only get more money if you provide useful service. You must focus first on the cause—useful service—rather than on the effect—the money.

Everyone Who Gets Paid Is an Entrepreneur

If you sell your services for money, you're an entrepreneur. It doesn't make the slightest bit of difference whether you own your own business, or work as an employee. Every employee is an entrepreneur with one exclusive customer—his employer. In order to *lead yourself*, and be able to see and harvest opportunities, you must think this way. Regardless of who you work for, *you always work for yourself!* However, because a business opportunity is always a two-way exchange of value, your mission must answer the question: *'What's in it for me?'* for your customer as well as for yourself. There must be a strong win-win in the relationship. Your opportunity is not to get rich. Your opportunity is not a niche in the market. Your mission should be defined as how you're going to serve others. As Peter Drucker said, *'The purpose of business is to create and keep a customer.'* The ideal mission is one in which you help the customer live up to his potential, so he loves you and can't do without you. For example, Google's mission is 'to organize the world's information and make it universally accessible and useful'. Amazon's mission is 'to offer our customers the lowest possible prices, the best available selection, and the utmost convenience'. These mission statements clearly convey the type of service provided to customers, while being broad enough to unlock huge areas of opportunity.

Many people provide their employers or customers with indifferent or poor service. They may feel that they have been forced to take a job that is beneath their dignity or capabilities, so they don't perform well. Many others feel that they have been pushed into a career or into a family business that doesn't suit them. *But regardless of your circumstances, if you provide poor service to your customers, you are an idiot.* Remember—you are the sole proprietor of your own business. Call it YOU Un-Ltd. There is no limitation on your own growth. But if you refuse to take responsibility for running your own business, blame others, and provide poor service to your customers, *you will never succeed.*

To unlock huge opportunities, you must provide nothing less than *fantastic service* to your customers, at all times. Regardless of where you are, where you work, or what your job title is, you can always look for ways of being useful. Early in my life, even though I had recently graduated from a good college, I was forced by circumstances to take the lowest level job in a restaurant—scrubbing pots and pans. But I was the best damned pot scrubber that restaurant had ever employed. The service I provided was so superb that my employer quickly offered me better opportunities for growth. Within less than a year, I had mastered every position in the restaurant, and was offered the job of manager.

Never forget this—*you are always the sole proprietor of your own business.* To succeed, you must lead yourself. It's up to you, and only you, to ensure that you can identify and provide the greatest value possible, so that both you and your customers can grow and grow together. *The hero's journey to success is never easy.* If you reach the 1 per cent, you will be one out of only 100 who succeed. You must choose a mission that is so meaningful to you that you will be relentless and persevering in overcoming obstacles. You must choose a mission that provides such tremendously useful service to others that you will attract the resources and customers you need to grow.

How to Start Defining Your Mission

In auditing your own opportunity environment, it's crucial to start with your mission. Why? Because you are leading your own opportunity journey. Your mission is your compass. *Don't worry,* you don't have to figure out your whole life's mission right away. It's enough to choose a general direction. As marketing guru Jagdeep Kapoor says, 'it's an evolution, not a revolution.' Your mission will evolve as you go along.

Consider: *What was your mission in the past? What is it now? How would you need to adapt it to create a better mission?* You don't have to entirely throw out your current mission, as this can be very difficult and disruptive. But if you hate your current mission as it is not giving you value, you can consider it, because you would be getting rid of a nopportunity—slaying the dragon.

Surendra Hiranandani is the billionaire co-founder of Hiranandani Constructions, one of India's largest and most reputed builders. When he started, Surendra knew only two things about his mission: 1) he didn't want to be a doctor, like his father and eldest brother; and 2) he aspired to be an industrialist, like the Tatas and Birlas. Surendra had no clue how to do this, but he did have a direction to start his journey. He dropped out of medical school in the third year, and with his meagre resources started a small textile unit.

For five years before leaving the US government, I struggled to define my own mission of service. At first it seemed an insurmountable task. At one point I fell into a deep depression, convinced that I would never discover a useful mission. Eventually, I realized that the first step to defining a mission properly is to focus on the *rules*. Rules dictate what you can and cannot do. Look back into the past. Consider: *what rules did you like to follow, and which do you want to rebel against?* This will help you to clearly define what you don't want to do.

For example, Surendra Hiranandani did not want to follow the family rule of becoming a doctor. His brother Niranjan had already broken it, and become a chartered accountant. Surendra decided that he would rather become a successful businessman. He succeeded; he's now a billionaire. Ritesh Agarwal, founder of OYO Rooms, dropped out of education at the age of seventeen. Five years later, he was already a millionaire. Travis Kalanick was breaking rules long before he founded Uber. When he dropped out of college it was to create a file-sharing network called Scour.

In defining your mission, it's also very useful to understand your own attitude toward rules, and the degree to which you need to control them yourself. I disliked working for the government because following their rules was more important than getting results, even if the rule was stupid, irrelevant and inappropriate. The rules were oppressive and pervasive in every facet of my job, and impossible for me to modify. In evaluating my experience, I realized that I am a very poor rule-taker. Because rules often create irritation for me, I notice them. My typical attitude toward rules is *extreme irreverence*. I am very good at not only noticing rules but also critically assessing their value. I understood that I needed a mission that allowed me to make and control as many of my own rules as possible. I also realized that I could provide useful service by analysing and improving other people's rules.

My friend Ajay Sharma is an irreverent rule-breaker. Not surprisingly, he's a creative designer and serial entrepreneur who's dabbled in many things. His daughter, on the other hand, is a highly reverent rule-taker. She enjoys pointing out all the rules that her parents keep breaking.

What sort of mission might she enjoy pursuing? Given her fondness for rules, Ajay has arranged for her to intern with a law firm.

If you're the person who likes to follow rules, you should consider a career in which rules govern most actions and change very slowly. These are professions such as lawyer, chartered accountant, engineer, scientist or a civil servant. You might appreciate a business such as hotels, which are typically run on hundreds of standard operating procedures. You might also like to own a franchise that comes with its own fixed rulebook, rather than start something new. *How do you understand your own rules?* By looking at what you've done and asking why you did it. *What patterns have you followed? Which ones have been dominant? Which rules do you like to follow? Which ones have given you the most value, and which ones have created problems and destroyed the most value for you?* Repeat the same exercise for your organization or your business.

Why is it so important to understand your rules? Because in order to identify the best opportunities for you, you must understand what rules you want to modify. These are rules you understand well. You could frame a convincing argument about why these rules in particular need to change. There will be an area in which you hold strong opinions about this. This area is your principal zone of adaptation. This is where you should focus your mission in searching for opportunities. Why here? Because in areas where you have the greatest expertise, you are more likely to be able to see and evaluate opportunities. Your mission need not be entirely new. It could be an adaptation of what you're already doing and know well.

For example, after a few years in real estate development, Surendra Hiranandani understood the rules that could create opportunities for him personally and for his business: 1) he hated having to constantly negotiate on small parcels. He decided to buy one big parcel and build a complete community; 2) he hated creating poor-quality buildings and public spaces, as most of his competitors did. He therefore decided to learn the best international rules of architecture, engineering and horticulture. To ensure compliance with these rules, he created his own construction team, rather than hiring contractors who had no clue of the rules he wanted to follow. These rules were also incorporated into his corporate mission and summarized in its tagline as '*creating better communities*'. This is certainly a better mission statement than 'building a housing complex in Powai' or 'maximizing the value of a parcel of land in Powai'.

Your mission statement should not only capture your own personal mission but also tell your customer how you are providing value. Pursuing this mission has created tremendous value for Surendra, his company and for his customers. His first community, Hiranandani Gardens, was built in a virtually inaccessible abandoned quarry in Powai. But because he followed the rules of his mission, Surendra transformed Powai from a backwater into one of the most sought after and elite areas of Mumbai.

In addition to focusing on rules you don't like, you can discover your mission by focusing on things you'd like to avoid. *Ask yourself:*

1. What do you hate most about my current (or past) job? If you eliminated the friction from your current job, what would it be like?
2. What do you most want to avoid doing?
3. What do you hate most about service provided to you by others? What is the biggest pain point? Is this a pain point suffered by many others?
4. What useful service do you or could you provide to relieve this friction? How could you fix it?
5. What friction suffered by your customers are you very good at removing? What friction isn't being removed? How could you do a much better job of removing it?
6. What would you most like to change in your life? What pains you, what are you most angry about? What are you most unsatisfied with? What can you do to fix it?
7. What do you imagine you want, and what's what keeping you from getting there?

What Can Happen When You Break The Rules?

It was the early 1990s, and Lord Snowdon was waiting. The Queen's brother-in-law and world-renowned photographer was sitting in the home of a client whose portrait he was shooting—and he had been waiting for some time.

Eventually, two hours late, Zaha Hadid came down the stairs. She was wearing an Issey Miyake top, as she often did, but she was wearing it upside down. The sleeves had been tied around her waist, and the waistband was now a ruff collar. That account, published in *Architectural Digest* in 2015, a year before Hadid's death, says much about the architect's attitude towards norms and rules.

Born in Baghdad to a UK-educated industrialist, Hadid attended a Catholic school even though her family was Muslim. She studied maths at the American University in Beirut, then architecture at the Architectural Association in London under Elia Zenghelis and Rem Koolhaas, two of the world's most famous architects.

Her first job was to design a fire station at the furniture company Vitra in Weil am Rhein, Germany. Instead of just giving the fire brigade a garage to park their fire engine, she created a giant building with sharp angles and strange protrusions.

And so her career continued. She designed the $300 million Guangzhou Opera House, inspired by two pebbles. The London Aquatics Centre that she designed for the 2012 Olympics looked like a single frozen wave. The Heydar Aliyev Centre in Baku contains not a single straight line. In 2004, Zaha Hadid became the first woman to win the Pritzker Architecture Prize, and in 2015, Dame Zaha Hadid was the first woman to be awarded the Royal Gold Medal from the Royal Institute of British Architects.

Rules can be like comfort spaces: good things happen just outside them.

Focus on What You Value

Focusing on what you hate will help you to define 1) what you don't want to do, or 2) ways you can provide valuable service by fixing what you don't like.

Next, you should focus on what you love doing, and where you are good at adding value. To identify a mission based on increasing value, focus on the job you have right now. If you're currently unemployed, focus on past jobs you may have had. If you're a student, focus on your studies. If you're a business promoter, focus on the job of running your company. *Ask yourself the following simple questions:*

1. What work have you done—past or present—that has been so easy and enjoyable that it was more like play to you? Even if the entire job wasn't pleasurable, what aspect of it did you particularly enjoy doing?
2. Why was the work enjoyable? What did you love about it?
3. Did this work provide service to other people? How? How did that make you feel?
4. What did you do in past that provided the most valuable service to others? What's special about what you can do? How? How could you do it even better if given the chance?
5. What are you happiest about in your work and your life? What would you least like to change? How could you be even happier?
6. What job are you getting done for other people? What valuable service are you providing them that gives both of you great satisfaction? What service do you provide better than all others?
7. What is your obsession? What do you like the most? What do you miss when you're not doing it? What do you focus on? What do you think about when you're bored?
8. How can you best be useful to others? How can you best be of service to others? How will this be valuable to others and what can they give you in return that you value?
9. What do you care about the most? How can you transform this into a useful and valuable service for others?
10. What changes would you make to your world that would most benefit others?

11. What is valuable to you? What do you consider to be valuable in the world?

From Blue-Sky Thinking to Blue-Sky Flying

How many violins are there in America?

That was a question posed to Mark Vanhoenacker when he applied for a job as a management consultant. He wasn't supposed to know the answer, but he was supposed to be able to show that he could reason his way to a good estimate. He thought about how many people had played violin at his school then tried to scale upwards.

He got the job, and when it was his turn to ask the questions, he had a good brainteaser of his own. He asked a candidate to estimate the percentage of the world's population that had been on an airplane. (There are no statistics to support the answer but Vanhoenacker himself estimates it's about 20 per cent.)

It wasn't the only time that Vanhoenacker had brought up planes at work. He had a habit of working aviation terms into his business jargon, arguing that the team should 'blue-sky this', warning against 'strong headwinds in Q2', urging everyone to take the '30,000-foot view' and reminding everyone that a new company has a 'good long runway'.

So when, at the age of twenty-nine, just three years after joining the firm, he told his colleagues that he was quitting a desirable job helping businesses to grow in order to learn how to fly commercial airlines for a living, no one was surprised. In fact, as he writes in *Skyfaring: A Journey with a Pilot*, he'd only taken the job because he needed to pay back his student loans, to save the money he'd need for flight training, and because the job required lots of travel on planes. He had always known that his mission was to fly passengers around the world. Not everyone is that lucky.

You can also ask yourself:

1. Who are your role models? Who do you consider to be a success? In whose shoes would you most like to live?
2. What sort of people do you look up to? Whom do you emulate?
3. What sort of accomplishments do you admire the most?
4. Imagine yourself getting plaudits and sincere appreciation from so many people whom you have helped. You are respected. For what? What have you done to help people?
5. Imagine that it is 100 years from now and a large group of people are commemorating your birthday. What mission of service have you carried out in your life that has led people to be grateful to you for so long after your death?

For me, Richard Branson is a good role model. Why? Because he leads himself; he has created so many different new businesses, he is open-minded and creative, and he doesn't run the companies himself. All these aspects appeal to me and helped me to create my own mission.

Some of the things about yourself you discover through this exercise are appropriate for a career mission, and others for play. For example, I have a strong need for physical exercise, and enjoyed working as a messenger and a waiter. But I realized that these careers would never satisfy me financially or intellectually. So, I made exercise a hobby, and designed a mission that provides me the time to walk two hours every day.

Avoid Mission Impossible!

There are some missions that are simply impossible. You may be trying to change rules that either can't be changed or that you cannot change. Or you may be trying to make an adaptation that is beyond anyone's capabilities. You're may be trying to slay the dragon, but it's either impossible because he can't be killed or because he exists only in your imagination!

Many people pursue missions that are impossible because they are not adequately valuable or useful. For example, in the late 1990s, the American company Iridium spent $6 billion setting up a global satellite phone network. The company collapsed within nine months. There were very few customers for its service as it only worked outdoors and was many times more expensive than standard mobile phones. The company had not bothered to integrate its mission or business model with the market and domain, which were adapting cheaper and more convenient mobile phone technology. Eventually the company was bailed out by the US military, which uses it in extremely remote locations where there is no mobile phone service available. Now that mobile phone service is available virtually everywhere in the world, these locations are increasingly few and far between.

My Own Mission of Service

In my own case, I first focused on what I loved about my job. I realized that I loved the following aspects of my job:

- Meeting with and helping people from many different sectors of business.
- Understanding and identifying opportunities for many types of people and businesses and helping them develop it.
- Living and working in developing countries, especially India. I love the people, the climate and the abundant opportunities in India.
- Managing consulting teams to achieve success.
  I then focused on what I hated about my present job, the sources of unhappiness:
- Working full time for others, especially for a government.
- Lack of freedom and the requirement to follow others' stupid and irrelevant rules.

Based on these factors, I was able to focus better on the type of *useful service* I could provide to myself and others. I decided to become an *Opportunity Consultant*. I checked online and was surprised to learn that there were absolutely no opportunity consulting companies in the entire world. So, I decided to start my own. But whom would I service and how? In order to assess the mission as an opportunity, I still had work to do.

The Opportunity Audit: Your Mission

1. We all need to be useful
We all need a sense of purpose. We want to be useful. We'd all like to be a hero. Whether we achieve that through helping others or building something that lasts, it's a drive more powerful than financial rewards.

2. Define your mission
Understanding your mission and the values that will keep your mission on track is one of the most important steps anyone can take. Focus on what you value and what you love. Understand what rules you'd like to follow as well as avoid. Use what you learn to guide yourself to the best opportunities for you, whether that's designing outlandish buildings like Zaha Hadid or flying planes like Mark Vanhoenacker.

3. Know what's possible
Some missions are easy. If you've always wanted to be a pilot, then plotting your path through flight school to the cockpit is straightforward. Some are hard. And some missions are impossible because the technology doesn't work, or the environment isn't right.

More tips, tools and templates to help you to focus on your own mission are available on my website at www.power-of-opportunity.com.

14

The Opportunity Audit: Your Model

What is your business model? Does your model match your mission? Can you scale it? How do you find the opportunities that lie within your model environment? What nopportunities does it contain that can break your business? What if you have nothing—knowledge or resources—when you start your professional journey?

Seventy-nine. That's how many countries have a branch of Starbucks. From China to Chile and from South Africa to Sweden, you can travel across the world and always find a nearly identical branch of the coffee chain with its signature Frappuccinos and its misspelt customer names.

But there's one country that Starbucks failed to conquer. In 2001, the company opened six outlets in Israel. Within two years, all of them had closed. Starbucks hasn't returned since. All sorts of theories have been put forward to explain the failure of the Starbucks model in a country with a strong coffee culture. Some analysts have pointed to a mismatch with its local partner, Delek, better known for its petrol stations than for its coffee. Others note that the coffee shops opened during a wave of terrorism that emptied cafes and made the chain slow to open in Jerusalem, the capital. Others have pointed to the chain's relatively high prices, its heavy decor that didn't match Tel Aviv, and its coffees that didn't cater to the local preference for 'backwards' coffee, a shot of espresso added to steamed milk instead of the other way around.

But despite Israel's unusual approach to coffee-drinking, the country's own chains have started to export their models. Four years after Starbucks pulled out of Israel, Aroma opened its first branch in Toronto, Canada. By the end of 2016, the company, which opened its first branch in Jerusalem in 1994, had thirty-five branches in Toronto, where it competes directly with Starbucks.

So why has an Israeli cafe model succeeded in Canada when an American model (as well as Canada's own Coffee Bean and Tea Leaf) failed in Israel?

The answers are complex, but they boil down to a mixture of the right model in the right environment. Unlike Starbucks, Aroma is a franchise business with local managers connected to the community. Each branch also has a full kitchen that prepares fresh food and bakes its own bread. Customers get a combination of casual, fast dining with good coffee and a choice of healthy dishes. The menu is 80 per cent the same as the menu in Israel. Aroma has already started to export its model to the US and has also opened branches in Ukraine, Kazakhstan and Romania. When a model fails to adapt to the environment, it fails. When it fits, it scales.

What Is the Environment of Your Business Model?

Your Opportunity Model can be as large as an entire business or as small as your current job function. For a nascent opportunity, it may be a model only in your imagination. Components of your model environment may include one or more of the following:

- Leadership and inside/outside team
- Culture, beliefs, WIIFMs
- Resources and capabilities
- Assets, money management and finance
- Products, services and solutions
- Sales, marketing and channels
- Operations and execution
- Intellectual property, technology and patents
- Investors
- Suppliers

You can audit your *model environment* from two directions: 1) from the perspective of improving a current business model, which could be your own or someone else's; or 2) from the perspective of building a new model for your newly defined (or redefined) mission.

In 1982, a close college friend, Anil Shah, invited me to visit India. I had never travelled to India before; in fact, Anil had been the first Indian I had ever met. Little did I know at the time that I would eventually make India my home. I spent two months in Mumbai and loved the experience. The winter weather was perfect. In addition to falling in love with the country, I also literally fell in love—with Anil's sister, Tabu. We secretly got engaged, pending my transition to a serious career. (We got married in 1984.) Prior to coming to India, I had been working as a waiter, cook and bartender, hardly a suitable career for Tabu's future husband. I had enjoyed working in the restaurant business, but it seemed to offer few serious prospects.

Not knowing what else to do, I accepted an offer from my uncle Joel Weinstein, who was the senior vice president in charge of manufacturing at Price Pfister, Inc., a $100 million Los Angeles-based manufacturer of taps and other plumbing products. The company had recently been purchased by KKR, a private equity company. It was investing in new products and running a consumer advertising programme for the first time. I was hired as a management trainee. For one year I did short stints in all the departments of the company. In those days, before the rise of China, the company still manufactured all its parts in-house. I worked in various areas of the vast manufacturing plant, which included the largest brass foundry in western United States, as well as extensive die casting, plastics, machining, polishing, plating and assembly operations. The company also made all its tooling in-house. I worked in every area of engineering, as well as in the sales and marketing departments in the front office. I got to know the fifty-odd managers who ran the company.

Finally, I was put in charge of the company's OEM division. OEM stands for Original Equipment Manufacturing. The OEM division made component parts for other companies. It was an *intrapreneurial* venture started by my uncle in order to monetize the plant's excess manufacturing capacity. Unfortunately, the unit was doing poorly. Its sales of approximately $1 million were stagnant. My predecessor in the job had been sacked because he couldn't get products made on time. I was given marching orders: fix the OEM unit's business model, and fast. *How would I do it? I had no idea.*

Auditing Your Current Business Model

If you have an existing business or work in a job as I did with Price Pfister, first identify the value in your current model. Your current model, as well as each of its main components, can be audited by running them through *the nine evaluators*:

1. *Does your model provide useful service that creates value?* If so, why, where, when and how? If not, why, where, when and how? Israel's Aroma coffee chain, for example, gave coffee-drinkers in Canada the chance to eat a fresh, healthy meal with their coffee. That was a service that other coffee chains had ignored.

2. *Does your model have substantial scale potential?* If so, why, where, when and how? If not, why, where, when and how? Howard Schultz, the founder of Starbucks, decided early to avoid franchising, preferring to retain control and to cluster stores, something he couldn't do with franchisees. Aroma has stayed with franchising, making growth easier with less capital. Both models provide scale potential. In addition, as coffee is a product virtually everyone drinks in many countries, the potential market is huge.

3. *Does your model add relevance to your mission and market?* Is it relevant with important changes in the domain? If so, why, where, when and how? If not, why, where, when and how? Aroma describes its goal as providing 'high-quality meals alongside fast-casual service with a strong "to-go" ethic and superior Italian-blend coffee'. Consumers in most countries are increasingly concerned about health and prefer to eat fresh food, as long as it can be served fast. Aroma's focus on freshness was therefore highly relevant.

4. *Is your model unique? Does its uniqueness add or remove value?* If so, why, where, when and how? If not, why, where, when and how? Most food chains have a central kitchen from where they deliver packaged food to branches. Aroma's model of including a kitchen in every branch in order to provide fresh food is unique in its industry.

5. *Is your model sustainable? Does it increase or decrease sustainability in other segments of the environment, especially the market?* If so, why, where, when and how? If not, why, where, when and how?

Existing coffee chains such as Starbucks would have great difficulty copying Aroma's fresh-food model as it would require more space and kitchens to be added.

6. *Is your model accessible? Is it well designed to sustainably overcome any barriers to entry?* If so, why, where, when and how? If not, why, where, when and how? By using a franchise model, Aroma has made entry— and scalability—reasonably simple. Franchisees must pay around CDA $50,000 in licensing fees for each location and expect to spend another CDA $600,000 to CDA $900,000 to build and equip the franchise. The company provides training and support as well as a model that's proven to work. The cost of opening a new branch of Starbucks isn't clear but a licence to run a store in a restricted location such as an airport has been put at $315,000 in the US. In practice, Starbucks has to use its own capital to open new stores and each new outlet is said to cannibalize one in every seven transactions at other nearby stores.

7. *Is your model suitable? Does it easily and efficiently align with the mission, market and domain?* If so, why, where, when and how? If not, why, where, when and how? Although Aroma doesn't hide its origins, it doesn't advertise them either, focusing instead on its 'Mediterranean menu' and renaming its Israeli Breakfast a Power Breakfast in Canada. By adjusting 20 per cent of the menu to match the local market, it's also able to repeat its model in the same way that McDonalds did in India but without losing its brand. Starbucks, too, matches its menu to its location. While customers everywhere can buy the giant milk and coffee blends that made it so popular in the US, Chinese outlets tend to have more tea-based drinks while customers in India can order Tandoori Paneer Sandwiches, Murg Kathi Wraps and Chole Masala Wraps, as well as Hawaiian Veg Club Sandwiches.

8. *Is your model actionable? Is it efficiently and effectively feasible at scale?* If so, why, where, when and how? If not, why, where, when and how? By following a franchise expansion model, Aroma has kept its business easy to act on but it's also rolling out its expansion relatively slowly. Starbucks, with nearly 15,000 branches in the US and nearly 4000 in the US, over-expanded and struggled for a period. Aroma is focused on efficient scaling.

9.   *Is your model profitable? Can it put you in the top 1 per cent?* If so,
     why, where, when and how? If not, why, where, when and how?
     Aroma hasn't released details of its profits but its continued growth,
     particularly across Canada, suggests that it's doing fine. Starbucks
     continues to have among the highest operating margins in the
     hospitality industry. In the US, for example, their net margins are
     over 20 per cent.

You should also ask: *what are the biggest threats to your business model
right now? What would put you out of business and destroy any profits you
have now?* If so, why, where, when and how? If not, why, where, when
and how?

     Within your business, you follow rules about what business you
are in, what products you sell, how you make money, how you treat
your customers, and so on. The rules that govern your key relationships,
particularly those concerning employees, operations, customers,
channels, suppliers and other key stakeholders need to be reviewed
very deeply. *How many of these rules, whether formal or informal, are
creating or destroying value? How many of them are helping to meet your
goals and which goals are they meeting?* You must hold nothing sacred.
God didn't write any of these rules. You can compare your rules with
those of competitors, using the same criteria. Modifying these rules
can sometimes unlock huge opportunities and help you to eliminate
huge nopportunities. You can also discover what key drivers of change
in other areas of the environment can destroy your current business
model, and which key drivers of change you could potentially create
new opportunities.

     In India, it makes sense to look at how your mission can evolve
by becoming more aligned with more relevant business models. For
example, in the 1990s, when Indian retail was still virtually all single-
unit mom and pop establishments, Future Group founder Kishore
Biyani noticed the trends in the environment driving the adaptation
of modern retail, such as urbanization, shopping malls, the ability to
advertise and scale brands, foreign brands entering the market, and
modern distribution systems that cut out the middlemen. He adjusted
his model to capture these opportunities and pioneered many successful
modern retail businesses such as Big Bazaar.

Avoid Falling into the Capabilities Trap

Very often companies fall into the *capabilities trap*, believing that their current capabilities are more than adequate to effectively capture opportunities created by changes in the market or domain. Often, companies refuse to adjust their legacy model because they've invested so heavily in it, and as a result miss opportunities. For example, Walmart's retail model was a game changer before the Internet appeared. In the space of a few decades, starting with a single store, it quickly grew to become the world's largest company, with sales of over $500 billion, and over 23 crore employees. Its model was based on its hyper-efficient logistics system, which allowed it to offer consumers everyday low prices. Secondly, it initially opened stores only in small towns in which it had very little competition. But for many years Walmart failed to take advantage of opportunities to sell through the Internet and was harmed by the emergence of Amazon, which offered even greater variety, even lower prices, and the convenience of shopping without leaving home.

The Benefits of Branching

Sometimes an audit of your current environment can uncover a loosely connected business model that you can adapt and use to drive your mission. This phenomenon is known as *branching*. Others may be taking advantage of drivers of change in the model, market or domain environments that you may not have noticed or appreciated. The model you are adapting from doesn't have to be in your current business but could be related to it, such as that of a channel, customer or supplier.

For example, in 1954, Ray Kroc was at, age fifty-two, selling milkshake mixers for a company called Prince Castle. When brothers Richard and Maurice McDonald purchased eight of his Multi-Mixers for their San Bernardino, California, restaurant, Kroc was so impressed by the size of the order that he visited them. Having previously viewed over 1000 kitchens, Kroc believed that the McDonald brothers had the best-run operation he had ever seen. Their restaurant was inexpensive, clean, efficient, mechanized and, above all, fast. Roadside hamburger restaurants were notorious for slow service and inconsistent quality. Kroc saw in McDonald's an easily replicable model that completely removed that friction and added tremendous value for both promoters and customers. In 1955, Kroc signed an agreement to sell franchises for the McDonald brothers, and in 1961 he bought them out for $2.7 million. Today McDonald's is the world's largest restaurant company, with over 37,000 outlets. The key to McDonald's success internationally has been to always adapt the model to the local environment. For example, in India, its menu is vastly different from the one in the US, as it includes a wide variety of vegetarian and spicy options. In addition, rather than franchising individual units, as it does in the US, the company has sold development right to only two Indian master franchisees, who develop all the units in their territories.

Branching can help you to build a new model, especially when your mission is still in its infancy. Over thirty years ago, Captain Percy Master decided to retire after two decades at sea. Initially, he had decided on only a couple of firm rules for his new mission: 1) he wanted to continue working in the shipping industry, but wished to stay on land, and 2) he wanted to work for himself. Other than that, the mission was fluid, as was the model. When he started examining the potential market for his services, he discovered that the shipping lines that previously employed him at sea were all experiencing significant friction in their operations on the ground. At that time, all shipping lines employed specialist companies called *surveyors* to inspect their shipping containers as they moved around India, and flag those in need of repair. In doing his audit, Capt. Master found that accurate data was needed by lines and their customers to prepare the numerous documents required in the shipping cycle. Collecting and collating this data was a nightmare for the lines. Captain Master spotted an opportunity for a valuable adaptation to the surveying business. He created Master Marine Services to 1) accurately collect this data and 2) do it on a nationwide basis. By eliminating this huge source of friction, Master Marine was able to quickly become India's largest surveying company and retain customers for decades.

You can adapt elements from other industries to create a branching model that meets your needs and harvests big opportunities. For example, one of my past clients is one of the pioneers of India's wine industry. The business has two major pain points for him: 1) the capital cycle is eighteen months from the time the grapes are bought until he gets paid by wine buyers; and 2) he dislikes marketing. He prefers to focus exclusively on product development and production. I suggested a model that focuses on his strengths and eliminates his friction. Adapting a practice of the hotel industry, he can set up and manage wineries for rich people who want one, have the money but don't know how to do it. The ventures will completely fit his mission and remove his pain as they will cost him nothing and not require him to do any marketing. Will he take advantage of this opportunity? Only time will tell.

Your Team Drives the Model

The key to your model is people, starting with you. The ideal model should be a *learning community* that harnesses the power of continuous, collective and cumulative learning. You simply don't have all the knowledge and capabilities required to audit all of your opportunity environment or make all decisions by yourself. Building a team is like putting together a jigsaw puzzle. Initial team members should ideally be disciples with complementary skills who are motivated by your mission of useful service. They can help you to build your model, develop proof of concept, and start testing with markets. They should ideally have reasonably good familiarity with the entire opportunity environment and be able to create a better alignment of mission, model, market and domain.

You can pay a high price for thinking you can do or learn everything by yourself. For example, my father was a genius at retailing, as I have shared in an earlier chapter. In the 1950s he set up one of the world's first self-service furniture stores. His superb merchandising skills allowed him to display three times the amount of furniture in the same space used by other stores. He was able to run the store with only two staff. But he was never able to duplicate this success because he refused to create a team. His store was located near Harvard University. One day a Harvard Business School graduate visited his store and offered to work for him for minimum wage, in order to learn the business and scale the model nationwide. Rather than hire this disciple, my father refused, and never learned how to grow his business beyond a single store.

Ideally, you would like to be part of a team of *Pareto Superstars,* the best of the best. How can you build one? By identifying and trading your own superstar skills. Everyone—including you—is very good at something. In this process, you'll learn how *you* best fit into the model, and you'll do it by identifying your greatest skills, strengths and areas of contribution. How will you get to know your greatest strengths? Others will tell you, by their willingness to trade their skills for yours. Who may be willing to trade? Those who have the same points of friction and care about the mission and want to help to develop it further. Or you can join someone else's team. You don't have to be the leader of the team. But you do need to lead yourself, always.

The Most Important Member of the Band

Lee Soo Man never made it big as a singer. His career in the entertainment industry started while he was a student at Seoul National University in 1972. He sang in a folk duet with a classmate before leaving to become a radio jockey and television presenter. By 1979 though, when he finally graduated, he'd had enough. He travelled to the United States to study for a master's degree in computer science. It was there, while watching MTV and listening to Michael Jackson, that Lee realized what pop music could be.

He returned to Korea and created a production company called SM Studio. His first act, a singer called Hyun Jinyoung, failed when Hyun was arrested for marijuana possession. But the failure led Lee to understand that the song and the singer were only part of the act—and in his opinion, not the most important part. At least as important were character and personality, as well as the look of the band, its image, its dance moves, and its match to market niches. All those elements could be controlled.

Lee abandoned the traditional entertainment model. Instead of scouting for talent in bars or at talent shows and then trying to guide unpredictable stars, he would host auditions around the world and then hire children as young as nine or ten who could be pushed together, formed into groups, and modelled into future celebrities. Recruits would be housed in dormitories, practise for twelve hours a day and learn foreign languages to appeal to different markets. They would even be banned from having relationships. The individuals who made up the band would matter less than how they were packaged and presented.

In 2011, SM Entertainment launched a band called EXO that came in two forms: EXO-K had five male singers from Korea; EXO-M had five Chinese members. Each band sang the same songs but in different languages for different markets. The members of the bands were almost interchangeable. The K-Pop model takes a special view of the role of the team in music production, one that makes the members of the team less important than the person who conceives and manages it. It's created a national entertainment industry that's now worth nearly $5 billion a year, and it has given Lee Soo Man personal wealth of more than $147 million.

How to Focus on Nopportunities in Your Model

Think about your current business model. *How are you trying to reduce friction? What is causing day-to-day problems? Where are you constantly firefighting? What are the specific problem areas? What is causing the failures?* You know what the problems are because you're always dealing with them. Chronic problem areas in your model can result in all kinds of consequences: poor quality, bad or inconsistent service, returns, low margins, customer and channel dissatisfaction, low morale and difficulty in recruiting good people. Most of all, you will be dissatisfied. Consider why you are dissatisfied. *What type of value are you failing to receive or deliver? What can be done to turn things around?*

I've had numerous clients who had market opportunities that were potentially huge, but which they were unable to scale properly because of issues with their model. One client in the healthcare space is a major player in an enormous, fast-growing market with little competition. It has a range of excellent brands. But it lacks the management bandwidth to execute the opportunity. It is now working to remove this friction by hiring team members with the required skills.

I had another client in the textile industry that was having chronic difficulties in supplying quality products to its clients on time. The reason was that most of its production was outsourced, and it found it difficult to find reliable vendors. In order to meet its aspirations, the company adjusted its model to increase its capabilities to produce quality goods in-house.

Sometimes both people and companies waste a lot of time and resources trying to fix nopportunities that are not worth the effort. There could be significant opportunities to increase value by closing down nopportunities, or outsourcing parts of your model that are non-critical. Similarly, if you have a job, consider: *What is the key driver of problems in your work environment? What can be done to reduce it?* It may be that you need to consider a new job or career. I massively increased the value in my own life and career by retiring early from the US Foreign Service and by pursuing a systematic process to see, evaluate and choose new opportunities.

How Chinese Tourists Sank a Cruise Liner

Visit a tourist location anywhere in the world now, whether it's the Taj Mahal or the Tower of Pisa, and you'll struggle to see the sites over the heads of Chinese tourists. In 2018, the China Outbound Tourism Research Institute predicted that Chinese tourists would make 160 million trips altogether that year. They'd see the landmarks and load up on luxury goods. According to the World Tourism Organization, Chinese tourists spent more than $257 billion in 2017, nearly double the spending of American tourists.

That change is an opportunity for businesses that can adapt to it. One industry that was quick to see the opportunity was cruise companies. In 2014, Royal Caribbean formed a joint venture with Chinese tourism company Ctrip to create the SkySea Cruise Line, running a ship called the Golden Era. In 2016, Chinese tourists overtook Germans to become the second-most popular cruise-goers.

The cruise companies made sure that they met their Chinese customers' needs. Recognizing that Chinese tourists wanted to eat familiar food, and shop and gamble, they filled the stores with luxury goods, added gaming tables, Asian restaurants and Karaoke machines. In 2018, passengers spent $3 billion on cruise ships.

But Chinese tastes changed quickly. Instead of looking to shop and gamble on the seas, passengers started to think more about experiences and rest. The gaming tables and luxury stores no longer appealed. Spending figures fell.

Norwegian Cruise Line was quick to act. It spent $50 million removing all of the Chinese extras it had added to one of its ships before relocating it to Alaska. After 300 trips and 500,000 passengers, Caribbean and Ctrip sold the Golden Era. What looked like an opportunity in the cruise model had quickly become a nopportunity.

What Can You Do if You Start With Nothing?

At the beginning of your quest, you may have no resources to pay team members or sufficient gravity to attract Pareto Superstars. That's fine. You can begin by recruiting *value partners*. These are advisors who are intrigued by your mission and are willing to provide expertise and connections that can help to move you forward. Value Partners can help you to understand the environment, and clarify, focus and test opportunities. Their presence on your team can also help you build the gravity you need to recruit more and better Partners.

On a broader level, *Value Partners are people who you exchange value with.* They are the other side of the value exchange. The most important ones are your customers and team. But to build an Opportunity Model, you need all varieties of Value Partners. They will help you not only with your Model but also with your Mission, Market and Domain environments. You will recruit new Value Partners in each segment.

For example, as mentioned earlier, in 1985 I was abruptly put in charge of the OEM business unit of Price Pfister Inc. and given orders to turn things around, quickly. I had no reason to consider myself qualified for the job. I had no useful experience or education in manufacturing, and I was given only four days training for this job. I had never run a business. I was suddenly responsible for making 100 products for our twelve B2B customers, getting them billed, delivered and paid, costing out new products, getting tooling designed and made and production run. Although I had been a management trainee for a year, none of the assignments on that job had even remotely prepared me to run this business. My predecessor had been fired for not getting the products made on time. Customers were unhappy.

On the first day on the job I entered my orders into the factory's production system and waited for my parts to get made. Nothing happened. Although there was a formal system in the factory, I soon discovered that absolutely everything in the company got done informally, based on personal relationships. I had huge responsibility but absolutely no authority. Unfortunately, nobody in the company had any incentive to make my products, as they were not part of the company's regular product line. Since being taken over by KKR, the company had invested in new products and better marketing. Sales of its regular product line were increasing rapidly. As a result, it no longer had much spare capacity available to make many of my products.

The only resources at my disposal were the relationships I had gained working as a trainee all over the company. I personally knew every one of the fifty key managers who could get my work done. Although I certainly didn't use this terminology at the time, I converted all of them into Value Partners. I spent two-thirds of my time walking around the company's 20-acre plant and meeting these key people. I turned these fifty managers into mentors and collaborators. I traded them value in terms of friendship, news, companionship, conversations or connections. My failed predecessor had fought with them. Instead, I co-opted them, and all my work got done on time.

How can you attract Value Partners? Identify experts and ask them for feedback on your mission and model. How would they suggest improving things? The people who pay attention and bother to answer you are really interested. You need to co-opt them to help learn together. That means you should constantly request for criticism from the most able commentators. These could be people within your company, or your current or potential customers, suppliers, your channels, even your competitors. They could be domain experts such as securities analysts. You need to build gravity to attract partners. The best way to build gravity is by explaining how your mission can decrease friction and increase value for large numbers of paying customers. Value Partners aren't only useful for entrepreneurs. They can be even more useful for employees.

For more tips, tools and templates to help you to focus on your model environment, visit my website at www.power-of-opportunity.com.

The Opportunity Audit: Your Model

1. Auditing your current business model

Take the time to examine your business model. Ask yourself whether and how it can scale, match your mission, stand out and be sustainable. As you review your model using the nine evaluators, be honest and make sure that your opportunity isn't a nopportunity.

2. The benefits of branching

Opportunities can often be found in a field related to one in which you're currently working. Ray Kroc found his opportunity in the buyer of his milkshake mixers. Patrick Byrne is finding his in the technology underpinning one of the currencies his website accepts. When you look for opportunities in a branch of your current work, you bring knowledge of the environment and the model.

3. Your team drives the model

Sometimes you'll start an opportunity with nothing but optimism and your personality. And if you can bring on others who share your vision and want to help, that might be enough. It was enough for Lee Soo Man who looked for exactly the people he needed and groomed them the way he wanted.

15

The Opportunity Audit: Your Market

What are the rules for defining market opportunities? Why are some of the established theories of corporate strategy incomplete or outdated? Why should you look for addressing pain instead of capitalizing on gains? What are the best ways to examine your market environment? Why should you look beyond your current customers? How do employees find market opportunities? Should you focus on providing products or delivering service opportunities?

Facebook is for old people. That's the conclusion you could draw from a 2018 Pew Research survey of American teens. Only 51 per cent of respondents aged between thirteen and seventeen said that they used the platform, a decline of 20 per cent since a similar survey conducted three years earlier. (In India, the most popular age for Facebook users is between eighteen and twenty-four, followed by twenty-four to thirty-four.) Leaving aside the idea that anyone aged over seventeen is old, Facebook's shifting demographic has created a new opportunity. The platform has always been protected by its network effect. Once all your friends and family were on the site, it was hard to leave for a platform where you didn't know anyone. That means that the best market for social media companies is the young people joining and engaging for the first time. It's the market that Snapchat tried to target. That company succeeded for a while, before Facebook copied many of its features and applied them to its own image-sharing platform, Instagram.

But when TikTok started targeting users around the world, it was already too big for even Facebook to swallow. The company started in China as Douyin and is part of ByteDance, a company that has been valued at more than $75 billion. ByteDance had no need for Facebook's money and was free to find its own place in the market. It did that in part by differentiating itself from other social media applications, but mostly by using technology to push past social media's pain point: finding content to show new users who haven't yet given any data to the company. Other platforms emphasize content from friends, family and people the user follows, making trending content and news secondary, and start up slow. Tik Tok throws algorithm-driven content directly at the user, then holds onto them with continued suggestions. The result has been that while Facebook has been losing its grip on young audiences joining social media for the first time, TikTok has been busy sucking up the new market. I've seen opportunities like that, and their use, in many different industries.

What Are the Dominant Rules for Defining Market Opportunities?

Over the past thirty years, most rules for defining the best market opportunities have been based on principles of *competitive advantage*. In order to capture the highest profits in your industry, leading strategy guru Michael Porter advises you to approach the market with either a low-cost or differentiated strategy.

Porter's Generic Strategy

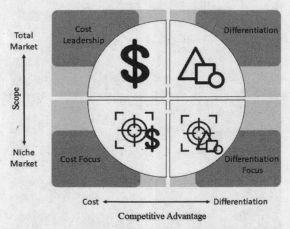

If you're pursuing a low-cost strategy, you go for a broad market, as Walmart or DMart do, with everyday low prices. If you're pursuing a differentiation strategy, you go for a higher priced exclusive niche market, as Tiffany and Tanishq do in the jewellery business. *Blue Ocean*

Strategy is another popular model for choosing a market. Its creators, INSEAD professors Chan Kim and Renée Mauborgne, advise you to avoid wasteful and bloody competitive battles, and only contest markets where there are no existing competitors or customers.

A recent example of a blue ocean strategy was Apple's release of the iPad. Although the tablet computer was effectively just a giant iPhone, its use was very different, and it appealed to a different market. No one was sure whether it would sink or swim—including Apple, which released a fairly basic first model. It was only after Apple realized that there was a market for a large screen that could be used to consume and share content, that it began to really develop the product, and other companies started following suit.

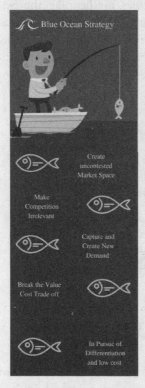

The *Disruptive Innovation Model* developed by Harvard University professor Clayton Christenson recommends that you create innovations that are cheaper, simpler and/or more convenient versions of what competitors offer. Some products are over-engineered, with more functionality than the average consumer wants or needs. That provides opportunities to develop simpler products that provide just enough functionality to get the job done for a large enough market. Can't afford an iPhone? Don't need all its bells and whistles? Disruptive innovators will provide you a simpler, cheaper phone with less functionality.

These popular strategy models can be useful for examining how to define your market opportunities. I recommend that you study them and understand them, *but avoid following them*.

Why are these models of limited use to you?

1. Because they define your market opportunities largely in terms of how you should be *different from competitors*. But the people who pay you—your customers—don't give a hoot whether you're different from competitors. If you sincerely work at providing your customers with extremely useful service with a fair value exchange, and if you are irreverent about existing rules and are willing to create your own, *you will be different*.
2. Because they all put you *in a tight box*. If you follow Michael Porter's rules, you have two choices: low cost or differentiation. If you follow Clayton Christenson's rules, you have one choice: disruptive innovations. If you follow Blue Ocean's rules, you have one choice: uncontested market space. Obviously, you have many more choices than those!
3. Because these models *have not evolved*. Porter developed his model over thirty years ago, yet he has never updated it. Has the widespread application of his model in the real world taught him nothing since then?

Another common model of defining your market is called *Positioning*. This advises you to define your market by *positioning yourself against* a competitor or competitive category. A famous example: the car rental company Avis positioned themselves against the leader Hertz with the statement: 'We're number 2, but we try harder.' Unfortunately, positioning can limit the definition of your opportunities as doing something different than your competitors. In addition to creating unnecessary competition for you, this can also lead you to define *useful service* incorrectly. For example, it can lead you to create insincere positioning statements such as HDFC Bank's *'We understand your world'*. After six years of dealing with HDFC Bank, although I'm reasonably satisfied with them, I'm quite certain that they are not striving to understand my world. They've been far more focused on selling me products that boost their bottom line.

Your competitors are never the cause of your failure. They are the consequence of your failure. As long as your mission is based on useful service, and you build and maintain and adapt your model to deliver service with growing relevance, then what difference does it make what your competitors do? If they deliver better service than you, or uncover markets that you never considered, you can learn from them. Everyone wants a moat that provides sustainable competitive advantage. But you don't build the moat. The market builds your moat. You may be able to defeat your competitors, but you can never defeat the market. Even when you're enormous, the market can easily defeat you.

How 'Tipping' Made Lei Jun One of the Top Ten Richest People in China

Think of 'tipping' and you probably imagine a small pile of change dropped into a bellboy's hand. For Chinese software engineer Lei Jun, though, it describes a business model that made him one of China's richest people. 'Tipping' is the name he gave to the business model he created for his company, Xiaomi. The idea was to produce top-quality hardware, sell it at a margin as small as 1 or 2 per cent, but earn revenues from the services, such as watching movies or playing games delivered through the device. 'I started Xiaomi after turning 40,' Lei told the *South China Morning Post*, 'and had figured out 90 per cent of the business model before starting the project.' The strategy worked especially well in developing markets where people were able to buy flagship-quality devices at budget prices. In India, Xiaomi quickly became the market leader, soaking up a 27 per cent market share.

The dominance didn't last. Xiaomi ran into supply problems, had organizational issues, and depended too much on online sales instead of retail sales. While Xiaomi fell back, rivals such as Huawei and Oppo took advantage, churning out their own low-cost devices. Xiaomi then adjusted its model. Responding to its lack of retail penetration, it opened its own retail stores. But it also branched into new products to sell in those stores and give the company an additional revenue stream. One of those products was air filters. Like many Indian cities, China's cities suffer from serious pollution problems. But air filters typically cost about $500. Xiaomi funded a start-up, providing help with design, supply chain management and production to create an air purifier that could sell for $105. The device connects to Xiaomi's smartphones, alerting customers when the filter needs changing.

Don't Look for Gaps—Look for Friction

Opportunities are not market gaps. A gap indicates empty space. Most of the universe is empty space. What value does it have? Opportunity is generally found in unmet customer needs that are creating friction. Is empty space full of pain? No. That's why looking at markets like blue oceans can be so difficult. The number of fish in the sea is not the main issue. The main issue is unaddressed pain. Your own pain is a good starting point for identifying opportunities. As India's leading angel investor Sacha Mirchandani said, 'The best businesses come from the personal pain point of the entrepreneur.' This advice applies equally to employees. You must look outside of yourself for pain that you can successfully relieve.

When There's Just Too Much Pain

If you've travelled to China recently, you would have given people pain. You'll have done it every time you reached into your wallet and tried to buy something. If you were using a foreign credit card, you can expect to be refused. For a long time, foreign credit companies were kept out of China. Few places now accept them. But if you tried to pay in cash, you'll have forced the seller to look around for change. Many places won't have any because the Chinese economy is now largely cashless. Whether they're buying a coffee, paying for a taxi, or sending money to a friend, Chinese people now perform all their transactions on their phones. They use WeChat or Alipay to scan a QR code or to send money digitally.

While anyone can send funds to anyone else using a Chinese app, funding a WeChat or Alipay wallet requires a Chinese bank account, which isn't available to people travelling to China for pleasure or business. They're stuck waiting for change while everyone in line waits impatiently, their phones already in their hands. The problem is even more acute for anyone trying to send money into or out of China. Banks have high fees and long lines, and require giant piles of paperwork.

That was the experience of Sandi Yu, one of several foreign students and expats who grew fed up with the difficulty of sending money home. Yu and her co-founders established Swapsy, a peer-to-peer currency exchange network. People travelling to China could send dollars to other people in the country and receive Renminbi (official currency of China) directly to their WeChat or Alipay wallets. People in China could make their Renminbi available and receive dollars.

It should have been a perfect solution, a way to beat a giant pain point. But the Chinese government required users to have either a Chinese bank account or a Chinese ID card to receive funds on Swapsy. Governments can always inflict pain.

Better Ways of Examining Your Market Environment

In auditing your market environment, your main job is to find friction that you can reduce through useful service. *Want to know what friction feels like?* How hard was it to make a phone call from outside your house before mobile phones were invented? How hard was it to get an air-conditioned taxi to come to your door before Uber was invented? Do you remember how hard it was to buy books before Amazon was invented? Bookstores were inconvenient and expensive, and still didn't have the book you wanted. Are you old enough to remember how difficult it was to find information before Google was invented?

Where is the pain? Where people need service, but have trouble finding it. Where the service is unreliable, inconsistent, overly expensive, hard to obtain, hard to customize. How do you find friction? The easiest way is to talk to your customers. Ask: *What challenges do they face? What do they need from you? Why are they buying from you? What useful service are you providing? Where are you and others failing? Where do you add value? Where is there pain that you're not removing? Where else do they have pain that you could possibly remove? What value exchanges with your current customers are positive for you? Which are negative? How can you add more value in order to receive more in return from your customers?*

You already engage in many value exchanges, both indirectly as well as directly. For example, I conducted an Opportunity Audit for a major Indian supplier of fancy yarn. This is a product that mainly goes into men's shirts to make them look more fashionable. My client's customers were all textile producers. I talked to several and asked them: *why do you buy fancy yarn? What do you need it for? What jobs does fancy yarn get done for you?* I discovered that the main reason they bought fancy yarn was to add *fashion value* to their products, so that *their customers*, the garment manufacturers, would give more value to their textiles. Given this finding, I advised my client to focus strongly on fashion as the key driver of their opportunities. Up to that point, they had focused only on all the generic factors that everyone in their industry thought customers cared about: low price, on time delivery and quality. But these factors were requirements, similar to a bed in a hotel room, they were not valuable drivers of useful service.

After you've talked to your customers, talk to *their* customers as well. In addition, you should talk to your channels and end users. Examine all the links in the value chain that connects you with the end user. Questions you could ask include:

- Do your customers have customers?
- Are you contributing to products or services they sell to their customers?

- How does your product/service add value to your customers' offerings? How does it remove pain? What pain does it remove?
- What friction doesn't it remove? Why? What are the consequences?
- How could you remove more friction and add more value for your customer's customer?
- Who helps you to reach your customers? Do you use channels?
- What are they buying from you? Why?
- How could you remove more of their friction and add more value?
- Are your end users the same as your customers?
- What do end users want? How are you reducing their friction and adding value?
- What pain are you not reducing for them? What additional value could you deliver?
- What, where, when and how?

See how people are using your product or service in ways that are not exactly what it was designed for. What jobs are they trying to get done and are finding that they get done imperfectly using your technology? For example, people use Google for problem solving, but it was not designed for this. Pay a lot of attention to unexpected people who are using your product or service. Find out why they're using it and what jobs they're trying to get done. You should always ask: *How can I extend useful service from what I'm already doing? How can I find more ways of making myself useful to the people I serve now?* Throughout its history, Amazon has done a great job of constantly extending utility to its customers, by selling more products in different ways, delivering faster, and providing other useful services, such as free entertainment.

Look Beyond Your Current Customers

In considering the useful service that you provide to your customers, next consider: *Who else could benefit from this service? How? Where else can you serve? Where else can your existing capabilities be applied to provide value through co-opportunity?*

For example, my former client Concept Hospitality specializes in building and running hotels on a management contract basis. This asset-light model that has allowed it to expand very rapidly. Its hotels are all environmentally friendly, making them less expensive to build and run and providing a good value exchange for investors. In only a few years it has built over sixty two- to five-star hotels all over India under its Fern and Beacon brands. Due to the strength of its model, Concept is also adept at attracting large investors. Can their strength in the *management contract model* be extended into other adjacent areas? For example, banqueting facilities? Retirement homes? Housing colonies?

You can uncover enormous opportunities by understanding why your customers buy things. As I shared in an earlier chapter, the MD of Asian Paints found out when he asked his customers, that nobody actually wants to buy paint. They want *the solution* the paint provides: a painted house. It's the same with all products. People buy products for the underlying services and solutions that they provide to them. Very often, companies are so fixated on the products they provide that they fail to realize how they can provide useful and potentially more lucrative services to customers.

Asian Paints could go even deeper by using the *Five Whys Analysis*. The next question would be: why do you want to paint your building? The two main answers might be: to protect it from the elements, or for beautification. The next question would be: why do you want to protect the building? That will give you a number of responses and you would again ask why. From asking why at least five times, you'll understand all the reasons why people buy paint. Next you should dig further and ask: how well are current solutions working for you? What are you happy with, what are you dissatisfied with? Which of your jobs are we getting done well, and which ones still creating friction? It's not enough to know: why do you like buying paint? It's even more useful to know: why do you not like buying paint?

Never settle for the first obvious answer. Look for second, or third or fourth right answers. *Always seek the truth:* look for evidence to back them up. For example, what does a manufacturer of playground equipment do? The simple answer is that he makes slides and swings. But why do parks buy them? Because they want to attract families to their parks. Why do parents think those playgrounds are attractive? Because they want their children to have fun. But those children could have fun sitting at home, playing with their mobile phones. Why do parents want them to have fun in the playground? Because they think that playing outside is healthier and better for their children's development. So instead of building simple swings and slides, why doesn't a playground manufacturer produce designs that are intellectually challenging and that teach children scientific principles?

That's exactly what some companies have done. Firms like Grounds for Play and ABA Science Play now design playground equipment that explain centrifugal forces and aerodynamics. Kids get to play outside and learn at the same time. And the parents can look at their own phones in peace.

How to Turn Products into Service Opportunities

If you sell products rather than services, ask: *what is the underlying service that my products provide to customers? How can I expand the range of services to create more value for both sides? How can I offer useful service for even more of the customer's journey?*

For example, my former client Essel Propack dominates the world market for flexible tubes, with over 50 per cent market share. Yet margins were very tight because raw material costs were eating up over 50 per cent of their revenue. It had little ability to bargain with its suppliers, as they were huge chemicals companies such as Dupont. The company felt it had limited pricing power, because its customers were all large FMCG and pharma companies, such as Colgate. In assessing its environment, I learned that Essel Propack's customers take up to two years to replace it as a vendor. Why? Because their packaging must be absolutely safe and secure and guarantee a long shelf life. Everything that goes into Essel's tubes is either ingested as food or medicine or applied on the skin. Essel has unique and valuable expertise in designing tubes that can keep sensitive products safe, with long shelf life. But it was not using this expertise to maximize the useful service it could provide. I therefore suggested that the company offer this expertise as a service.

Based on my advice, Essel Propack rebranded itself as a *concept to tube solutions provider* and within five years has been able to expand its customer base to small- and medium-sized manufacturers who lack this expertise. Services are a higher margin business because no raw materials are required, and smaller companies have weaker bargaining power. The company's stock price has tripled since it started to offer this service.

Every product should be considered a service. And every service should be considered potentially universal. Ask: *How could everyone in the world benefit from my service?* Uber and Airbnb started small but provided such useful service that they were able to spread worldwide and create completely new categories. Don't think that these were exceptional. All markets began this way. There are literally millions of areas of service in the world without markets of exchange—*you can create one.* Over 60 per cent of the Indian economy is service, yet the vast majority of it is disorganized. There are enormous opportunities to create universal business models that can provide useful service for millions of people.

For example, finding a servant in major Indian metros is often difficult because there are few organized established players who can handle service with speed and efficiency. Eventually, someone will develop a useful service that can transform pain into pleasure. UrbanClap, a start-up founded in 2014, tapped into a similar opportunity that it discovered in Indian households—the need for reliable plumbers, carpenters, electricians, etc. for odd jobs. Over the last five years, they have expanded to providing appliance repair, home cleaning, pest control, music training, photography, salon, fitness and yoga services through nearly 1,00,000 background-verified professionals across eight cities of India. They claim 3 million happy customers and have Ratan Tata as an investor. They identified a pain point and have discovered a market that includes nearly 20 crore middle class and upper middle-class households of India.

What If There's No Demand for What I Do?

Although there may be no current demand for your products or services, don't let that stop you. There could still be enormous friction that you can provide a solution for. Before the iPhone was invented, there was absolutely no demand for smartphones. But the phone provided so much useful service that it became the world's most popular product. What types of service are provided by a smartphone? I use it as a phone, watch, alarm clock, voice recorder, calendar and mobile office. I read all my books on it. When I go for a walk, I can transcribe the notes I left on my voice recorder on the phone's Dragon transcription app. What service does the phone provide me? So much that I'm probably only benefiting from 1 per cent of its utility!

When I set up shop as the world's first and only Opportunity Consultant, there was absolutely no demand for my services. That's not surprising. No one had ever heard of an opportunity consultant. Yet my services immediately addressed enormous pain points. I didn't create the Open Mind Process for the sake of being different, or because I wanted to look different. I did it because for the past twenty-nine years I had witnessed the friction suffered by thousands of my clients, and I felt I could provide useful service to address it.

From Booze to the Bunker

There are all types of needs in the market. You may be in an industry in which all products provide the same functional benefit. For examples, all whiskies provide you with the same functional benefit—inebriation. But whiskey can provide other types of useful service as well. My former client Deepak Roy built Officer's Choice into the largest-selling whiskey brand in the world by volume by providing emotional benefits to his customers, most of whom are day labourers—the feeling of *being an officer.*

In order to open your mind to new market opportunities, consider how you could provide out-of-the-box solutions to all kinds of needs. Be irreverent and throw away the rulebook. For example, some people have a very high need for security. For those people, imagine building a hotel called *The Bunker.* It will have no windows. It will be made of solid concrete capable of withstanding a nuclear attack. It will have deep underground rooms that are even safer. It might be ideal for particularly vulnerable companies, people or foreign governments that do not want electronic surveillance or any possibility of a terrorist attack. Sound crazy? Maybe. But maybe not!

What if You're an Employee? How Do You Find Market Opportunities?

If you are an employee, your boss is your customer. You need to consider: *How can you create value for him? What friction does he suffer from which you can help to relieve through useful service? What and how? What does your boss's boss want from him? Why? How can you help your boss to provide useful service to his boss?* If you are low on the totem pole, you can keep asking how, what and why as you go up the company hierarchy. To climb the corporate ladder, you need to create value at the highest levels possible. Reach for the stars, and you can at least rise from the bottom to middle management.

The Rise and Rise of Satya Nadella

Two of America's biggest tech giants are currently led by Indian emigrants. In Silicon Valley, Sundar Pichai heads Google, the search giant at the heart of Alphabet Inc. And in Redmond, Washington, Satya Nadella has led Microsoft since taking over from Steve Ballmer in 2014.

Nadella was born in Hyderabad in 1967. His father was a civil servant, and his mother was a scholar of Sanskrit. Nadella studied electrical engineering at the Manipal Institute of Technology but moved to the United States for his master's degree in computer science at the University of Wisconsin–Milwaukee in 1988. His first job was at Sun Microsystems, but in 1992 he applied for a job at Microsoft. He was then single and in his mid-twenties.

At his interview, the interviewer asked him a simple question: what would he do if he saw a baby fall down on the street and cry? 'I answered thinking this is some trick question,' Nadella told the Freakonomics Radio podcast. 'Maybe there is some algorithm that I'm missing and said, "I'll call 911" [the emergency assistance service in the US] only to have that manager get up and walk me out of the room saying, "That's [an] absolute bullshit answer."' He was supposed to say that he would pick up the child and hug it.

Nadella got the job anyway. He rose through the company. He ran Microsoft bCentral, a suite of Web services for businesses. He became corporate Vice President (VP) of Microsoft Business

Solutions and landed the job of senior VP of Microsoft Online Services, which put him in charge of Bing, Xbox Live, and the online versions of Office. From there, he was made president of the Server and Tools Division, the part of the company that sold server space and hosted Microsoft Azure. Within two years, the division's revenues climbed from $16.6 billion to $20.3 billion.

By the time Nadella was given Steve Ballmer's job as chief executive, and an $84 million first-year salary, he was married, the father of three children, one with cerebral palsy and another with some type of learning disability. He also understood the question he had been asked at the interview. What he had developed in his time at the company was empathy.

'Most people think empathy is just something that you reserve for your life, your family and friends, but the reality is that it's an existential priority of a business,' Nadella told Bloomberg. 'I think empathy is core to innovation and life's experience.'

For example, when I began as US Trade Commissioner in Mumbai in 2000, our lowest level professional employee was a young man in his late twenties named Ali Motiwala. He had recently been hired to run our commercial library. By 2000, commercial libraries were becoming obsolete, as most information was already readily available on the Internet. Rather than sit around passively and wait for his job to become irrelevant, Ali constantly identified and pitched ways our operation could expand its market. When I challenged him to turn these opportunities into reality, he went ahead and effectively implemented many of them.

I became so dependent on Ali's suggestions that he literally did my thinking for me. Whenever I had to adjust our mission, I would take his advice first. As a result of the useful service that Ali consistently provided, I promoted him five times. Before the age of forty, he reached the highest level possible for a non-American employee of the US Consulate.

For more tips, tools and templates to help you audit your market environment, visit my website at: www.power-of-opportunity.com.

The Opportunity Audit: Your Market

1. Don't look for gaps, focus on useful service
Businesses often look for gaps in the market. But being different from competitors just because you can is rarely worth the effort. When Lei Jun created Xiaomi, he wasn't thinking of Apple or Samsung. He was thinking of an entirely new way of providing useful service to customers.

2. Look beyond your current customers
An opportunity is one link in a value chain of opportunities: you supply your customer, they supply someone else, and so on. When you understand what the end-buyer wants, whether that's a nicer shirt or educational fun, you can add value that extends all the way through the chain.

3. Employees can find market opportunities too
Employees are their own CEOs and they have to look for their own opportunities. They have to look for them in the job market, but they also have to look for them at the workplace. They find them when they outperform, look to over-deliver, and understand why they've begun a task, as well as how to perform it.

16

The Opportunity Audit: Your Domain

What is your domain, and why is it a big source of opportunities? How can you understand the key drivers in your domain? What major trends are taking place in your domain, and how can those changes provide opportunity?

If you have ever used FreeCharge to charge your phone or pay a bill, you're not alone. About 52 million people own wallets on the platform and use them to make cashless transactions. In China, the opportunity in cashless payments has proved even bigger. The country's billion daily users of WeChat use the service to chat with their friends but mostly, they also use it to pay for . . . everything. Each user has a barcode connected to their WeChat wallet. The wallet is connected to their bank account so that with just a wave of their phone, they can buy anything. Taxi drivers rarely carry change any more.

Whether you're buying a drink in Luckin Coffee, stepping out of a taxi in Chongqing, or picking up a bunch of bananas in Beijing, you'll be looked at with surprise if you open your wallet and take out a banknote. Cash is so twentieth century.

And yet the same system hasn't taken off in the US or Europe despite the best efforts of companies as big as Apple and Google. Why not? Because those domains already had cashless systems called credit cards. About 183 million Americans own credit cards. Indians owned little more than 20 million credit cards in 2016 and while more owned debit cards, they mostly used them to withdraw cash from ATMs. In China, too, credit cards arrived much later than they did in the West.

Western markets are also concerned about privacy. Cities, including New Jersey, Connecticut, Philadelphia and San Francisco, have banned cashless stores. New York may join them. The difference in their domains meant that entrepreneurs in India and China were in a much better position to accept the opportunity provided by digital payment technology. In the West, they faced a much tougher struggle.

Your Domain: A Rich Source of Opportunities

Most businesspersons worry about their competition. But it's generally not your competitors that are out racing you. It's more likely that your environment is out racing you. Competitors come and go. Your environment remains, all around you, changing all the time. An awareness of the market allows you to see the market now. *An awareness of your domain helps you to harness the opportunities that will create the market of the future.* What is your Domain? It is *everything* in your opportunity environment that doesn't fit neatly into your Mission, Model or Market, yet can strongly influence all of them. Your Domain includes:

- Technology
- Fashions
- Industry trends
- Societal trends
- Economic trends
- Legal and regulatory trends
- Trade relationships and barriers
- Political trends
- Cultural trends
- Potential substitutes
- Emerging needs
- Changes in the physical environment—natural and human-made
- Everything else, outside your mission, model and market

As domain trends can be long lasting, they can be a very rich source of opportunities. On the other hand, if you miss domain trends, you can be wiped out, just like the makers of fancy hats, buggy whips and slides rules.

Easy Ways to Explore Your Domain

These days, because of the Internet and Google, doing desk research on any domain is quite easy. First identify the key existing players in the industry you're looking at. For example, if you were exploring the domain of India's auto industry, you could easily begin by identifying the leading companies, such as Maruti. Read news articles about the company. These may be linked to more analytical articles that explore the trends affecting the entire sector. Look for reports written by research analysts employed by financial services firms. Next, you can branch out and look at media reports on other companies in the sector, such as Tata Motors, Hyundai, Honda or Mahindra. After exploring them in depth, look at their main suppliers. Consider: *what trends are affecting them? What new technologies, regulatory changes or social trends are driving change? How, why, when, where?* For example, the auto industry could be impacted by the introduction of electric vehicle technology, or by government regulations requiring stricter pollution controls, or by changes in taxation, or by any number of other factors in the domain. *Which ones are the key drivers of change?*

To get a more focused view, talk to your employees (if you have them), your customers, as well as to their customers, and to your channel partners. You can also seek out experts in the industry and speak with them. These include research analysts for financial services firms, industry executives or consultants. Getting time with experts is not necessarily a difficult task. Simply approach meetings with a learning orientation. When you ask people for advice, many are happy to give it. Leverage whatever contacts you may have to get introductions. If you don't know anyone, simply research the right contacts and contact them by email or LinkedIn. Make these people your Value Partners. You'd be amazed how many people would be happy to give you advice, expecting nothing in return but gratitude. For tech sectors that are attracting a great deal of venture capital, meeting with the founders of start-ups is a good way of understanding domain trends and how people are capturing market opportunities from them. Lists of start-ups in numerous sectors are easily available from research companies such as Tracxn.

For example, my former client Atul Goel, MD of E-City Ventures, hired me to look at market opportunities in the digital media space. Goel had just sold his Fun Republic cinema chain and was exploring new opportunities. We spent six months meeting with various start-ups in all areas of the digital media space and finally reached the conclusion that it would be very difficult to find operational opportunities for Goel that would meet his criteria. But in looking at the periphery of the digital space we found opportunities in fintech that matched his mission criteria. After assessing that space by meeting with dozens of fintech start-ups, Goel eventually purchased a controlling interest in a fintech company.

There can be many aspects to your domain environment, and obviously the key drivers of your domain will depend on where you choose to play. In the remainder of the chapter, I will provide examples of how changes in the domains of various sectors have created opportunities.

Technology: Domain Trends Foster the Creation of Microbrands

While the world is increasingly becoming a single global community, advances in technology are increasingly providing opportunities to create millions of new products and services that provide service at a far more personal level than ever before possible. For example, an 8 November 2018 article in *The Economist* reported, 'the growth of microbrands threatens consumer goods giants'. Thanks to the ability to sell directly to consumers online, as well as the growth of just-in-time manufacturing and cloud-based services, tiny new brands can effectively compete with giant consumer-good companies. Between 2001 and 2015, while large food and beverage companies grew sales by less than 1 per cent in the US, microbrands grew sales by over 6 per cent.

Microbrands have been popping up in all categories. They include companies such as Casper, which sells mattresses, Warby Parker, a spectacles brand, and Glossier, a cosmetics firm. In India, the micro brand Bira has successfully pioneered the market for craft beer.

Consider: *What trends in your domain could encourage the creation of microbrands in your sector? How are online channels or new technology allowing you to further personalize the useful service you could give to customers?*

Technology: Apple Marries Diverse Technologies to Transform its Model

Advances in domain technology often create opportunities for *branching* your services from a hyper-competitive category to an adjacent category in which you can become the innovative market leader. For example, when Steve Jobs returned to run Apple in 1997, he took advantage of new technologies, most of which were developed outside the computer industry, to shift the company's focus from computers to the adjacent consumer electronics sector. In the process, Apple Computers was transformed into the much larger and more profitable Apple Corporation. All the new products Jobs introduced combined computer technology with other emergent domain technologies to provide different types of useful service. The iPod, iPhone and iPad all married existing computer technology with numerous new technologies developed outside the computer industry, such as touch sensitive glass and cloud storage. In the process, Jobs also ensured that Apple benefited from the availability of 3G and 4G bandwidth by selling digital content, such as music. The marriage of computer technology and mobile bandwidth also created new service categories: the App Store and the iTunes Store. None of these new technologies were invented by Apple, but the company became their main beneficiary.

Explore: *What new technologies in your domain can you combine with your current products or services to provide better, more useful service for your customers or potential customers?*

Technology: Mobile Phones Transform Drug Distribution

In the 1990s, criminologists were unable to understand why murder rates suddenly fell by over 50 per cent in most US cities. In some cities, such as New York, murder rates fell by up to 90 per cent. New research by the US National Bureau of Economic Research (reported in the *Economic Times* in June 2019) claimed that the introduction of mobile phones may have made the US safer by reducing gang wars. Rather than having to use muscle to control physical territory to sell their drugs, dealers could now easily connect with buyers 24/7 over the phone and hand over drugs at any safe location.

Consider: *How are changes in technology impacting distribution in your industry? Could they eliminate the need for fixed physical points of distribution?*

Technology: Can Western Union Reinvent Itself to Keep up With the Domain?

Since its founding in 1851, Western Union has consistently been able to reinvent its business to keep up with changes in its domain environment. Western Union once had a near monopoly over telegraph service in the United States. However, it made a colossal error when it refused to buy Alexander Graham Bell's telephone patents for only $100,000. Even though telegraph services declined in importance in the coming decades, its services were still essential for conducting international trade. Many businesses around the world used Western Union telex services. However, the development of the fax machine in the 1980s completely wiped out its telex market. The company once again reinvented itself as *the fastest way to send money*, exploiting the growing flow of international remittances by people working all over the world. It set up the world's largest international agent network for money transfers. In India alone, the company has over 60,000 agents. However, Western Union's remittance business has attracted strong competition from new fintech companies which are exploiting new technologies that dramatically cut the cost of remittances. The emergence of mobile phones and digital payments is also challenging Western Union's business model.

Think: *How could Western Union once again overcome domain trends to survive and thrive? How are technological trends threatening to disrupt your business model?*

Technology: Are Domain Trends Shaking up the Humble Kirana Shop?

Since the 1990s, domain trends such as the creation of shopping malls and the growth of the Indian middle class have changed the Indian retail landscape. Major Indian corporates such as Reliance, Tata and Future Group have set up thousands of modern retail stores across India. At the same time, the spread of smartphones and cheap bandwidth have led to the creation of a giant e-commerce market, led by Flipkart and Amazon. Yet, despite it all, India is still largely a nation of independent shopkeepers. Almost 90 per cent of India's $700 billion retail market remains unorganized, in the hands of ubiquitous *kirana* shops that seem to be on every corner of every city. They provide customers with friendly, personalized service, credit and easy home- delivery. Within a one-minute walk of my Mumbai home, there are six kirana shops selling the same items, and all seem to be thriving.

However, domain trends are finally starting to shake up the kiranas and adapt their business models to modern times. As the *Economic Times* recently reported on 9 June 2019: 'They (kiranas) are the focus of two transformational forces—one that seeks to modernize (them), using technology to bestow the efficiencies and tactics of modern retail, and another that seeks to make them the pulsating nerve centres of a coming ecommerce and digital payments revolution.' Corporates such as Walmart India, Reliance and Metro Cash & Carry are offering the kiranas low-cost point of sales solutions that allow them to track their customers' sales and offer them promotions. Start-ups such as PhonePe are offering kiranas an app to help them more efficiently manage their inventories. Fintech companies such as BharatPe are offering kiranas digital payments platforms and lending solutions. It is already used by 5 million small retailers.

Think: *How are new technologies shaking up the traditional ways of doing things in your world? How can this create opportunities for you, your company and your industry?*

Infrastructure: Domain Trends Shift Goods from Air to Road

We can see the impact of change when people start asking: *why should we put up with this anymore?* Why should it take five days to move a truck between cities? Why should we have to pay for air freight when much faster new highways have been built?

Changes in the domain, particularly a massive nationwide highway-building campaign, have drastically reduced transit times between major Indian cities. While a few years ago it took a truck four days to travel between Mumbai and Delhi, it can now take only thirty hours. GST has created a national market and changed the way companies organize logistics. E-Commerce, another emergent trend in the domain, has massively increased demand for intra-city shipping. In the past, shippers were often forced to use expensive air freight. High-speed trucking is one half the cost. Trucking is a highly disorganized industry, with immense price competition. How can a model be created and scaled that aligns well with domain trends and can be a win-win for the trucker as well as the shipper?

One Indian start-up, Rivigo, thinks it has the answer. It believes the key driver of the model is driver happiness. Drivers' main complaint over the years was the number of days they have to spend on the road, sleeping in miserable conditions. Rivigo's answer is to run a relay system. Drivers go only up to a certain point, and then get on another truck to return home. This system requires fine coordination and control, so Rivigo owns its entire fleet of 2500 trucks. Although the company has attracted enough venture capital to scale quickly, it is still losing money. Industry critics say that the driver happiness model is too expensive to be feasible in a value-driven market in which 95 per cent of the industry is still unorganized.

The owners of Mituj have a different answer. This Delhi-based company owns a much smaller fleet of 250 trucks. It doesn't use a relay system, believing it is too expensive. It uses the traditional two-driver model. Mituj focuses instead on economics, which helps it to continuously discover routes that provide maximum margin and value arbitrage against both air freight and unorganized players. However, because of the capital requirements of its model, Mituj believes that it can only scale nationwide if it also creates an affiliate network of independent truckers. Therefore, it is planning to spend Rs 4 crore to create a technology platform to organize independent truckers. The objective is to arrange more full truckloads on both ends of each trip and raise capacity utilization. Critics have commented that organizing India's independent truckers is like herding cats; nobody has ever succeeded.

Consider: *How are changes in your domain environment creating opportunities to provide better service to customers? Which new business models are being tested in the market to provide these services? How are they relevant to you or your business? What can they teach you?*

Health: Can Domain Trends Help Organize the Diabetic Footwear Market?

In 2014, I was hired by the US company *Foot Solutions* to find it a partner in the Indian market. The company is a retailer that specializes in shoes for people with chronic foot problems. One of their largest and fastest-growing segments worldwide is shoes for people who suffer from diabetes. A 2018 study published in the medical journal *Lancet* predicted that India would have 98 million diabetics by 2030. The Indian industry supplying shoes for diabetics is completely disorganized, with inconsistent service, few styling choices and poor-quality products. There could be a huge market for an organized retailer of diabetic shoes. A specialized retailer could also supply a range of profitable services to diabetics and people with other foot maladies.

I first offered the opportunity to partner with Foot Solutions to major Indian shoe retailers. Rafique Malik, the MD of Metro Shoes, declined to participate because he thought the segment to be incompatible with its market focus, mission and model. Rajeev Gopalakrishnan, MD of Bata Shoes, first had his team do some market research. They found an enormous and fast-growing market for diabetic footwear. Gopalakrishnan was therefore quite interested but never took the opportunity forward. I then took the opportunity to Lifespan, India's second-largest chains of specialized diabetic clinics. It is 50 per cent-owned by the Times of India Group. Its MD, Ashok Jain, was interested enough in the opportunity to seriously examine if he could convert a small space in all his clinics to a shoe display area. But he delayed because he said he had other projects to complete first.

Therefore, this opportunity still exists in the market. *Are you the one to take it? Ask yourself: do you believe in the diabetic footwear market? How well would it integrate with your current mission, model and market? Are there any health trends impacting your industry? How would you explore them?*

I recently offered this opportunity to a small footwear company that sought my advice. They make stylish sandals with soles made from cork. Their products are unique but expensive. I suggested that they consider the much larger market in diabetic footwear. The company has two promoters, a brother and sister. The sister, who designs the sandals, was initially unenthusiastic, because normal diabetic sandals completely lack style. I pointed out that she could make diabetic sandals in all sorts of designs, as there is surely a market for everything. The brother was more enthusiastic, as he sees the opportunity to be the first organized mover in a potentially enormous nationwide industry. He believes his production model can easily adapt to this segment. But he will need additional resources to scale it up.

Ask yourself: *If you were the promoter of this small sandals company, would you take advantage of this opportunity? Why? Why not? How?*

Health: Trends Make Comfort Foods Uncomfortable

Why do Americans eat hot dogs in buns made from white flour? Whenever the marriage of hot dog and bun began, it must have been a valuable adaptation, otherwise it would not have become the market norm. But things change, creating opportunities.

Hot dogs in traditional white buns were always full of calories and carbs. Many people consciously avoid eating white flour, as it has no fibre and little nutritional value. The image of hot dogs also took a huge hit in 2018 when the World Health Organization announced that cured meats, including hot dogs, contain cancer-causing carcinogens. To avoid irrelevance, manufacturers are experimenting with alternatives to both the traditional hot dog and the traditional white bun.

Similarly, Coca-Cola and other fizzy drink companies are being roundly criticized for the sugar and calories in their beverages. They have been blamed for causing the worldwide epidemics of obesity and diabetes. Some local governments in the US have already imposed high taxes on sugary drinks. As a result, Coca-Cola and its competitors are increasingly introducing new products that are in the health category, such as flavoured waters or juice drinks. Colas are increasingly becoming a drink of the past.

Consider: *What health trends in the environment are affecting or could affect demand for my products or services? If not health, what other domain trends are having an impact, and how is this creating opportunities I could pursue?*

Politics: Can Domain Trends Help Nokia Win Capture the 5G Market?

In 2013, Nokia completely exited the mobile handset business and acquired Alcatel-Lucent, one of the world's largest manufacturers of telecom equipment. Rather than selling handsets to consumers, Nokia now supplies network equipment and software to telecoms operators.

It bet its future on the hope that it could capture a significant share of the billions of dollars that telecom companies worldwide were expected to spend on next generation 5G telecoms networks in the coming decade. *Would this bet work out?*

Nokia's early years in the telecom equipment business were not particularly promising. Although it stood at number two in the world, between 2015 and 2018 its market share fell from 20 per cent to 17 per cent, and it was barely profitable. Meanwhile, market leader Huawei of China grew its share from 24 to 28 per cent, and it seemed to be best poised to benefit from the creation of 5G networks. Huawei was spending over $13 billion annually on research and development and was widely regarded as having the best technology and the lowest prices in the industry.

However, in 2019, the US government placed Huawei on an export blacklist because of concerns that all traffic over Huawei equipment could be monitored by the authoritarian Chinese government. This ban came amidst a trade war launched by President Donald Trump between the US and China. The ban has forced companies that supply to Huawei, such as Google, to limit or cease their relationships with Huawei. The US government also pressured all its allies to refrain from buying Huawei equipment. Although Australia and New Zealand agreed to ban Huawei equipment, both Germany and the UK have thus far refused. On 16 June 2019, Huawei's founder and CEO Ren Zhengfel announced that he expected the US ban to slash its revenue by up to $30 billion in 2019. Some market observers doubt that Huawei's problems will help Nokia gain market share. Many believe that several telecom companies around the world are so dependent on Huawei equipment that they will delay the introduction of 5G networks rather than turning to alternative suppliers. Most of Europe's roughly 200 operators of mobile networks already use Huawei's 4G gear.

Consider: *Are there any political or regulatory trends that could impact your market? How can they harm your current business model? How can you benefit from these trends?*

Remember this: the trend is your friend. Domain trends can a very rich source of opportunities for you and your company. But to see these opportunities, you must first understand and keep track of the trends that affect your business. It's especially important to understand the trend of domain elements because they can have a big influence on entire industries.

Think: *Which trends are becoming more relevant in which less in your industry? Which are closely connected to your service offerings?*

For more tips, tools and templates to help you audit your domain environment, visit my website at: www.power-of-opportunity.com.

The Opportunity Audit: Your Domain

1. Explore your domain to find a rich source of opportunities
Your domain makes up much of your opportunity environment and includes technology, fashion, changing needs, trends in industry, society, economics, politics and culture, and much more. It can be a rich source of long-lasting opportunities. However, if you miss domain trends, you can be wiped out.

2. Read, research and understand your domain
To understand your domain, start by listing the key players in your industry. Read news articles about the companies, then dive into more analytical articles that cover the sector's trends. Speak with your employees, customers and channels. Expand into suppliers and subsidiary businesses to understand the trends that affect them too. Finally, look for experts and industry leaders to speak with personally.

3. Identify the trends in your domain
Once you know the main players in your domain, focus on the trends that affect them. Look for the challenges that new technology poses for them, how they're trying to adjust to new tastes or new demands. It's in those changes that opportunities lie. Look for the key drivers of change that can create opportunities or nopportunities for you.

17

Create Your Opportunity Inventory

What steps do you need to take to create a complete inventory of your opportunities? How do you identify and rank the key drivers and draggers of opportunity in your environment? What kind of opportunities should you put in your inventory? Should you also include nopportunities? How do you identify new opportunities that you've never considered before?

It was autumn 2005, and disaster had struck for a small start-up in San Francisco. Odeo was the work of an entrepreneur called Noah Glass. He believed that he had found an opportunity turning voice messages into MP3s hosted on the Internet. One of the first investors in the company was Evan Williams, who had recently sold his blogger platform to Google. Williams took over the project and shifted the company's direction. Instead of making voice messages available online, it would produce a podcasting platform.

By July 2005, the product was ready. A few months later, it looked dead. Apple had announced that iTunes would now come with its own podcasting platform. No one with an iPhone would have any need for Odeo's product. The environment had changed. The company needed a new opportunity.

Williams told the company's thirteen employees to start considering new directions for the firm. They held 'hackathons' at which they would spend an entire day working on their own projects. One engineer had an idea. He thought there might be a demand for a platform that people could use to share their current status. Instead of sending a single message to a friend, they could send a public message to anyone who wanted to see it. How that idea was shared and evaluated is the stuff of legend. The engineer, Jack Dorsey, told CNBC that he had pitched it to his colleagues one afternoon as they ate burritos in a San Francisco playground. He then pitched the idea to Williams and to the rest of the team, who set to work creating the product that would become Twitter.

The Twitter team were lucky. Most Silicon Valley ideas go the same way as Odeo. No one evaluates the opportunity, assesses the environment or conducts an audit. They build and hope, burning through other people's money. You can do better. Let's say that you've carefully examined all four segments of your environment. What's next? You need to make an inventory of your opportunities. This inventory should be as large and thorough as possible. After all, in order to pick the golden egg from the basket, you must have the largest possible basket of eggs to choose from.

Simulation Exercise: Creating Your Own Opportunity Inventory

In the next three chapters, you'll be taken through a *simulation exercise* that will help you to understand how to create, evaluate, choose and implement your best opportunities. In order to benefit from the simulation, you must open your mind a bit and pretend that you are completely immersed in a new work environment, which is entirely fictional. In this chapter, you will conduct an Opportunity Audit and create your Opportunity Inventory.

Your simulation begins now. Put yourself in a different pair of shoes:

The company dates back to 1948, when Jehangir Irani, a Zoroastrian who had migrated from Iran, founded the small but thriving *Rule Britannia Restaurant* near the famous Gateway of India in Mumbai's Colaba district. This cheap and cheerful establishment was open every day from 7 a.m. to midnight. It was a favourite of local residents as well as the crowds that visited the Gateway every weekend. Over the years, through hard work and thrift, Jehangir and his three sons were able to buy the entire 10,000 square foot, three-storey building, *Mehta Bhavan*, that housed their restaurant on the ground floor. The family lived on the first floor and rented out the rest of the building. When Jehangir died at the age of ninety-one in 2002, he and his sons still ran the restaurant, which had fallen into a sad state of disrepair. By that time most Irani restaurants had been converted into fast food joints or branded clothing shops.

Jehangir's three sons had only two children between them: the cousins *Cyrus and Xerrxes*. Both joined the business, and by 2005 they were in complete operational control. The two men were opposites. Cyrus was a born opportunity-seeker. He saw the growth of Mumbai's middle class, and understood that there was a hunger for modern, air-conditioned branded chain restaurants that offered good-quality food (*ghar ka khana*) at reasonable prices. Xerrxes was more conservative. While he appreciated the opportunities in the market, he handled the finances, and well understood how easy it was to lose money in the restaurant business. In contrast to Cyrus' persistent enthusiasm, Xerrxes was usually the voice of caution. In 2006, Cyrus was able to convince Xerrxes to finally shut down the decrepit Rule Britannia. Rather than rent the space to someone else, they opened a new restaurant format that was Cyrus's brainchild: *Comfortwala*. It offered a full range of delicious vegetarian and non-vegetarian foods in air-conditioned comfort at comfortable prices. The new concept was a huge hit. By 2018, the Irani cousins operated twenty-two Comfortwala restaurants in Mumbai, Pune, Ahmedabad and Surat.

Congratulations! You've Just Been Promoted.

You've just been appointed to the position of *vice president of new ventures* of Irani Restaurants. You've done very well for yourself, so far. You grew up in a chawl in Kalbadevi, an old, crowded neighbourhood not far from Colaba. Although you managed to finish school, your grades were poor. Fed up with education, you took a job as a dishwasher at the original Comfortwala, mainly because it was your favourite restaurant. To your surprise, you excelled at the restaurant business. You soon mastered every job in the restaurant and happily worked eighty-hour weeks. Within two years, you were managing the restaurant. Within three years, you were put in charge of opening new restaurants, a job which you'd done very successfully.

Cyrus is obsessed with offering consistent quality. He has always refused to sell restaurant franchises as he is concerned that other owner operators will cut corners and destroy his brand. Xerrxes is obsessed with conserving cash. He refuses to risk the company's limited capital on new restaurants.

Both policies limited the growth of the chain until you found the solution by borrowing a model from the hotel industry. You learned that Marriott Hotels, the largest chain in the world, doesn't own a single one of its 5000 properties. Rather than own them, it manages them, and in return takes a fee and a percentage of sales. This transfers the risk to the hotel owner and ensures that Marriott always makes money. It also ensures that the hotels are run to a consistent quality standard, protecting the value of the Marriott brand. By applying the management contract model to Comfortwala, you've successfully opened twenty-one new locations, with very little capital. You recently arranged a block deal with Eveready Capital, a private equity firm that invests in restaurants, to fund new outlets in Pune and Gujarat.

Is Your New Job a Big Opportunity?

The two Irani cousins didn't want to give you a new position. They were delighted with your work and wanted you to continue scaling Comfortwala. But you've already groomed a worthy successor and want to start something new. But you like working with the Iranis. You offered to stay with them if they let you develop new concepts and compensate you with sweat equity. They have agreed. As vice president of new ventures, your mission is to create new concepts. The only requirement is that you focus on adaptations to the company's current restaurant operations. Therefore, opportunities that don't involve food will not be considered. In addition, Xerrxes will only consider new concepts if they are funded through cutting costs in the existing Comfortwala chain. Therefore, you are also responsible for identifying nopportunities in current operations which can be eliminated.

Your Opportunity Audit

As a first step, you wisely decide to do a thorough Opportunity Audit of your Mission, Model, Market and Domain environments.

Opportunity Audit Part 1: Mission

You: would like to build and own a part of a new nationwide food business. You don't care what segment of the industry it's in, but it should be able to make you a lot more money.

Cyrus: would like to improve the company's reputation. He would one day like to be recognized as a successful player in the global restaurant industry. Therefore, he'd like a new concept with international potential.

He's been toying with the idea of opening a fine dining restaurant in Mehta Bhavan.

Xerrxes: is willing to go along with Cyrus's plans, as long as they don't require any debt. He is only willing to develop new businesses by using cost savings from the existing business or other people's capital. Remain *asset and capital light* is his mantra.

Opportunity Audit Part 2: Model

Your audit uncovers three potential concepts for new restaurant models, all of which you have been considering for the past year:

New Venture Concept 1: Bigwich

The most popular item sold in most Comfortwala outlets is a gigantic vegetarian sandwich called *The Bigwich*. It's over twice the size of a normal sandwich, covered in butter and chutney, and stuffed with vegetables and cheese. A non-veg version adds chicken or eggs. It's so big that it's usually shared. The Bigwich is also very profitable, with a food cost of only 19 per cent, far below the chain's average of 28 per cent. You believe that this sandwich could become the signature dish of a QSR (quick-service restaurant) chain called *Bigwich*. A few company-owned restaurants could be opened for proof of concept, after which the concept would be franchised. Master franchises could be sold in various parts of India. Although these types of sandwiches are very commonly sold in the disorganized market all over India, there is no nationwide chain. You feel that the popularity of the product, the high margins, and the lack of organized competition are very positive factors.

However, Cyrus is reluctant to endorse this concept as he feels that fast food will damage the company's reputation. He would prefer to move upscale rather than downscale. Xerrxes, on the other hand, is open to the Bigwich concept, as it can be scaled with other people's money. He is not opposed to entering the low-end market, as long as it can be profitable. Although he is open to using a franchise model, he is concerned that it will be expensive to set up a sales team to sell franchises as well as a control team to train and continuously monitor franchisors to ensure that they follow quality standards. He's also concerned that a low-end model may have low margins, and therefore minimal franchise fees, because salaries have been increasing rapidly due to a shortage of qualified restaurant labour.

New Venture Concept 2: Banquetwala

After years of litigation, the Irani cousins have finally managed to evict all the tenants from Mehta Bhavan. A Comfortwala outlet is on the ground floor, but the first and second floors are now vacant and available. The area has become a popular hub for upscale restaurants such as Indigo Deli and The Table.

One option would be to rent out the space as a banquet facility. A local caterer, Farouk Khambata, had made a fortune a few years earlier by running a banquet facility in a similarly sized space.

In your new role of VP for new ventures for Irani Restaurants, you have a bigger opportunity in mind. India's banqueting industry is very large, but almost entirely disorganized. Demand for banquet space has been growing quickly in urban India, for weddings, corporate events and other functions. You would like to create India's first national brand of banqueting facilities, called *Banquetwala*. You would run the brand under management contracts, just as you do with *Comfortwala*. Eveready is interested in investing in the concept, pending proof of concept. Xerrxes likes this idea, as he's comfortable with the management contract model, and it requires little or no capital. Cyrus, however, feels that a banqueting brand may not enhance his reputation or further his dream of expanding internationally.

New Venture Concept 3: MasterChef Studio

A local entrepreneur has asked to rent the first floor of Mehta Bhavan to operate a pop-up restaurant (a temporary restaurant often operated from a private home, former factory or similar space, and during festivals). Every month he would like to install a new restaurant concept. This has given you a bigger idea. You would create the world's first permanent pop-up restaurant. The restaurant would feature ten to twelve different chefs cooking for customers, creating a new category of *Dinner Theatre*. Every two weeks the restaurant would feature a different theme of cuisine with a different group of chefs. The uniqueness of this concept would make it easy to promote. You would set up a YouTube channel with videos of the chefs cooking in your restaurant. You would also allow other aspiring chefs to post videos on the site. The ones that get the most likes will be invited to cook. You could also hold national and international competitions. Irani Restaurants could then arrange funding for the best chefs' restaurants and potentially manage them as well under contract.

Cyrus loves this concept. He believes that it will enhance the group's reputation and could be duplicated in major cities worldwide. It would also benefit from two trends: 1) the huge growth in rich Category A consumers in urban India hungry for better food and unique dining experiences and; 2) the emergence of many new gourmet chefs who are selling their food and catering through Internet delivery services such as Swiggy. MasterChef Studio would give them an ideal venue to demonstrate their skills and reach their target market. Xerrxes considers it an untested pie in the sky idea and won't get excited until he sees proof of concept.

Nopportunity 1: Comfortwala Conveyor

On a trip to Singapore five years ago, Xerrxes ate in a Japanese sushi restaurant featuring the famous kaiten-zushi system. Kaiten-zushi is a sushi restaurant where the plates with the sushi are placed on a rotating conveyor belt that moves past every table. Xerrxes thought the conveyor belt system would be ideal for Comfortwala. Snacks and other dry starters could be placed on the conveyor, and patrons could start eating immediately. This would reduce the number of waiters required and allow them to turn tables faster.

In the past three years, six *Comfortwala Conveyor* restaurants had been opened. They were the first restaurants of this type in India.

Unfortunately, while the concept was popular, the restaurants using the conveyors have lost money. The conveyor systems were expensive, had to be imported from China and needed constant servicing. The manufacturer had no distributor or servicing capabilities in India, resulting in costly and chronic breakdowns. Second, the inventory of food needed on the conveyor proved difficult to manage. Since every restaurant seemed to have a different demand profile, often the food available on the conveyor didn't match demand and got cold. Third, Indians prefer hot food, and complained if food got soggy. Up to 15 per cent of food taken off the conveyor was returned by customers, and complaints were frequent. Fourth, Indian customers prefer service to self-service, so the number of waiters remained the same.

You believe that Comfortwala Conveyor restaurants should be converted into regular Comfortwala outlets. After paying for conversion, this will save Rs 3 crore in the first year. These funds can be redeployed to fund new ventures, providing you with an initial operating budget.

Going, Going . . . Gone!

The Christie's auction house has been selling furniture and artworks for more than 250 years. On the face of it, little has changed at the company in that time or at its main rival Sotheby's. Suited experts still evaluate Old Masters, antique chairs and impressionist art. They state an estimate, and then charge a commission on whatever sale price the artwork reaches at auction. The model has barely changed since 1766.

But the domain *has* changed, and it's changing even more now. More purchases are taking place online while more new buyers are emerging in places like Mumbai, Shanghai and Dubai than in London or New York. As those changes have become clear, the venerable old auction houses have had to explore new opportunities to adjust their model in order to make the most of market and domain trends. Their options have included:

1. Closing salesrooms in shrinking markets and opening new salesrooms in the new markets.
2. Conducting more sales online, like on eBay.

3. Changing the commission structure to encourage sales and increase the profits of high-value artworks.
4. Focusing on lower-value items, where the profit margins can be higher.

Each of these opportunities has benefits and drawbacks. Closing historic salesrooms makes the company look like it's in trouble and costs the company prestige but gives the auction better access to today's buyers. It moves the company from its old centre to a new centre. Online auctions allow anyone to take part in the sale easily, but they don't have the theatre of a live sale and they don't suit every kind of piece.

Buyers tend to want to see furniture, for example, before they buy it. Auction houses have experimented with guaranteed prices in order to bring in high-prestige, high-value items, but that's produced limited sales and sometimes no profits. Lower-priced goods are more plentiful and provide more scope for profit but could scare away big-walleted buyers. These are the models that Guillaume Cerutti, the chief executive of Christie's, has to assess before deciding which concept, or concepts, to adopt.

Similarly, Cyrus and Xerxxes have several models to explore before they find one that meets both their expectations.

Opportunity Audit Part 3: Market

India's food services market is growing quickly at every price point and in every category, from QSR to high-end to delivery and banqueting. Growth is expected to continue indefinitely, as the average Thai or Malaysian dines out four times more than the average Indian. Consumer spending on dining out is expected to quadruple per capita over the next 15 years. In general, however, because of increased competition, particularly in the low to mid markets, the industry suffers from hyper-competition and declining margins.

The Market Opportunity in Vegetarian Foods

'Our findings indicate that these markets represent high-value opportunities for plant-based and clean meat producers, most of which are US-based,' was the conclusion of a group of researchers who had surveyed consumer perceptions of plant-based and clean meat (food grown from animal cells without the use of a slaughterhouse.) They had conducted an opportunity audit of a market—the market for meat substitutes—and found a high likelihood of purchase in China, India and the US. Nearly 60 per cent of people in China and 48.7 per cent of people in India were 'very or extremely likely' to buy clean meat. More than 62 per cent of both Chinese and Indian respondents said that they would buy plant-based meats.

Currently, it's American firms like Beyond Meat and Impossible Foods that are building an adaption to a market that's less tolerant of the environmental cost and animal suffering involved in meat production. But businesses outside the US have seen the opportunity as well. China has a long history of using meat substitutes in its Buddhist cooking. Qishan Foods, a Chinese producer of meat substitutes, has partnered with Walmart to place its products across the retail firm's 400 locations in China. Within a year of launching its vegetable-based Omnipork, Hong Kong's Right Treat saw sales triple. The company has started selling in Singapore, Macau and Taiwan, and plans to sell in mainland China too. Market audits are a vital part of identifying opportunities.

Opportunity Audit Part 4: Domain

Technology has increased demand, as numerous delivery companies have provided a new consumer channel. Many new formats are delivery-only, providing a distribution outlet for independent chefs working on a part-time basis, part of the emerging gig economy. Wealth is increasingly concentrated in India's westernized middle and upper classes. This is driving demand for higher-end dining and western cuisine. It is also driving increased demand for banqueting by both individuals and corporates. Increased rural prosperity and welfare schemes has reduced the flow of labour from farms to cities. This trend, combined with the increase in the number of restaurants, has created a labour shortage in the industry.

Results of Your Opportunity Audit

By examining your Opportunity Environment, you've identified *Key Drivers and Draggers* of each quadrant. Key Drivers are important areas of focus in your mission, model, market and domain that help to create successful performance for you. In contrast, Key Draggers are *things you actively avoid doing because they lead to failure*. For the purposes of this simulation, each dragger begins with the word 'avoid'. It's essential to identify your drivers and draggers because they need to be aligned through all four quadrants for you to be able to effectively and efficiently implement an opportunity. These include:

1. Key Drivers of Mission:
   - Expand Comfortwala to all metros
   - Make a lot more money
   - Improve reputation

2. Key Drivers of Model:
   - Remain asset and capital light
   - Improve skills continuously
   - Maintain strict quality control
   - Maintain management contract model only
   - *Avoid franchising model*
   - Exploit popular high margin products

3. Key Drivers of Market:
   - Enter high-end market
   - *Avoid low-end market*
   - Expand corporate market
   - Expand catering and banqueting
   - Enter international markets

4. Key Drivers of Domain:
   - Benefit from growth in Category A
   - Benefit from trend to gig economy
   - *Avoid qualified labour shortage*

Please note that the drivers and draggers identified by you, Cyrus and Xerxes are not necessarily completely accurate. You may have completely disregarded important drivers. You are human beings and are therefore prone to make decisions incorrectly based on all kinds of biases. This process is designed to identify a solution that works best for you, but not necessarily for others. A group of three different promoters might identify a vastly different list of drivers. Readers are therefore advised to critically question all the decisions made by the promoters in this simulation. Irreverent questioning of all assumptions and rules will help you to discover better opportunities. In order to get the best results, it is best to always seek the truth through the collection and examination of evidence, rather than simply relying on your own opinions.

Next: Rank the Key Drivers and Draggers

The next step of the process is to identify and rank the Key Drivers and Key Draggers. Each driver will be considered separately by the three people in the management team. The drivers that score the lowest will be removed from future evaluation exercises, allowing us to better focus on essential criteria to rate opportunities. For the purposes of this particular exercise, I've already removed drivers that fail to add up to a score of at least 10, based on the addition of the points given by you, Cyrus and Xerxxes. Each driver and dragger is rated on a five-point scale by each promoter. The scale is as follows:

5: Essential
4: Important
3: Neutral
2: Less than neutral
1: Not needed at all

Results of the Key Driver and Dragger Ranking exercise are summarized in Table 1.

Table 1

	OPPORTUNITY AUDIT				
	For Irani Restaurants				
	Key Driver and Dragger Rankings				
Quadrants					
Mission	Key Drivers	You	Cyrus	Xerrxes	Total
	Expand Comfortwala to all metros	5	5	5	15
	Make a lot more money	4	2	4	10
	Improve reputation	3	5	2	10
Model	Remain asset- and capital-light	5	5	5	15
	Maintain strict quality control	5	5	5	15
	Exploit popular high margin products	5	3	3	11
	Continuous skills improvement	5	5	3	13
	Avoid franchising models	2	5	4	11
	Maintain management model only	2	4	5	11
Market	Enter high-end market	4	5	3	12
	Avoid low-end market	3	5	2	10
	Expand corporate market	3	4	3	10
	Expand catering and events	4	4	4	12
	Enter international markets	3	5	2	10
Domain	Avoid qualified labour shortage	5	5	5	15
	Benefit from growth in Category A	3	5	3	11
	Benefit from trend to gig economy	4	4	3	11

Next: Create Your Opportunity Inventory

Types of Opportunities to Put in Your Inventory

The opportunities you put in your inventory must come from all four segments of your Opportunity Environment: mission, model, market and domain. Opportunities fall into six broad categories:

1. *Opportunities you're currently pursuing*

Examples: your career in information technology, your current job as a business analyst, your existing business, your current product line, your current customers.

2. *New opportunities you're thinking of pursuing but haven't implemented*

Examples: Bigwich, Banquetwala, and MasterChef Studio

3. *Old opportunities you pursued in past but abandoned*
4. *Old opportunities you thought of pursuing in past but never implemented*
5. *Nopportunities you should reduce or abandon*

Examples: Comfortwala Conveyor

6. *New opportunities discovered through the Opportunity Audit*

To identify opportunities in Categories 1 through 4, consider all the opportunities that might come from valuable adaptations to change in your mission, including your purpose, goals, aspirations and beliefs. Next, consider opportunities that you're pursuing, or have considered or pursued in the past in your model, including your own skills, your team, your investors, your suppliers, your assets, your capabilities, your resources, your products and services, your intellectual property, and your systems and processes. Next, consider all opportunities that you're pursuing, or have considered or pursued in the past in your market, including current and potential customers, consumers, channels and competitors. Next, consider all opportunities that you're pursuing, or have considered or pursued in past that was created by changes in your domain. Your domain includes technology, industry and macro trends, political trends, government regulations, fashions, industry beliefs, potential substitutes, and emerging needs, and everything else influencing change in your mission, model and market.

To identify nopportunities in Category 5, consider everything you've been pursuing in your mission, model and market that has been unproductive, negative, and a waste of time and resources. A thorough audit of your entire Opportunity Environment should easily identify dozens of opportunities in Categories 1 through 5.

How to Identify New Opportunities

Dieter Mateschitz was a toothpaste salesman. The Austrian had taken ten years to complete his degree in marketing, and after spending a short time working for Unilever, had moved to Blendax, now part of Proctor & Gamble. His job included finding new markets for the company's toothpaste. That meant taking frequent trips to Thailand . . . which also meant frequent bouts of jetlag. During one trip, Mateschitz noticed that Thai truck drivers and manual workers would drink a tonic to keep themselves awake during long shifts. He wondered if the tonic could also help him beat his own post-flight exhaustion. The tonic was called Krating Daeng, or Red Bison in Thai, and it was made by a Thai business-owner called Chaleo Yoovidhya.

Yoovidhya had been born to poor Chinese immigrants. He had almost no secondary education. His first job had been helping his parents raise their ducks and sell their fruit. He had worked as a bus conductor, then as a salesman for a pharmaceutical company before noticing that an energy tonic the company sold was popular with truck drivers. He decided to make his own version, adding taurine, an extract from bovine bile, to the drink. This was the tonic that Mateschitz tested. When he found that it worked, he believed that he had discovered an opportunity. If the tonic gave him energy when he was tired, maybe it could do the same for others.

He approached Yoovidhya about a partnership. Yoovidhya agreed, and Mateschitz set about changing the flavour of the tonic to match Western tastes. The taurine and the clashing bull logo he kept, but he changed the name of the product to Red Bull. He had found a new opportunity—one that he'd never considered.

Category 6 opportunities are those that you've never considered before. The best new opportunities are valuable adaptations to what you're doing now. This is exactly how nature gradually adapts to change: *it's always an evolution, not a revolution.* The difference is, you are now adapting to change by using a conscious process. The best way to identify these adaptations is through *branching* from your existing key drivers and considering options for combining them with new key drivers. Consider the smartphone. Although it was a revolutionary product, it was simply an adaptation that combined the existing telephone with the new technology of the mobile computer with a touchscreen. The marriage of the two created an enormous new category that conquered the world.

The key drivers highlighted in grey in Table 2 are the ones you currently are following or wish to avoid. Look for ways to combine higher- and lower-ranking drivers to create valuable adaptations.

Table 2

	OPPORTUNITY AUDIT				
	For Irani Restaurants				
	Branching Key Drivers				
Quadrants					
Mission	Key Drivers	You	Cyrus	Xerrxes	Total
	Expand Comfortwala to all metros	5	5	5	15
	Make a lot more money	4	2	4	10
	Improve reputation	3	5	2	10
Model	Remain asset- and capital-light	5	5	5	15
	Maintain strict quality control	5	5	5	15
	Exploit popular high margin products	5	3	3	11
	Continuous skills improvement	5	5	3	13

	Avoid franchising models	2	5	4	11
	Maintain management model only	2	4	5	11
Market	Enter high-end market	4	5	3	12
	Avoid low-end market	3	5	2	10
	Expand catering and events	4	4	4	12
	Expand corporate market	3	4	3	10
	Enter international markets	3	5	2	10
Domain	Avoid qualified labour shortage	5	5	5	15
	Benefit from growth in Category A	3	5	3	11
	Benefit from trend to gig economy	4	4	3	11

For example, the *Management Contract model* is one of the current key drivers of the Irani Restaurants' model. How could this be branched to identify new opportunities? By combining it with a new key driver: *Expand Catering and Events.* Your Banquetwala concept is simply an adaptation that is a combinate of old and new key drivers, branching the business into a new category in which it gets to create many of the rules.

Irreverently consider as many options as possible. Don't just settle for the first *right answer*, consider second, third, fourth and fifth *right answers*. It's wise to look for branching opportunities that allow you to create a potentially large new categories, which you can lead. However, don't start by looking for vacant categories. There are an infinite number of these, and the vast majority are of no use to you. You should ideally start from the lens of current key drivers and match them with new drivers. For example, Bigwich is a combination of two key drivers: the current '*Remain asset- and capital-light*' and the new '*Exploit popular high-margin products*'. It creates a new category of QSR restaurants based on toasted cheese sandwiches.

There are numerous other methods of identifying new opportunities for your inventory. In my previous book, *Master Opportunity and Make it Big*, I identified Sixteen Opportunity Activators used by the Opportunity Masters profiled in the book.

Opportunity Inventory for Irani Restaurants

For the purposes of this simulation, you are only considering potential opportunities in Category 2: *new opportunities you're thinking of pursuing but haven't implemented yet*, as well as a potential nopportunity in Category 6. Your audit identified three new opportunities in Category 2:

1. Bigwich—a new QSR fast-food restaurant chain
2. Banquetwala—India's first nationally branded banquet hall chain
3. MasterChef Studio—the world's first permanent pop-up restaurant

Your audit identified one nopportunity in Category 6:

1. Comfortwala Conveyor—reconfigure all six restaurants without the conveyor, saving Rs 3 crore in the first year

Congratulations! You've finished your Opportunity Audit and created your Opportunity Inventory. Next, you'll move on to evaluate these potential opportunities in the next stage of the Process.

For an exhaustive list of Opportunity Activators, as well as more information on the Irani case and tips, templates and tools to help you to identify opportunities in all categories, please visit my website at: www.power-of-opportunity.com.

Create Your Opportunity Inventory

1. Audit your mission, model, market and domain
To see opportunities, you must first conduct a thorough audit of your mission, model, market and domain environments.

2. Rank your key drivers and draggers
Score each driver and each dragger for each interested party. Give each one a score from 1 to 5 from 'not needed' to 'essential'. Once you've counted the scores, you'll be able to assess the opportunities based on how well they match with key drivers.

3. Create your opportunity inventory

Finally, create your Opportunity Inventory by listing the opportunities you're currently pursuing; the opportunities you're thinking of pursuing but haven't implemented; the opportunities you previously pursued but have now abandoned; the opportunities you thought of pursuing but never implemented; the nopportunities you should reduce or abandon; and the new opportunities you discovered in your Opportunity Audit. You should find that, whether you're expanding a restaurant business or growing an auction firm, you have a number of opportunities that you can identify.

18

Evaluate Your Opportunities

How do you rank your opportunities' Key Drivers and Draggers? What conclusions can you draw from a Key Driver Alignment exercise? What are the nine evaluators that reveal the potential value of an opportunity? How do you evaluate nopportunities and focus on the opportunities with the biggest potential?

The year was 1963 and men would never smell the same again. It had been seventeen years since Estée Lauder had launched her four basic beauty products, placing them exclusively in high-end department stores and giving personal demonstrations to create a buzz. It had been three years since the company opened its first international account, in London's exclusive Harrods store, and a year since it had released a package of products for evening wear. But now Estée Lauder was about to do something completely different. All her company's products had been aimed at women. They had all relied on women's desire for clear, young-looking skin, and the marketing had assumed that women would tell each other when they found a product that worked. Now though, the company was going to launch its first product range for men. Starting with a scent called Aramis, named after a Turkish aphrodisiac, it was entering a whole new market. Could a company that had always been aimed at women, succeed in a new environment? Was there an opportunity in male grooming? Was the opportunity compatible with the company's mission, market, model and domain? The decision had been made. The results? Fifty-five years after its launch, Aramis, still sold in its tortoiseshell packaging, remains one of the world's leading male grooming products.

Whether you're assessing a male fragrance in the 1960s or a new technology in the first decades of the twenty-first century, the questions are the same as are the methods of answering them. The process of evaluating potential opportunities has two steps: first, align the opportunities in your inventory with your Key Drivers and Draggers to measure how well they would work together with all four quadrants of your environment. This step will quickly weed out opportunities that won't align well with your mission, model, market and domain. Second, put opportunities that align well through the nine evaluators to determine whether they are valuable enough to pursue.

Evaluation Step 1: Key Driver and Dragger Alignment

Your first step is to use your Drivers and Draggers to quickly focus on opportunities that align well with your entire opportunity environment. Opportunities that align well can be successfully implemented. There is no point in focusing on an opportunity, regardless of how potentially valuable, if you cannot implement it.

You, Cyrus and Xerrxes must come to a consensus answer to the question: *Will this opportunity help to promote the Key Driver, or will it help to remove the Key Dragger?* The only acceptable answers are Yes, No or Maybe. Maybe means that the answer could be Yes or No, depending on how the opportunity can be adapted and implemented. Results are in Table 3.

Table 3

		Irani Restaurants		
	Alignment with Key Drivers and Draggers			
Drivers and Draggers	**Comfortwala**	**Banquetwala**	**MasterChef**	**Bigwich**
Expand Comfortwala	Yes	Maybe	Maybe	Yes
Make a lot more money	Yes	Maybe	Maybe	Maybe
Improve reputation	No	Maybe	Yes	No

Remain asset- and capital- light	Yes	Yes	Yes	Yes
Maintain strict quality control	Yes	Maybe	Yes	Maybe
Exploit high margin products	Yes	Maybe	No	Yes
Skills improvement	No	Yes	Yes	Yes
Avoid franchising models	Yes	Yes	Yes	No
Expand catering and events	Yes	Yes	Maybe	No
Maintain management model	Yes	Yes	Yes	No
Enter high-end market	No	Maybe	Yes	No
Avoid low-end market	Yes	Yes	Yes	No
Expand corporate market	Maybe	Yes	Maybe	No
Enter international markets	Maybe	Maybe	Yes	Maybe
Avoid labour shortage	No	Maybe	Yes	No
Benefit from Category A growth	Maybe	Maybe	Yes	No
Benefit from gig economy	No	Maybe	Yes	No
No	5	0	1	10
Yes	9	8	12	4
Maybes	3	10	4	3

Your promoter group draws three conclusions from the Key Driver Alignment exercise:

1. *Bigwich* is eliminated from consideration, as it scored ten *No*s and therefore aligns very poorly with your drivers. While it may be a big opportunity for others, it simply will not work well with your mission, model, market and domain environment.
2. *Banquetwala* has zero *No* scores, meaning that it could potentially align well with your entire environment. However, it has ten *Maybe*s. These ideally should be converted into *Yes*es for the opportunity to be aligned with your entire environment. Because Banquetwala has the potential to align well with your environment, it will move to the next stage, to determine whether it can provide you with enough value.
3. *MasterChef Studio* aligns the best of all. It has only one *No* and only four *Maybe*s. The only question is: can it provide you with enough value to be a Golden Opportunity? You will answer that crucial question in the next stage of evaluation.

Visit my website www.power-of-opportunity.com to read more about how key driver & dragger alignment decisions were reached for these four opportunities.

Evaluation Step 2: The Nine Evaluators

Next, your team will each rate *Banquetwala* and *MasterChef Studio* on all of the nine evaluators. They are called evaluators because they are indicators of *potential value*. They include:

1. Opportunities should provide *useful service*. This service should ideally be provided to all stakeholders, including you, your customers, channels, employees, and investors. Useful service is the key driver of value and is therefore more important than all the other evaluators.
2. Opportunities should be *substantial*, with large-scale potential.
3. Opportunities should be *relevant*—needed now.
4. Opportunities should be *unique*—those that are relevant but not unique are commodities.

5. Opportunities should be *sustainable*—have durable competitive advantage.
6. Opportunities should be *accessible*—with low barriers to entry, at least for you.
7. Opportunities should be are *suitable*—fit your mission, model, market and domain.
8. Opportunities should be *actionable*—feasible to execute at scale.
9. Opportunities should be *profitable*—with the potential to be in the top 1 per cent of their category.

You will rate each opportunity on evaluators on a five-point scale. You are not measuring actual value, which obviously would not be known yet. The scale is as follows:

5: High potential value
4: Moderately high potential value
3: Average potential value
2: Below average potential value
1: Low potential value

For example, would Banquetwala provide useful service? If you give this a rating of 5, you believe that it is has the potential to provide a high value of useful service. As *Useful Service* is the key driver of value, it receives a double weighting, with a high score of 10. The other eight evaluators have a high score of 5. The total score for all nine evaluators is 50. To be considered adequately valuable, an evaluator must receive a score of at least 10 out of 15, or 66 per cent. Obviously at this point you're only estimating potential value. Ratings can be readjusted later based on modifications you make to improve value.

What a Lifetime of Evaluating Opportunities Can Bring

When your uncle owns a company and offers you a job as soon as you finish your diploma in business management, two things are true. First, you're very lucky. Second, you still have to prove yourself. You have to show that you deserve the job and that you're capable of making the decisions that increase the company's value.

That was the challenge that faced Yusuf Ali when he left India in 1973 to work for his uncle's EMKE Group in Abu Dhabi. The group consisted of a small trading centre in the old souk in Abu Dhabi. Ali and his uncle, M.K. Abdullah, did everything: they drove the delivery van, loaded and unloaded stock, and stood in the market to sell the goods. Ali soon saw an opportunity though. He began importing frozen products from Europe and the United States, distributing them to the interior of the Emirates. The company grew. Profits rose, and in the mid-1990s, the environment in the UAE began to change. The country opened to investors. European companies such as Continent, now Carrefour, entered the market, opening modern, air-conditioned supermarkets with a wide range of goods.

Ali, who was then in charge of the company, faced a difficult decision. He had managed to grow his uncle's wholesale and import business, expanding it to include cold storage, food processing plants, and retail too. But should the company go head-to-head with the international supermarkets and build its own retail chain? Was that a direction the company wanted to take? The move marked a shift from import towards real estate development. Did that align with the group's mission?

In 1995, Ali Yusuf's LuLu Group International opened its first supermarket in Abu Dhabi. The chain expanded quickly, spreading across the Middle East. From hypermarkets, it was a small branch towards malls, and in 2013, Yusuf Ali opened the LuLu International Shopping Mall in Kochi, India. The store cost Rs 16 billion to build. With 1.7 million square feet of retail space, it was the largest in India. The ability of Yusuf Ali, chairman and managing director of LuLu Group, to evaluate and implement opportunities has made him the twenty-fourth wealthiest Indian and given him a fortune estimated at more than $4.4 billion.

Your Evaluation of Banquetwala

1. Does Banquetwala provide very *useful service*?
Cyrus and Xerrxes each give Banquetwala a *useful service* score of 6 out of 10. There are already many banquet facilities available nationwide. Would a nationwide branded chain provide a much higher degree of useful service? They are not sure. You argue that a chain under your management could provide the same degree of consistently high quality and value for money that Comfortwala has achieved. Currently, consumers have to use expensive five-star hotel facilities to receive that level of useful service. Banquetwala will fill a gap and provide consistently superior service at lower prices. You see an analogy with the hotel industry. You will create a three- to four-star chain of branded banquet halls, just as others have created three- and four-star chains of branded hotels. You give a score of 8 out of 10. The total score for useful service is 20 out of 30, or 66 per cent.

2. Is Banquetwala a *substantial* opportunity, with large-scale potential?
You believe that the opportunity is mammoth and score it 5 out of 5. Weddings alone are an enormous industry in India. According to a May 2017 report by KPMG, the marriage services industry in India was estimated to be worth approximately Rs 3,68,100 crore in 2016. Hotel aggregator OYO Rooms has launched a wedding services aggregator business, OYO Auto, in eight Indian metros. You prefer to stick to banquet facilities, as these can be used by the corporate market as well. Cyrus and Xerrxes are also bullish about the size of the overall banquets market, but not completely confident that a national brand will be compelling enough to capture a substantial share. They each score substantial at 4 out of 5. The total score for substantial opportunity is 13 out of 15, or 86 per cent.

3. Is Banquetwala a *relevant* opportunity, with a large market now?
All three of you give a relevance score of 3 out of 5. Although banquet space is certainly relevant now, you cannot be sure that a national brand will be particularly relevant to consumers until you launch it. Since the business is new to your company, a learning process will be required

to understand what aspects of relevance are particularly compelling to consumers. Total score for relevance is 9 out of 15, or 60 per cent.

4. Is Banquetwala a *unique* opportunity?
You believe that the concept is somewhat unique, as a national brand has not been done before in this segment. However, you are unclear whether it would be perceived as unique by consumers, corporates or investors. You give it a score of 4 out of 5. Both Cyrus and Xerrxes believe that the opportunity is unique but will not be perceived as such by consumers until it can be promoted and scaled to some extent. They each give a score of 3 out of 5. The total score for uniqueness is 10 out of 15, or 66 per cent.

5. Is Banquetwala a *sustainable* opportunity? Does it have durable competitive advantages?
All three of you give a score of 3 out of 5. The reason? On the face of it, there are no competitive barriers to entry. Many others could attempt to set up a national chain of banquet halls on a management contract basis. However, you will have the first mover advantage, and you have a track record of consistent excellence in the restaurant industry. As long as you can scale quickly, your brand and head start may be able to give you sustainable advantage. But can you scale quickly? That is unclear, given your dependence on the management contract model. Eventually, others will copy you, but there is certainly room for many brands in this space, just as there are in the hotel industry. The total score for sustainability is 9 out of 15, or 60 per cent.

6. Is Banquetwala an *accessible* opportunity? Are there any major barriers to entry?
There are no major barriers to entry in this space, just the normal hassles of licensing in India. You all score 5 out of 5, and the total score is 15, or 100 per cent.

7. Is Banquetwala a *suitable* opportunity? Is it compatible with the company's mission, model and domain?
You believe that Banquetwala is highly compatible with your company's mission, model and domain. The alignment exercise with key drivers

found no area in which the concept did not align. You score suitability as 4 out of 5. However, both Cyrus and Xerrxes point out that the alignment exercise also found 10 Maybes for this opportunity. For example, there are serious question marks about whether Banquetwala will help the company to *Expand Comfortwala, Maintain strict quality control, Exploit high margin products, Enter the high-end market, Enter international markets or Benefit from Category A growth.* If the opportunity can be better aligned with some of these key drivers, they would give it a higher suitability score. For now, they both give 3 out of 5. The total score for suitability is 10 out of 15, or 66 per cent.

8. Is Banquetwala an *actionable* opportunity? Can it be efficiently and effectively scaled?

Both you and Cyrus give an actionability score of 4 out of 5. The company is already highly skilled at cooking and serving food. Preparing food for banquets is even easier. In addition, current investors in Comfortwala could be tapped to invest in Banquetwala. Xerrxes points out that banquet customers won't just want Comfortwala food, they'll need a much wider selection, which will require the use of other vendors. Secondly, outside cities in which Comfortwala already operates, the company will not be able to supply any food. He doesn't think investors will bite until they see proof of concept. He gives a score of 3 out of 5. The total score for actionability is 11 out of 15, or 73 per cent.

9. Is Banquetwala a *profitable* opportunity? Can it put you in the top 1 per cent?

One thing is sure: banqueting is usually more profitable than the restaurant business. Preparing food in bulk is more economical than for individual orders. Xerrxes points out that banqueting still requires a lot of labour, and costs are increasing rapidly. All three of you are uncertain about whether the creation of a nationwide chain would provide the higher margins and capacity utilization required to achieve industry-leading profits. You each give a score of 3. The total score for profitability is 9 out of 15, or 60 per cent.

In aggregate, Banquetwala scores 106 out of 150, or 70 per cent. This is barely above the minimum hurdle rate of 66 per cent. Will MasterChef Studio do better?

How Amazon Came to Serve the Internet

In 2003, Jeff Bezos, founder of Amazon.com, called his team to an executive retreat. The retreat took place at his house, and once there, he asked them to identify the retail giant's core competencies. The exercise was expected to last just thirty minutes. It was pretty clear that Amazon was very good at selling stuff online. They could fulfil orders quickly and send them to customers. What else was there to say?

But the meeting dragged on. Andy Jassy, then Bezos's chief of staff, told *TechCrunch* that the leaders realized that in addition to taking and fulfilling orders, they had also become very good at building and running data centres. They had put together infrastructure capable of computing and storing data that was endlessly and easily scalable. That ability had never been a plan but as the company had built new functions, it found that each team would create its own infrastructure from scratch. Projects that were supposed to take three months would take that long just to build the server systems. Eventually, the company had realized that it made more sense to create a common infrastructure system that any team could use. As Amazon's executives sat in Jeff Bezos's house, they started to see that infrastructure as a new opportunity, a kind of operating system for the Internet. Any company would be able to rent part of the structure to run their own technology applications.

Looking back, that should have been a light-bulb moment similar to Bill Gates' conception of an operating system for personal computers. But it wasn't. Even though Amazon had already built most of the product, it was three years before the company launched Amazon Elastic Compute Cloud. That was three years spent evaluating the opportunity, checking the drivers and draggers, scoring the benefits and the costs, and building the offer. Now known as Amazon Web Services and led by Andy Jassy, that infrastructure product had sales of $25.6 billion in 2018.

Your Evaluation of MasterChef Studio

1. Does MasterChef Studio provide very *useful service*?
Cyrus is so convinced that this concept can provide useful service that he has scored it as a perfect 10. He feels that westernized, upper class Indians are hungry to experiment with diverse cuisines, which are still in short supply. This concept will allow them to try the cuisine of up to twelve different chefs in one meal, with a new theme every two weeks. It adds utility by having each chef cook for you individually, a form of performance theatre. For the chefs, many of whom are only catering now or selling through delivery services, it will provide a prestigious promotional outlet. For the Irani's it will provide a huge reputation enhancer, a bold move above and beyond comfort food. You agree but are not as passionate as the concept is yet to be tested, so score an 8 out of 10. Xerrxes sits on the fence, pending a test. He scores 6 out of 10. The total score for useful service is 24 out of 30, or 80 per cent.

2. Is MasterChef Studio a *substantial* opportunity, with large-scale potential?
Cyrus believes that the MasterChef Studios has limited scope in India; outlets could be opened in Mumbai, Delhi, Bangalore, and possibly a couple other cities. However, internationally the concept has enormous potential. Outlets could be opened in all major European and Asian capitals. He believes that in the US and Canada, the company could open at least 50 restaurants. He scores it 4 out of 5. You see this potential also but would prefer to first see a proof of concept. You score 3 out of 5. Since the concept is still untested, Xerrxes is even more sceptical, scoring 2 out of 5. The total score for substantial opportunity is 9 out of 15, or 60 per cent.

3. Is MasterChef Studio a *relevant* opportunity, with a large market now?
You and Cyrus both agree that the concept is highly relevant with high-end Indian restaurant patrons and score this 5 out of 5. Cyrus' friends are constantly comparing and discussing new restaurants offering new cuisines, just as they are discussing new overseas travel venues. They have broken away from the standard Punjabi and Chinese restaurant fare of earlier generations. Many of them have lived or travelled extensively in

the US or Europe and have been exposed to new and better-quality food. Xerrxes would prefer to test the concept for relevance first, and scores 3 out of 5. The total relevance score is 13 out of 15, or 87 per cent.

4. Is MasterChef Studio a *unique* opportunity?
All three of you give a score of 4 out of 5 for uniqueness. The pop-up restaurant concept is already well known. This will be unique only in the sense that it will be the first to combine up to 12 chefs in one restaurant. The total uniqueness score is 12 out of 15, or 80 per cent.

5. Is MasterChef Studio a *sustainable* opportunity? Does it have durable competitive advantages?
All three of you give a score of 3 out of 5. This concept will be easy to duplicate by others, there are no competitive barriers. However, you will have first mover advantage. In order to benefit from that, you would need to create powerful brand loyalty through top-notch execution and would have to scale quickly. You have accomplished this with Comfortwala, can you do it with a high-end concept? The jury is out. The total sustainability score is 9 out of 15, or 60 per cent.

6. Is MasterChef Studio an *accessible* opportunity? Are there any major barriers to entry?
There are no major barriers to entry in this space, just the normal hassles of licensing in India. You all score 5 out of 5, and the total score is 15, or 100 per cent.

7. Is MasterChef Studio a *suitable* opportunity? Is it compatible with the company's mission, model and domain?
Cyrus conducted the alignment exercise and found that the concept is highly compatible with twelve of the company's key drivers, and only incompatible with four maybes. He therefore scores it 5 out of 5. While you're convinced that it is compatible with mission and domain drivers, you're unsure whether the company is capable of executing a high-end business model. You score 4 out of 5. As usual, Xerrxes sits on the fence, waiting for proof of concept. He scores 3 out of 5. The total score for *suitability* is 12 out of 15, or 80 per cent.

8. Is MasterChef Studio an *actionable* opportunity? Can it be efficiently and effectively scaled?
Both you and Cyrus score 4 out of 5 for actionability. You feel the concept is relatively simple. Xerrxes is concerned about your ability to recruit and qualify chefs and ensure quality and variety. Is there enough cooking talent out there to tap? Will chefs be as enthusiastic about the concept as we are? Can the company develop the skills needed to manage this? Will you be able to execute this in cities where you currently have no operations, such as Delhi, Bangalore and overseas? These are big question marks. He scores 3 out of 5. The total score for *actionability* is 11 out of 15, or 73 per cent.

9. Is MasterChef Studio a *profitable* opportunity? Can it put you in the top 1 per cent?
All three of your score 3 out of 5 for profitability. High-end restaurants can be very profitable, or spectacular failures. The cost structure and pricing for the model is not yet clear. The total score for profitability is 9 out of 15, or 60 per cent.

In aggregate, MasterChef Studio scores 114 out of 150, or 76 per cent. Although this is above the 70 per cent score of Banquetwala, it is still far from perfect. Total scoring for both concepts is given in the table below. Those that are below the hurdle rate are highlighted in grey in Table 4.

Table 4

Irani Restaurants Evaluation					
Banquetwala	**You**	**Cyrus**	**Xerrxes**	**Total**	**Per cent**
1. Useful (double weight)	8	6	6	20	66
2. Substantial	5	4	4	13	86
3. Relevant	3	3	3	9	60
4. Unique	4	3	3	10	66

5. Sustainable	3	3	3	9	60
6. Accessible	5	5	5	15	100
7. Suitable	4	3	3	10	66
8. Actionable	4	2	3	11	73
9. Profitable	4	3	2	9	60
Totals	40	32	32	106	
Percentages	80	64	64	70	

MasterChef Studio:	You	Cyrus	Xerrxes	Total	Per cent
1. Useful (double weight)	8	10	6	24	80
2. Substantial	4	3	2	9	60
3. Relevant	5	5	3	13	86
4. Unique	4	4	4	12	80
5. Sustainable	3	3	3	9	60
6. Accessible	5	5	5	15	100
7. Suitable	4	5	3	12	80
8. Actionable	4	4	3	11	73
9. Profitable	3	3	3	9	60
Totals	40	42	32	114	
Percentages	80	84	64	76	

How to Evaluate Your Nopportunities

Nopportunities are destroyers of value. As they are the exact opposite of opportunities, they should be evaluated based on the opposite criteria:

1. Nopportunities should provide *useless service*. Useless service is the key dragger of value and is therefore more important than all the other evaluators.
2. Nopportunities should be *unsubstantial,* with small-scale potential.
3. Nopportunities should be *irrelevant*—not needed now.
4. Nopportunities should be *standard*—commodities, commonly available.
5. Nopportunities should be *unsustainable*—lack competitive advantage.
6. Nopportunities should be *inaccessible*—with high barriers to entry, at least for you.
7. Nopportunities should be *unsuitable*—a poor fit with your mindset, model, market and domain.
8. Nopportunities should *not be actionable*—not feasible to execute at scale.
9. Nopportunities should be *unprofitable*—with average to below average profit potential in their category.

When Sir Richard Branson Fell for a Nopportunity

There must have been a moment, as Sir Richard Branson shaved off his beard and pulled on his bridal dress, when he thought: 'I've made a mistake here.' The occasion was a charity catwalk organized to promote Virgin's new venture: Virgin Brides. Sir Richard would be photographed wearing make-up and dressed as a bride.

The idea for the business had come from Ailsa Petchey, a member of the cabin crew of Virgin Atlantic. Petchey, who had a business degree, had put together a plan for a bridal business. The industry, she said, was worth £3 billion and had a gap for a reliable brand. Offering brides a single stop where they could buy everything they needed for their special day was an opportunity. Sir Richard gave her five minutes to make a pitch and had been impressed by what he'd heard. He gave her space in Virgin's offices to research the business then, in 1996, opened Europe's largest bridal emporium just off Trafalgar Square in London. Over the next ten years, the company sold about 10,000 wedding dresses and 40,000 bridesmaid dresses. In 2007, though, Virgin Brides closed the last of its outlets.

Sir Richard has mused that a picture of him wearing a wedding dress might have put off customers and also suggested that there just weren't enough virgin brides to justify the business. In a blog post though, he noted that while 'the team, the service and the products were all excellent . . . the cost of growing the business was not proportional to the slice of the market such an effort would attract. We had misjudged the business model, and Brides needed to scale to work for the Virgin brand.' Even Sir Richard Branson gets his evaluations wrong sometimes and makes a commitment to a nopportunity.

Your Evaluation of Comfortwala Conveyor

Comfortwala Conveyor is clearly still relevant, unique and accessible. However, it is also judged to provide useless service, particularly to the promoters and investors, who are losing money due to the failure of the model. In addition, it is highly unsubstantial, unsustainable, unsuitable, not actionable and unprofitable. With an overall score of 71 per cent, it is a clear nopportunity, and should be eliminated. Scores are in Table 5.

Table 5

Comfortwala Conveyor	You	Cyrus	Xerrxes	Total	Per cent
1. Useless (double weight)	8	8	10	26	86
2. Unsubstantial	4	4	5	13	86
3. Irrelevant	2	1	4	7	46
4. Standard	1	1	1	3	20
5. Unsustainable	4	3	5	12	80
6. Inaccessible	1	1	1	3	20
7. Unsuitable	4	4	5	13	86
8. Not actionable	5	5	5	15	100

9. Unprofitable	5	5	5	15	100
Totals	34	32	41	107	
Percentages	68	64	82	71	

Results of the Evaluation

Both MasterChef Studio and Banquetwala have scored above the hurdle rate of 66 per cent for opportunities and Comfortwala Conveyor has scored above the hurdle rate for nopportunities. They therefore can all move into the implementation phase of the opportunity process.

For tips, tools and templates to help you evaluate opportunities and nopportunities, visit my website www.power-of-opportunity.com.

Evaluate Your Opportunities

Evaluation Step 1: Key driver and dragger alignment
Start your evaluation by making sure that your key drivers and draggers align with your opportunity environment. Ask yourself whether each opportunity promotes your key driver or removes a key dragger.

Evaluation Step 2: The nine evaluators
Give the potential value of each opportunity a score from 1 to 5 according to whether it provides a useful service; is substantial; relevant; unique; sustainable; accessible; suitable; actionable; and profitable.

Evaluate your opportunities . . . and your nopportunities
Once you've scored your opportunities, compare the results. Then move on to score potential nopportunities on the opposite criteria. Even Richard Branson could make a commitment to a nopportunity like Virgin Brides. So, beware!

19

Implement Your Opportunities

Once you've assessed an opportunity, how do you implement it? What should you focus on for greatest success? How do you align multiple opportunities so that they complement while also competing against each other? How do you quickly raise the value of your opportunities? How do you align your team and resources with your opportunity in order to test them properly?

The story of Microsoft is a tale of alignment. The company was formed with a single product: a graphical interface that allowed anyone to interact with their computer without having to write code themselves.

When the first version of Windows came out in 1985, the operating system represented one kind of opportunity. It also created a second opportunity. Now other software companies could build their products on top of Windows. Microsoft had provided a platform into which they could plug their own services.

Bill Gates was quick to see that opportunity. The company soon released two additional products: a spreadsheet application called Excel; and a word-processing application called Multi-Tool Word for Xenix systems. The name of that application would be edited down to Word. In 1990, the company bundled together Word, Excel and PowerPoint to create the first version of Office.

Looking back at that early Office, the lack of alignment becomes clear. Each product was made by a different team working independently. Not only did each application have a different design, it also made different demands on the customer. Word placed its files in the computer's C drive; Excel required customers to create folders themselves and build their own paths. Today's Office Suite is installed with nothing more than a click on a website and the look and feel of each product is the same. The products are aligned and work together smoothly. A user of Word feels at home with the ribbons whether they're on Excel or on PowerPoint. A customer who switches to a different product has to learn again the functions available and their placements. Microsoft didn't think about alignment when the company initially implemented its opportunity. It feels the benefits of that alignment now.

That alignment is something that you will also have to bear in mind as you implement new opportunities for Irani Restaurants, under the watchful eyes of Xerrxes and Cyrus. Based on the results of the evaluation phase, Xerrxes has issued orders to remove the conveyor systems from six Comfortwala restaurants. This will save Rs 3 crore in the coming year and provide you with an operating budget to fund your new opportunities. In addition, the empty space available on the first and second floors of Mehta Bhavan is available to you. To recap, your two new opportunities had the following evaluation scores:

MasterChef Studio: 76 per cent
Banquetwala: 70 per cent

Since neither opportunity has achieved a large margin over the 66 per cent hurdle rate, and since their scores are so close, you decide to let them compete with each other, to see which would be best to focus on. As you consider how to move forward into the process of implementation, you recall the *Success Equation*:

$$Your\ Success = Opportunities + Resources + Action$$

You've already identified the opportunities. Next you need to answer the following questions: *What actions should we focus on? How we determine these? What resources will we need, how will we identify them, and how will we get them?* In answering these questions, you must always strive to focus on the *Pareto Leaders*, the key drivers that can get you the best results for the least effort.

The Key Driver of Opportunity Implementation

Your family, like everything in nature, grows by reproducing—by having babies. Opportunities are very much like babies. Imagine that you have two babies of your own. The world is always changing and may be very different when they grow up. You would like them to be super successful

Pareto Leaders in whatever fields of endeavour they choose to pursue. In order to achieve that success, how would you prepare them? What would you have them focus on? As a priority, you would obviously focus your babies on learning. Learning what? Learning to adapt successfully to their environment. Learning is the key driver of adaptation, and adaptation is the key driver of success. You would test the kids on a regular basis to measure their progress and skills, and you will continuously adjust their lessons to increasingly focus them on their individual strengths. If your two children compete with each other, will they learn faster? Competition may help to improve their skills and identify weaknesses. If one of them were much more successful, would you give up on the weaker one and dump him in an orphanage? Of course not. You want both children to thrive. Should they compete so hard with each other that they start fighting? Of course not. Although a certain degree of competition will help them adapt better, fighting will be destructive and teach them the wrong lessons. You would like them to cooperate, so that they can grow together, and complement and learn from each other, just as Cyrus and Xerrxes have done. They will each have different skills. They would ideally learn to balance and align with each other.

If you have multiple good opportunities, you can make them compete with each other. But remember, your best opportunities are like your children. You don't want them to die. You want them to live and thrive.

Implementing a New Coffee Opportunity

The first phase began in 1986. Nestlé, the Swiss food conglomerate, tasked five employees with the mission of enabling anyone to create a perfect cup of espresso coffee, just like a barista, but in their own home. It was a bold move for the company.

Nestlé had pioneered home coffee-making since the 1930s, when it had created Nescafé to use surplus coffee beans left unsold after the Wall Street Crash. The instant-coffee powder was included in the ration packs of US soldiers who brought it into their homes after they were demobilized. But customers were soon becoming fussier about their coffee. They wanted to know where their morning Java came from and what kind of beans it contained. Nespresso would take aim at a new premium market that wanted both quality and convenience.

What Nespresso calls the 'Pioneering Years: Trial and Error' lasted between 1986 and 1994 and covered the release of the first machine and the first Grand Cru coffee varieties. The next period, 'Start-Up Phase: Laying the Foundation', lasted until 2000. Nespresso machines with their coffee capsules became available in the US, France, Switzerland, Italy and Japan. Nespresso launched B2B services, a club and a website. The company started making a profit. Between 2000 and 2005, it focused on creating a brand. The machines were redesigned. The company launched surprising new coffee varieties and opened boutiques that turned Nespresso into an experience as well as a product. Over the next six years, Nespresso set out to shape 'the global coffee culture'. It hired Hollywood actor George Clooney as a brand ambassador, sponsored events and rolled out environmental programmes to show its commitment to sustainability, an important interest for the company's customers.

The company, an autonomous part of the Nestlé Group, doesn't usually isolate its revenues from the rest of the group. However, in 2011, it reported sales of around $3 billion. It now employs 13,500 people in seventy-six countries and, by serving premium coffee to customers who now want much more than just Nescafé, continues to grow at a rate of around 5 per cent each year.

After much effort, you have identified Banquetwala and MasterChef Studio as your best potential opportunities. Wouldn't it be great if both could be hugely successful? How can you manage that with your limited resources? First, by focusing them on learning the lessons they need to grow. Second, by not only testing them but also aligning them, not only with each other but also with the existing environment. By working on their own, Cyrus and Xerrxes might be able to achieve a certain degree of success. By aligning their diverse skill sets, they are able to achieve much more. Opportunities work in the same way. *Alignment* is a key driver of successful opportunity implementation. The first and most important type of alignment is *environmental alignment.* If your opportunity is fully aligned with its mission, model, market and domain environments, it can be successfully implemented. When a great opportunity is fully and consistently aligned with its environment, you have created a *moat*—a durable competitive advantage. Ironically, this advantage has very little to do with besting your competitors. It is based on your ability to consistently supply a high quality of useful service because your opportunity environment is fully aligned.

If even one quadrant of its environment is not aligned, you will fail to provide a high-quality of useful service. For example, I recently ordered food through *Scootsy*, an online food-delivery service. The food did not show up. This was the second time in a week that Scootsy failed to deliver my food, blaming it on *technical failure*. Clearly, Scootsy's model is not well aligned with its mission, market and domain. The result for the customer is *useless service*. The result for Scootsy is the creation of an unhappy customer who is seeking alternatives. Like Scootsy, most companies fail to build a moat not because of what their competitors have done, but because of their own failure to align properly or to stay aligned with their environment.

For example, when I headed the OEM division at Price Pfister, I had to align my own operations with the opportunity environment of the rest of the company. Rather than fighting with the other parts of the company as my predecessor had done, I focused on cooperation. That's the only way I was able to get my work done and provide my customers with useful service.

How to Align Your Opportunities

When you're implementing an opportunity, your time and resources are limited. You must focus on what matters most. The easiest way to align your opportunities with their environment is by *focusing on key drivers and aligning them with each other*. What are key drivers? Key drivers are *essential* elements. To put it simply, a key driver is a thing you can't live without. A key driver is a *Pareto Leader*, with the largest influence on your results. Your opportunities are valuable adaptations. Key drivers increase their value the most. Let's say that your opportunity is to build a capital-intensive business. What key drivers would you need to align with each other in order to achieve success? For example, when Dhirubhai Ambani scaled up Reliance Industries, his opportunities were based on creating gigantic industrial capacity with their huge-scale economies. In order to implement these successfully, what other key driver did he need to align this with? The ability to raise staggering amounts of money.

Irani Restaurants: Aligning Your Opportunities

The ideal scenario for your company would be to align its potential new opportunities with its existing business—Comfortwala. This would allow all three to share resources and learn and adapt together, a phenomenon known as *opportunity synergy*. If you don't seek alignment right from the beginning, the new opportunities could clash with your current business model. This conflict could not only doom the new opportunities to failure but also damage your current business. A restaurant is a factory in which sales, production and consumption all happen in the same place. What is the most important element among these? The answer is: all of them. Everything needs to work well. As in the example with Scootsy, when even one critical area fails, useful service is transformed into useless service.

The drivers and draggers of your environment are below. The three opportunities already seem to be aligned on four key drivers and draggers, as highlighted in grey in Table 6.

- Remain asset- and capital-light
- Avoid franchising models
- Maintain management model
- Avoid low-end market

Table 6

Quadrant	Drivers and Draggers	Irani Restaurants		
		Alignment with Key Drivers and Draggers		
		Comfortwala	Banquetwala	MasterChef
Mission	Expand Comfortwala	Yes	Maybe	Maybe
	Make a lot more money	Yes	Maybe	Maybe
	Improve reputation	No	Maybe	Yes
Model	Remain asset- and capital-light	Yes	Yes	Yes
	Maintain quality control	Yes	Maybe	Yes
	Exploit high margin products	Yes	Maybe	No
	Skills improvement	No	Yes	Yes
	Avoid franchising models	Yes	Yes	Yes
Market	Expand catering and events	Yes	Yes	Maybe
	Maintain management model	Yes	Yes	Yes
	Enter high-end market	No	Maybe	Yes
	Avoid low-end market	Yes	Yes	Yes
	Expand corporate market	Maybe	Yes	Maybe
	Enter international markets	Maybe	Maybe	Yes

Domain	Avoid labour shortage	No	Maybe	Yes
	Benefit from Category A growth	Maybe	Maybe	Yes
	Benefit from gig economy	No	Maybe	Yes
	No	5	0	1
	Yes	9	8	12
	Maybes	3	10	4

For implementation to go smoothly and attract resources, you initially focus on aligning the other key drivers. You go through each quadrant of your environment separately and consider alignment opportunities.

Table 6A

Quadrant	Drivers and Draggers	Comfortwala	Banquetwala	MasterChef
Mission	Expand Comfortwala	Yes	Maybe	Maybe
	Make a lot more money	Yes	Maybe	Maybe
	Improve reputation	No	Maybe	Yes

First you look at your mission. The key driver of the mission is to *Expand Comfortwala*. How can your new opportunities help to expand Comfortwala? Alternatively, how can the expansion of Comfortwala to more Indian cities help to attract investors for Banquetwala and MasterChef?

All three concepts are already aligned to use the management contract model. Investors own all the restaurants, while Irani Restaurants owns the brands and manages operations under exclusive contract. You could offer the two new opportunities to the existing Comfortwala investor network on the same basis. For important investors, such as Eveready, you can offer block deals to develop

Banquetwala and MasterChef in new cities, along with Comfortwala. For new investors, especially larger ones such as Eveready, who require scale, the menu of three offerings should prove more attractive.

Think: *In what other ways could you align the three opportunities so that they can help each other to expand?*

Table 6B

Quadrant	Drivers and Draggers	Comfortwala	Banquetwala	MasterChef
Model	Remain asset- and capital-light	Yes	Yes	Yes
	Maintain quality control	Yes	Maybe	Yes
	Exploit high margin products	Yes	Maybe	No
	Skills improvement	No	Yes	Yes
	Avoid franchising models	Yes	Yes	Yes

Next, you align the key drivers of model, as show in Table 6B. All three concepts are already aligned to *remain asset-light* and *avoid franchised operations.* You're concerned that Banquetwala may have problems maintaining quality control. Why? Because a banqueting facility needs to have a range of food offered to customers. These facilities won't just be serving Comfortwala food. Secondly, you'd like to open Banquetwala outlets in cities where Comfortwala doesn't operate. How could you control quality in these places? Clearly, it will make sense to first develop Banquetwala in the four cities where Comfortwala already operates. Second, it will be necessary to create a team to carefully vet and qualify outside caterers. MasterChef could be an excellent proving ground for new chefs who can cook in Banquetwala's facilities. The concept could include a YouTube channel to which current and aspiring chefs all over India (and ultimately the world) could submit cooking videos. This could help to identify chefs who would be invited to 'try out' in MasterChef's restaurants. If their cuisine is popular, they can be empanelled to cook in Banquetwala facilities nearby.

Consider: *In what other ways could you align the three opportunities so that they help each other to ensure quality control?*

Table 6C

Quadrant	Drivers and Draggers	Comfortwala	Banquetwala	MasterChef
Market	Expand catering and events	Yes	Yes	Maybe
	Maintain management model	Yes	Yes	Yes
	Enter high-end market	No	Maybe	Yes
	Avoid low-end market	Yes	Yes	Yes
	Expand corporate market	Maybe	Yes	Maybe
	Enter international markets	Maybe	Maybe	Yes

Next, consider how to align the key drivers of market, as show in Table 6C. MasterChef can easily be aligned on the key driver of *expand catering and events*, as its chefs could offer catering sold by the company under the MasterChef brand. Clients using Banquetwala facilities could also be offered the use of popular MasterChefs. By offering catering by MasterChef, Banquetwala could branch into the high-end market, by servicing rich wedding and corporate customers who would otherwise use five-star hotels. If MasterChef can be expanded into international markets, it could create a base of investors who might be interested in considering localized versions of Comfortwala and Banquetwala. These concepts might first be attractive in geographies with large Indian diaspora communities, such as areas of the US, UK, Canada, South Africa, Australia and the Middle East.

Ask yourself: *In what other ways could you align the three opportunities so that they help each other to expand catering and events, and enter high end and international markets?*

Table 6D

Quadrant	Drivers and Draggers	Comfortwala	Banquetwala	MasterChef
Domain	Avoid labour shortage	No	Maybe	Yes
	Benefit from Category A growth	Maybe	Maybe	Yes
	Benefit from gig economy	No	Maybe	Yes

Finally, you align the key drivers of domain, as show in Table 6D above. By offering catering by MasterChef in Banquetwala facilities, you could help the company to benefit from the massive growth in the number of wealthy Indian consumers. Popular dishes served by both Banquetwala and MasterChef could potentially be tested on the Comfortwala menu, keeping it fresher and more relevant, and allowing more pricing power.

Think: *in what other ways could you align the three opportunities so that they can benefit from growth in Category A consumers?*

How Disney Turned a Cartoon Mouse into a Massive Business

It was a notepad that did it. Walt Disney had released *Steamboat Willie*, the third Mickey Mouse cartoon and the first with sound, to general acclaim. As Disney sat in a hotel lobby in New York in 1929, a man approached him and asked if he could buy a license to place Mickey Mouse on the cover of a children's notepad that he wanted to produce. He offered Disney $300. Disney took the money and started to look for new merchandising opportunities. A deal with George Borgfeldt & Company gave the company the right to produce figurines of Mickey and Minnie Mouse in return for royalties of 2.5 per cent for goods under 51 cents and 5 per cent on more expensive products. In 1932, a new agreement with Herman Kamen, an advertising executive, split revenues on a 50/50 basis and spread the black-and-white mouse across products, including bedspreads, toys, wallpaper, napkins and more. When Kamen signed an agreement with the Ingersoll-Waterbury Clock Company, his partner was on the edge of bankruptcy. Weeks later, it had tripled its workforce. The revenues generated by the merchandising funded Disney's next movie, *Snow White and the Seven Dwarfs*, which in turn created a whole new set of merchandising opportunities.

Since then, Disney has found ever more ways to capitalize on its assets, including theme parks and resorts, a club, television shows, and a host of additional brands from Star Wars to sports. A company that started with a single animated mouse on movie screens has evolved into a complete entertainment business in which ideas can be sold in a variety of different forms and through a range of different channels. In 2018, the Walt Disney Company generated revenues of nearly $60 billion.

Your Next Step—Value Alignment

Next you need to look at *value alignment*. There are nine sources of value in your model. Although the most important source of value is Useful Service, you would ideally like all nine to score 100 per cent. In evaluating the opportunities, you've already ascertained where you feel the opportunities are strong, and where they need improvement. See the scores in Table 2 of Chapter 17 on page 271.

Focus first on areas of weakness that need to be improved. For example, for Banquetwala, the key areas requiring improvement are:

1. There are many other banqueting options available. How can opportunity be designed to give more *useful service*, and be more *relevant*? Not only to customers but also to investors, channels and to Irani Restaurants?

2. Although Banquetwala may become India's first national brand of banquet halls, the concept is easy for others to copy. How can the opportunity be designed to be more *sustainable* against competitive attack?
3. The profitability of the concept is unclear. How can the concept be designed to be highly *profitable* compared to comparative services in the market?

For each one of these focus areas, you must answer these questions:

*   What would be required as proof of concept?
*   How can we economically test this opportunity? Who, what, where, when and how?
*   How can we assess our results? What are the best metrics?
*   How can we create more value in this area? How can we do so while better aligning it with the other sources of value?

Next, focus on how evaluators that are already strong—such as suitability, actionability and uniqueness—can be further strengthened and aligned. Repeat the questions above.

Your Next Step—Team Alignment

Ideally, you would build a team of Pareto Superstars. They need to be aligned to fill all gaps in your model, just like the pieces in a jigsaw puzzle. Ideally, your team should be made up of people who are so passionate and interested in the mission that they would do the work for free if they could afford it. Successful implementation of opportunities is all about learning. To be effective, learning must be continuous, conscious, collective and cumulative. It's crucial that the people that you are learning with are as dedicated as you are to provide useful service; and have the specialized and complementary skills needed to design your model and test your market. They have a strong personal interest in the service you're offering, as well as reducing the problems and pain faced by customers. Such people can learn well and fast.

Why Budweiser's Eagle Crashed and Burned

Kevin Bowler, president of US beer company Anheuser-Busch, was looking for an opportunity. The country's beer industry was growing at a rate of just 1–2 per cent in the 1980s, and he wanted to move his company into a space that could deliver faster growth. The company chose to branch out. Bowler knew its customers tended not to just drink beer. They also ate snacks as they drank, gulping down nuts, pretzels and potato crisps. The market was the same. The production process was similar. The distribution networks could be shared. The company's snacks subsidiary, called Eagle Snacks, could be a perfect complement to its beer and give it access to a better and faster-growing opportunity.

Eagle Snacks started selling its products across the US in 1988. Backed by a comprehensive marketing campaign, sales grew quickly, increasing by 25 per cent every year. Soon, the company had 6 per cent of the market for salty snacks. Within three years, it had almost 10 per cent of American supermarket sales of potato crisps. But while Eagle's market was similar to Anheuser-Busch's beer customers, the opportunity's environment was very different. The snack industry was dominated by Frito-Lay, a Pepsico subsidiary, and it wasn't going to let Anheuser-Busch steal its customers. The company had advantages of scale that let it cut prices to preserve market share. According to the *New York Times*, it reduced its profit margins from 21–17 per cent and increased its distribution. Borden, another competitor, soon followed suit in a bid to block Eagle's growth. 'We can't allow them to achieve their goal at our expense,' George Wado, the head of Borden's snack division, told *The Times*. 'We are doing everything we can to prevent it.'

To compete, Eagle Snacks had to cut its own prices. Although analysts described it as having good products, marketing and packaging, its profitability was entirely dependent on its competitors' willingness to absorb lower margins. By 1991, Eagle was selling between $400 million and $500 million of goods a year, but was losing more than $12 million. Four years later, those losses had increased to $25 million. In 1996, Eagle Snacks, a victim of its failure to accurately evaluate its environment, was sold off to Procter & Gamble by Anheuser-Busch.

It may be that none of your team members report to you. For example, when I ran the OEM division at Price Pfister, my team consisted of fifty managers in all areas of the company, none of whom reported to me. I had no authority over any of them, yet I aligned them to share my goals and get my work done. The ability to build a good team has nothing at all to do with your position or the resources available to you. Many people with abundant resources waste them on poorly aligned and unqualified teams. Even if you have no resources to pay a team, and no authority to hire a team, you can recruit and align a team of unpaid advisors who are enthusiastic about your opportunity.

Think: *What sort of initial team members would you need to test and implement the Banquetwala and MasterChef Studio opportunities? What skills would they have? How could you get them to help you without paying them initially?*

Your Final Step—Resource Alignment

Just as your children won't grow without food, your opportunities can't grow without resources. Your team members would ideally be people who can help to attract resources due to their experience and expertise. Resource providers would ideally have the credibility to help you to attract a more extensive group of advisors and potential customers and channels who can help you to test the opportunity economically and effectively. For example, my client Zaka Group was pursuing an opportunity to launch the world's fastest courier service. We first had to test for *actionability* and *relevance*. *Was the service feasible? Would it be relevant for a large enough market?* This required the consideration of numerous operational options. To test the market for this new service, which was completely unknown, Zaka partnered with a concierge service that had corporate customers who sometimes needed a service of this type. This cost nothing and gave us access to hundreds of his customers. Within a few months, the weaknesses of the opportunity were overcome, and proof of concept tested to the point where the promoter was able to attract the resources required to launch.

Consider: *What sort of resources would you require to test and implement the Banquetwala and MasterChef Studio opportunities? Where would you find them? How would they help you?*

Implementation Decisions for Irani Restaurants

You decide to test both the Banquetwala and MasterChef opportunities using the vacant second floor of Mehta Bhavan. You create a budget for renovation of the space, so that it can be flexibly used to test both opportunities. The first issue you want to tackle is relevance. On alternate weekends, you will invite target customers to dine or hold events either for free, or on a deeply discounted basis. You will test various chefs and cuisines. You plan to meet with many of them afterwards to get their feedback. If initial feedback is good, you will hire managers for each opportunity, and begin selective selling. This will allow you to test market and profitability. If response is positive, you will begin to build team and operate more days per week.

Think: *Could there have been an alternative decision? Why? Why not? What would you do?*

For tips, tools and templates to help you evaluate opportunities and nopportunities, visit my website: www.power-of-opportunity.com.

A Final Note

The case study of Irani Restaurants and the methodology used may seem very simplistic to some readers. In the real world, there would be many complexities and dynamics that would affect decisions at various stages of the opportunity process. The objective of using this fictional case is to help readers and practitioners to actually use the tools that have been developed through years of work by the world's only opportunity consultancy. They are being shared with you in order to help you to make the most of the opportunities in your environment.

For thousands of years, most people have hoped and prayed for providence or good fortune to provide them with wealth. However, by now we know that prosperity is not something that will descend on us from the heavens. We can only create success by taking tangible action to see, evaluate, choose and implement the best opportunities in our environment. We are truly fortunate to live in the Age of Opportunity, when opportunities are not only free, but freely accessible by everyone.

My own mission is to help you to achieve success by providing you with a process of opportunity, which is based on my several decades of experience working across countries and continents. The theories, techniques and tools in this book are by no means that only ways of seeing, evaluating, choosing and implementing opportunities. Like every process, the opportunity process must continuously improve through continuous, collective and cumulative learning, and everyone's contributions are welcome. I hope that we can create a community of like-minded people who would further improve this process by learning together. I welcome you to your journey into the world of *opportunities* and do hope to share with you.

You're invited to learn more and contribute to the opportunity process, by visiting our website at www.power-of-opportunity.com.

Implement Your Opportunities

1. Value alignment
Before you start implementing your opportunity, list the values you want the opportunity to deliver. Score the opportunity on its ability to deliver those values. You want each value to score 100 per cent. They won't score that highly, but where the values are weak, understand what you need to do to strengthen them.

2. Team alignment
To take action, you'll need a team—ideally, a team of people who are passionate and interested in the mission. They must care about the service and the people who receive that service, and they should want to find ways to address the customers' pain points. They should also be willing to learn continuously and collectively as the opportunity grows

3. Resource alignment
A good opportunity can attract resources. It brings in money, but it also draws a good group of advisors, customers and channels that can help you to deliver more effectively.

Epilogue: Thirteen Takeaways

What do you think are the thirteen top takeaways from this book? Here are my choices:

1. **Opportunity is the essential element for success.** Success has always been defined as control of resources. Opportunities are free and available to absolutely everyone, including you. Better yet, the best opportunities are like powerful magnets that attract all the resources you need.

2. **Opportunities are valuable adaptations to change.** Change is the only constant in our world and the greatest source of opportunities. All humans can consciously adapt to changes in their environments through continuous, collective and cumulative learning.

3. **To succeed, you must carefully focus.** Although we all work hard, a few of us reap almost all the benefits. To join the top 10 per cent, you must carefully focus only on your key drivers of value, and defocus on the key draggers, which destroy value. You must focus on the best opportunities and defocus on nopportunities, which lead you to failure.

4. **You live in the Age of Opportunity.** You live in a golden age in which there are no barriers to success. As long as you understand and follow the rules of the Now Era, you have complete access to all opportunities. But in order to succeed you must be able to see, evaluate and choose the best ones.

5. **To stay relevant, be irreverent.** If you unconsciously follow all the rules, you'll end up with average opportunities and average results at best. To capture big opportunities, you must be irreverent, question all assumptions, and be willing to break and remake the rules of your world.

6. **Opportunities require a fair exchange of value.** In the Now Era, all business opportunities require win-win value exchanges. Both sides must win. Therefore, in order to gain, you must provide extremely useful service to others, as well as to yourself, and always seek mutual benefit and co-opportunity.

7. **Increase your gravity to attract value.** Even if you start with nothing, there are many ways for you to increase the perceived value of your opportunities, in order to attract the resources you need to cross the bridge from aspiration to realization.

8. **Where you feel friction, you'll find opportunities.** Other people's pain can be your gain. When people are unhappy, there may be an opportunity for you to provide useful service by converting friction into value.

9. **You need to use a process.** Should you let a blinded folded monkey choose your opportunities? Of course not. Using systematic processes creates better outcomes. You need to use a systematic process to see, evaluate and choose your opportunities, and fortunately this book provides one to you!

10. **First know your location.** Opportunities are all around you. However, if you don't know where you are now, any route will get you lost. In order to see opportunities, you must audit all four segments of your Opportunity Environment: Mission, Model, Market and Domain.

11. **Opportunities are golden on the inside, not the outside.** That can make them hard to see. You can ensure that you won't miss the golden eggs by first creating a complete inventory of your opportunities, past, present and future.

12. **Use the nine evaluators to choose opportunities.** Your best opportunities are a mission of service to both yourself and to others. This service should ideally also be relevant, unique, scalable, sustainable, accessible, suitable, actionable, and profitable.

13. **Implement opportunities and eliminate nopportunities.** Test and align your opportunities with their environment by focusing on ways for them to work together, create value and attract resources and team.

And finally: This is a living book, and you are now a live part of it. Join our online learning community, share insights, get tips and tools, and help to make the Power of Opportunity even more useful for more people. We can make opportunities bigger for everyone by learning together. I welcome your cooperation and contributions. *Visit www. power-of-opportunity.com to join in.*